RICHARD RUSSELL

LIBERATION THROUGH HEARING

Rap, Rave & the Rise of XL Recordings

WHITE
RABBIT

First published in Great Britain in 2020 by White Rabbit
This paperback edition published in 2021 by White Rabbit
an imprint of The Orion Publishing Group Ltd
Carmelite House, 50 Victoria Embankment
London EC4Y 0DZ

An Hachette UK Company

10 9 8 7 6 5 4 3 2 1

A CIP catalogue record for this book is available
from the British Library.

ISBN (Mass Market Paperback) 978 1 4746 1635 5
ISBN (eBook) 978 1 4746 1636 2

Printed in Great Britain by Clays Ltd, Elcograf, S.p.A

MIX
Paper from
responsible sources
FSC
www.fsc.org   FSC® C104740

www.whiterabbitbooks.co.uk
www.orionbooks.co.uk

Contents

Dedicated to the memory of Keith Flint

PRELUDE 1: SALFORD
17 APRIL 2019

CASISDEAD
Everything's For Sale
(feat. Alexander O'Neal)

Track Information

Artist	**CASISDEAD**
Track	Everything's For Sale feat. Alexander O'Neal
Genre	Rap/RnB
Year	2020
Label	XL Recordings
Country	UK

1st Part (Steps 1—16)   **2nd Part (Steps 17—32)**

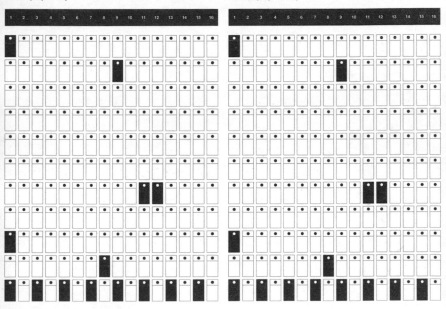

Tempo

The TEMPO dial controls how fast the drum sequence plays. Set to the correct dial position as shown below.

Pattern Write

The PATTERN WRITE dial selects which part of the sequence is being edited. To set a 32 step sequence, set the dial to 2nd PART, hold down the RED BUTTON and press Key 16.

23

Program Your 808 Series

By Rob Ricketts
www.robricketts.co.uk

Instructions

Use the diagram above to program the steps into your Roland TR-808 drum machine, then sit back while memories of your favourite 808 beats from the past are brought back to life.

■ Key On   □ Key Off

It's an overcast early spring afternoon. I'm in a recording studio on an industrial estate on the outskirts of Manchester. I've been here for an hour. It would have been hard to locate but I was collected at Manchester Piccadilly by a professional who had researched the destination and got us here easily. He used to drive Keith Flint during The Prodigy's UK tours, and having picked me up we spent the short journey reminiscing about Keith, who passed away less than a month ago, at the age of forty-nine.

I arrive in a sombre mood. There are three musicians here. A man known as CASISDEAD has just arrived from a stopover in Nottingham. He is the most idiosyncratic, articulate and fluent British rap lyricist I have heard since Dizzee Rascal emerged from Bow E3 in 2002. CAS's themes are typically the underbelly of street life, drug sales and sex work. In the first really classic song he has made, 'Pat Earrings', he tells the apparently heartfelt and melancholy story of his ill-fated relationship with a prostitute. At the conclusion of the song, he finds she has continued to see clients despite telling him she has stopped. 'Heartbroken, I'm at wits' end / She's never accepted by my friends / That's cool 'cause I never liked them'. The narrator is bereft.

As is often the case with those who make disturbing art, he seems a person of integrity. Those in the public eye who go out of their way to seem benevolent, the supposedly squeaky-clean ones, are the ones to beware of. Nasty pretends to be nice, and vice versa. CAS has his face covered at all times when in public. Oscar Wilde said, 'Give a man a mask and he'll tell you the truth.' CAS has a taste for the analogue synthesiser sounds of the 1980s, music that soundtracked my youth and was popular around the time he was born.

I have programmed my Roland TR-808 drum machine in order

to echo the feeling of the year that the machine was first released: 1980. This item is my favourite material possession. Its sounds and groove have been enjoying a renaissance in popularity since the James Brown samples of classic East Coast hip-hop made way for the more electronic palette that was being used by rap artists from the South. Its distinct sonic character is still a crucial part of the hip-hop production landscape.

Drums are only part of the story. In creating music for this session, I have enlisted someone who not only has the ability to craft unforgettable melodies but owns a collection of the vintage analogue synthesisers necessary to sonically execute this job properly. He sits behind one of these while his daughter Missy and his best friend Remi potter around. His name is Damon Albarn and, as frontman of Blur, mastermind behind virtual band Gorillaz and all-round musical polymath, he has scaled every imaginable height of creative and commercial success.

Damon and I are both fortunate to have benefited enough from our musical endeavours to each have our own first-class recording facilities in west London. We are in this particular location because of the third musician. We want him to record a hook for the song and this is where he wished to do it. He possesses a deep, deep soul voice that evokes not just the specific time we wish to reference, the mid-eighties, but the theme CAS wants to explore in this song, which is intended for his debut album, for release on XL Recordings.

This theme is the ephemeral nature of fame. The song is to be called 'Everything's For Sale'. It may become a worldwide hit. Or it may never be released, or even completed. At this formative stage of the creative process uncertainty is a given.

This third musician's name is Alexander O'Neal, and he is a sixty-five-year-old former Prince associate from Natchez, Mississippi, by way of Minneapolis, where he was the original lead singer for The Time, before making three solo albums with legendarily great production and writing duo, and fellow Prince acolytes, Jimmy Jam and Terry Lewis. These albums were quite successful in the US, but in the UK he became a huge crossover pop star, scoring Top 10 singles with his songs 'Criticize', 'If You Were Here Tonight' and his duet with Cherrelle, 'Saturday Love'. His second album, *Hearsay*, went triple platinum in the UK, and he sold out three consecutive nights at Wembley Arena.

His appetites were always legendary. Along with most other eighties success stories, his star faded through the nineties. With each new decade music changes irrevocably and only a tiny number of musicians can transcend the decade they found fame in. In recent times Alexander has appeared on reality TV programmes *Just the Two of Us*, *Wife Swap* and *Celebrity Big Brother*.

When CAS gave me a list of the eighties voices he wished to try to feature on his album, I knew that Alexander O'Neal was the one to pursue. My guess was that we would find him in LA, perhaps living near the airport, but it turns out he lives in Manchester.

We're here to capture the voice of this weathered soul survivor, and prior to the session he has been supplied with a map in the form of a recording, a guide version of the song that Damon, CAS and I made in London. Our preparation and planning have been exemplary and, while I have experienced enough 'best-laid plans' scenarios to know that nothing is ever guaranteed, an hour into the session we have a heartbreakingly soulful performance from Alexander O'Neal on our hard drive. CAS says to me that it is important to absorb moments like this. I agree. I have had many of them but they always feel dreamlike. Alexander says he needs to buy a bed, inexplicably, and with that he is gone.

PRELUDE 2: HOLLYWOOD
4 MAY 2019

Two weeks have passed. I'm driving down Sunset listening to the recordings I've been working on with CAS. I text him to say how good they sound. He texts back:

It's mad u should say that I've been playing bits we made all week/weekend

Another text:

I have never played my music so much Rich, man. It's exciting beyond comprehension

And a third:

Got my new mask fitting Thursday

I'm in LA with Esta for Adele's thirty-first birthday party. It takes place in the house where the *Godfather* horse-head scene was filmed. Adele has rented the property for the occasion, but should anyone be house-hunting, it's on sale for $135 million.

It's approaching midnight when I hear Esta urgently beckoning. I wander over to where she's standing and she introduces me to a tall, tuxedo-clad man sporting shades and dreadlocks. He exudes a megawatt charisma. His real name is Shawn Carter but the world knows him as Jay-Z. He is arguably the greatest rapper of all time and definitely one of my favourite artists, period.

Since making a failed attempt to license his first album for UK release in 1996, I have spent a great deal of time listening to his music over a period now spanning nearly twenty-five years. As well as being one of our greatest living storytellers, he is also a wildly successful entrepreneur, a former drug dealer who now has businesses encompassing the worlds of fashion, beverages, real estate and sports, not to mention his Roc Nation record label and management company. He would be able to purchase the property we are in should he so desire. He has a light energy yet possesses an intensely commanding presence.

There is a third member of the huddle. I've never met her either but she is intensely familiar. She is Beyoncé Knowles, and alongside our host tonight she is the world's most beloved female artist, or perhaps artist overall.

Before I have formulated my first words to say to Hova, perhaps a 'thank you' for the lifetime of enjoyment and inspiration I have got from his music, he begins to talk to me. He is immediately intimate and engaged, aware of me and what I do, and full of enthusiastic praise for XL. I'm wrong-footed and not sure what to say.

The awkward silence is broken by Esta. 'Look how much he's smiling. It's pathetic,' she says, of flattered and starstruck me, to the billionaire B-boy genius christened Shawn Carter, originally of Brooklyn's notorious Marcy housing projects. Her bullshit detector ever switched on, she has decided to challenge Jay-Z, saying to him, 'I bet you can't even name three acts on the label.'

But he can.

PART 1

Part 1 Playlist

CASISDEAD 'Pat Earrings' (XL Recordings)

Gorillaz 'Stylo' (Parlophone)

Alexander O'Neal 'Criticize' (Tabu)

Pusha T 'Drug Dealers Anonymous (feat. Jay-Z)' (G.O.O.D Music)

The Beatles 'Taxman' (Parlophone)

Wham! 'Everything She Wants' (CBS)

Teardrop Explodes 'Tiny Children' (Mercury)

Fun Boy Three 'The Lunatics (Have Taken Over The Asylum)' (Chrysalis)

Adam and the Ants 'Kings Of The Wild Frontier' (CBS)

Mike Steiphenson 'Burundi Black' (Barclay)

Joni Mitchell 'The Jungle Line' (Asylum)

Curtis Mayfield 'The Makings Of You' (Curtom)

Bobby Womack 'Across 110th Street' (UA)

Gil Scott-Heron 'The Bottle' (Arista)

Blondie 'Rapture' (Chrysalis)

Grandmaster Flash 'Adventures Of Grandmaster Flash On The Wheels Of Steel' (Sugar Hill)

Malcolm McLaren 'Buffalo Gals' (Charisma)

Carson Robison and His Old Timers 'Buffalo Boy Go 'Round The Outside' (Columbia)

Herbie Hancock 'Rockit' (Columbia)

Art of Noise 'Beatbox' (ZTT)

Beastie Boys 'Cookie Puss' (Ratcage)

Schoolly D 'P.S.K.' (Schoolly D Records)

LL Cool J 'Rock The Bells' (Def Jam)

Beastie Boys 'Hold It Now, Hit It' (Def Jam)

SOS Band 'Just Be Good To Me' (Tabu)

23 Skidoo 'Kundalini' (Fetish)

Coldcut 'Beats + Pieces' (Ahead Of Our Time)

Bernard Wright 'Who Do You Love' (Manhattan)

Meli'sa Morgan 'Fool's Paradise' (Capitol)

Zapp 'Computer Love' (Warner Bros)

Grandmaster Flash and the Furious Five 'The Message' (Sugar Hill)

Eric B. & Rakim 'Eric B. Is President' (Zakia)

Fonda Rae 'Over Like A Fat Rat' (Vanguard)

The Mohawks 'The Champ' (Pama Records)

James Brown 'Get Up, Get Into It, Get Involved' (King)

Mountain 'Long Red (Live)' (Windfall)

Audio Two 'Top Billin'' (First Priority)

EPMD 'It's My Thing' (FRESH)

Public Enemy 'Rebel Without A Pause' (Def Jam)

JB's 'The Grunt' (King)

Kings of Pressure 'You Know How To Reach Us' (Let's Go)

Son of Bazerk 'J-Dubs Theme' (SOUL)

Biz Markie 'Pickin' Boogers' (Cold Chillin')

De La Soul 'Plug Tunin'' (Tommy Boy)

Mantronix 'King Of The Beats' (Capitol)

Salt-N-Pepa 'My Mic Sounds Nice' (Next Plateau)

BDP 'South Bronx' (B-Boy Records)

BDP 'P Is Free' (B-Boy Records)

Super Lover Cee & Casanova Rud 'Do The James' (DNA)

Melvin Bliss 'Synthetic Substitute' (Sunburst)

Ultramagnetic MCs 'Travelling At The Speed Of Thought' (Next Plateau)

Ultramagnetic MCs 'Give The Drummer Some' (Next Plateau)

Max Romeo 'Chase The Devil' (Island)

London Posse 'Money Mad' (Justice)

Demon Boyz 'Vibes' (Music Of Life)

She Rockers 'Give It A Rest' (Music Of Life)

Lizzy Mercier Descloux 'Funky Stuff' (Ze)

Grace Jones 'Slave To The Rhythm' (ZTT)

Cameo 'She's Strange' (Phonogram)

Trouble Funk 'Let's Get Small' (Island)

Luther Vandross 'Never Too Much' (Epic)

Supreme DJ Nyborn 'Versatile Extension' (Payroll)

Derek B 'Get Down' (Music Of Life)

EVEN WHEN YOU'RE HEALTHY AND YOUR COLOUR SCHEMES DELIGHT

The Beatles were my gateway.

When I was seven years old, I used to get my grandma to take me to a shop dedicated to the Fab Four, a small room above another shop in Carnaby Street. She would buy me a badge, or a copy of *The Beatles Book* monthly magazine. I loved being there with her, not yet embarrassed by the company of a parent or grandparent. She bought me Hunter Davies's biography of The Beatles and I studied it from yellow cover to cover. There was something in there for me, something I needed to learn, and my childhood Beatles fandom gave me an incalculable amount of inspiration. From as early as I can remember, music meant escape. Freedom.

I cherished my first electric guitar, an eighth birthday present from my parents, purchased from Edgware Music Centre on the high street, and took guitar lessons until I was told that in order to progress further, I would have to do exams. I point-blank refused and never took another lesson. From an early age I wished to reject any institution I came across. I was committed to this approach.

I was astounded by the visions I witnessed on *Top of the Pops* every Thursday evening. It was so utterly different from what I saw around me.

My first and last gig as frontman was at a local Jewish youth centre, playing my guitar and singing a song that started 'Big men, little men, houses and cars', to an audience of mostly Israeli exchange students who'd come over to stay in Edgware for a week. I was ten. I think the words were from some biblical source and I'd put the lyric to three chords: G, C and D.

Me and an older boy tried to form a band. He had a girlfriend and she was in the band too. We split up during the rehearsals for our first gig, after he told me that I didn't know how to sing in tune, and that I had in fact been singing out of tune at my debut youth-centre gig. I told him that lots of great bands had singers who couldn't sing. We were both right.

But at age eleven my career as a frontman was over. This particular job, I have since learned, is partly about having the resilience (generally born out of intense desire and not a little insecurity) to withstand brutal rejection. The more different and bizarre your onstage appearance and performance, the more outlandish and unlikely, the more you are risking, the more spectacular the results are likely to be. Or the more ignominious the failure. That's part of what an audience responds to.

They don't realise it but they are seeing a high-wire act. If you are actually afflicted with the type of mental condition that could threaten your entire existence, it might help you succeed should you find yourself in the role of frontman. Stability is not a qualification for this post. Great performers make it look easy but it is in fact almost impossible and can go wrong at any moment. Like a prizefight, the glory is there for the taking if you can take the blows.

I couldn't.

My desire for front-of-stage glory seemed to wane at the first hint of negative feedback, meaning it was not the place for me. I had a feeling that music was for me, but this was one future job option ruled out.

My stint as frontman being so short-lived only intensified my admiration for the pop stars of 1981. Every issue of *Smash Hits* was a journey into the barely comprehensible universe of these fantasy creatures, each the front of a musical unit. George Michael from Wham!, Julian Cope from the Teardrop Explodes, Terry Hall from The Specials (and then the Fun Boy Three).

None seemed more fantastic than Adam Ant, lead singer of Adam and the Ants. My room became a shrine to him, the images carefully cut out of *Smash Hits* magazine and Blu-tacked to the walls. His performances seemed angry and somehow this was part of the appeal. There I was, on the sofa in the living room at my parents' house. Thursday night, 7pm. There was he, on *Top of the Pops*, on the TV in the corner. Adam Ant, formerly Stuart Leslie Goddard, bassist in pub-rock hopefuls Bazooka Joe. Sporting warpaint, a military jacket and feathers, gyrating wildly, while his band, the Ants, provided support like the loyal soldiers that for now they were. He was beautiful and somehow indecipherable.

These were the Ants mark two and they had recently replaced the whole original line-up of the band, who had abandoned Adam to back fourteen-year-old singer Annabella Lwin and become Bow Wow Wow. This coup was engineered by their manager, Malcolm Robert Andrew McLaren. This Jewish punk Svengali, former art student and proprietor (with his partner Vivienne Westwood) of Kings Road clothing store Sex, had grown up, unbelievably, in Edgware, and attended the same comprehensive school as my sister, a few years before her. He was present in Paris for the 1968 student riots, witnessing the Situationists and their tactics: chaos, spectacle and slogan.

Adam Ant saw Malcolm McLaren, the manager of the Sex Pistols, as a genius. But the feeling may not have been mutual. And Malcolm seemed to have had dubious ethics. He was a trickster. A talented thief. But he had both courage and deep insight. In a *Face* magazine interview I read in June 1983, he summarised his philosophy: 'You can get away with anything if you've got enough neck.'

Adam sported the same type of hussar jacket that Jimi Hendrix had worn, and the militaristic theme was apt. Adam Ant was at war not just with the former manager who betrayed him and stole his band, but more damagingly, due to his mental health issues, with himself.

As a ten-and-a-half-year-old record buyer in Edgware, I was delighted by the free poster that came folded around my 'Stand And Deliver' 7-inch single, but given the deep creasing the folding caused - it is not easy to fit a 30 x 20-inch pin-up around a 7-inch square - I deemed it unworthy for Blu-tacking to the wall, and instead kept it as vinyl packaging. The free gift, like many other aspects of the Adam and the Ants scenario, was disappointing and not quite right.

Adam had a history of behavioural disorders dating back to early childhood. The son of an alcoholic, abusive and mostly absent father, the terrifying attacks on his mother that Adam witnessed his father carrying out as a small child had prompted hallucinatory dissociative episodes. Adam Ant, my favourite pop star, a god on my bedroom wall, had recently been discharged from a psychiatric ward at nearby Friern Barnet hospital after a suicide attempt. The whole character of Adam Ant was part of a life-or-death personal reinvention.

Adam's dream of being managed by Malcolm McLaren turned out to be a nightmare, but it provided impetus. Before hotfooting it with all Adam's musicians to form Bow Wow Wow, McLaren, in the curator mode which he would shortly go on to occupy to inspirational effect in his own artistic career, had given Adam a mixtape he had compiled which included Buddy Holly, the Village People, Egyptian oud music by Farid Al Atrash and a 1971 song called 'Burundi Black' made by French composer and producer Michel Bernholc, working under the pseudonym Mike Steiphenson.

'Burundi Black' incorporated an East African field recording from 1967 of twenty-five drummers in a commune called Bukirasazi, who would go on to tour the world as the Royal Drummers of Burundi. Bernholc had overdubbed guitar and piano on top. 'Burundi Black' would become the basis of the new Adam and the Ants sound.

The plundering was actually second-hand. Joni Mitchell had already borrowed 'Burundi Black' some five years earlier for her song 'The Jungle Line'. Prince would later cite the album that 'The Jungle Line' was part of, *The Hissing Of Summer Lawns*, as a major inspiration, the last thing he heard before he embarked on creating his unmatchable run of eighties albums.

What was invisible to fans like myself was that much of the untethered nature of Adam Ant's creativity, his ambition and his performances was related to his mental condition. He suffered from bipolar disorder. His musical partner Marco Pirroni said that he had a response to the mental state of his famous and successful friend and colleague that was typical of the time: 'What's he got to be depressed about? And then you realise they're not depressed about anything. They're just depressed.' Adam had plenty to be depressed about, even in the midst of his success.

I wondered how I'd had the astonishing good fortune to find a copy of Adam's solo debut 'Friend Or Foe', which was actually signed by him, casually sitting in my local record shop display rack, the week it was released. Turns out Adam had of his own volition signed thousands of copies, in a frantic attempt to increase sales, and my treasured souvenir was evidence of his desperation.

I had wanted to be a frontman like Adam Ant, to receive that level of attention and validation, but frustratingly I wasn't built for it. However, I did have an understanding of what the role entailed, and could relate to the people who played it, and that would be a useful attribute in my future endeavours. Perhaps I was lucky to have not had the necessary constitution to pursue this line of work myself.

IT WAS ALL A DREAM

40p (Eire ir 59½p inc. VAT) JANUARY 6 - 19 1983

Smash HITS

ALL-STAR REQUEST ISSUE

MALCOLM McLAREN coming up to scratch

MODERN ROMANCE • THE TUBE • THE JAM

SPANDAU BALLET • SHAKIN' STEVENS • TOYAH and lots more

Religion was ever-present in my childhood. My family were observant Jews with a rigorous adherence to traditions that was more moderate than those of the Hassidic sect but just as ingrained. For many people who grow up in a family with strict religious beliefs, it's entirely possible, natural in fact, to accept these beliefs without question; that's how institutionalised religions have thrived for centuries, providing comforting answers to unfathomable mysteries.

But I struggled to embrace the unlikely-sounding things I was taught in Jewish primary school and Sunday Hebrew classes. The whole version of God that they explained, and how we were supposed to behave so as not to displease this punishing, judgemental entity, did not appeal. I felt like I was being pushed around. When I was seven, I announced in Hebrew class that God was not real. Edgware United Synagogue was not happy with me. We were there to offer praise to God, not to doubt his existence.

Initially, I inherited my parents' beliefs, then rejected them (and in turn all organised religion) and embraced an atheistic worldview. Eventually, I began to develop an awareness of the beauty and truth inherent in all religions, and an interest in gaining some understanding of them. The esoteric parts of most belief systems are not made that apparent. They have become the fringe, pushed to the margins so the more mainstream versions can be marketed. Much like the entertainment industry.

Mainstream entertainment, like mainstream religion, is used to control people. But there are threads that run through all religions and I see music in similar terms. Both religion and music provide ways of seeing the unseeable and a necessary escape from the sometimes unbearable harshness of reality. Ideas can be communicated about death and the worlds beyond the one we inhabit.

There is the same amount of great music being made now as

there was in 1967 or 1988 or whenever your 'golden age' was. Equally, most people will never again get the thrill of the music they heard when they were teenagers, and so they assume that was the best music ever. To them it was.

It's hard to comprehend now just how important the music press of my youth was. These publications, along with *Top of the Pops*, were our internet. As a small child there was *Look-in*, a sort of junior *TV Times* with wonky cover paintings of the likes of Abba and Bryan Ferry. This was a gateway to the drily witty *Smash Hits*, the militant and political *NME*, and both *Record Mirror* and *Blues & Soul*, where I discovered more about the myriad forms of black music I was increasingly interested in.

NME especially had a powerful and formative effect, its punk ethic still intact when I began reading it in 1981. It used its stance to connect naturally with reggae, soul and hip-hop: all music that was opposed to The Man. The anti-establishment stance of the paper and many of the artists it wrote about deeply resonated with me.

Its 1982 best-of-the-year top 30 included albums by Curtis Mayfield, Bobby Womack and Gil Scott-Heron. I could not imagine that I would one day interact with all of these soul legends, writing and producing with Gil, producing and touring with Bobby, sampling Curtis Mayfield in a recording I made with Sampha.

As far as I could see, Jews from north-west London didn't make records. Pop culture offered no reflection of how and where I grew up, but this made it all the more alluring. It represented total escape. While my childhood played itself out in Edgware, influences from the music that soundtracked clubs like The Wag, places I would attend a few years later, would begin to be heard in the music made by the fledgling pop stars in attendance. On their records 'Wham! Rap' and 'Chant No.1', Wham! and Spandau Ballet made well-meaning but lightweight and disconnected attempts at rap. These emerged, alongside Adam Ant's 'Ant Rap', some years before the UK had an actual hip-hop scene, the pop artists beating the underground to the punch, with mixed results.

It was down to former Sex Pistols, Adam and the Ants and Bow Wow Wow manager Malcolm McLaren, of all people, to make the first really impactful UK contribution to hip-hop with 'Buffalo Gals'. He was not a producer of any recognisable type, and he took the sensible step of working with a master craftsman, the producer who went on to define the pop sound of the eighties, Trevor Horn.

McLaren, casting himself as artist/curator, conceived of the notion of combining two indigenous American art forms in one short song: hip-hop and hillbilly square dance music. The refrain of Carson Robison's 'Buffalo Boy Go 'Round The Outside' was set to a street-friendly rhythm courtesy of Trevor Horn. I was enthralled. McLaren was clearly not a frontman. But his audacity – his chutzpah – allowed him to do whatever he wanted.

Malcolm was dabbling only briefly in the then underground culture of the Bronx but he did it with a punk edge. At the end of the song we hear a female caller to the World's Famous Supreme Team late-night radio show answering the question of how come she was up so late: 'too much of that snow white'. That wasn't the only thing getting up people's noses. McLaren had an unfailing ability to annoy people.

He appears on the cover of the 6 January 1983 issue of *Smash Hits* with a pair of turntables. I eyed them up. Vinyl is flying all around him. The DJ equipment was very much a prop and Malcolm would have had no idea what to do with it. On the letters page Graham Nickson from Truro writes his own review of 'Buffalo Gals': 'A nauseating drivel that insults the human ear with its monstrous gibbering shrieks and vile noises.'

Regardless of his Cornish critic, 'Buffalo Gals' would earn the respect of the world that spawned it. It's a catalytic recording that has been sampled hundreds of times by rap producers from J Dilla to RZA, and had a spectacular and unforeseeable influence on other musicians. In making it Malcolm McLaren became a mainstream pop star, appearing on *Top of the Pops* and the cover of *Smash Hits*. Some people may have found him irritating. But he was on my wall and in my growing record collection.

Later, I would develop the viewpoint that there is no greater achievement in music than to inspire other musicians. Only the most original work tends to do this.

'Buffalo Gals' found itself on a mixtape Herbie Hancock was given by his godson. Hancock thought the scratching in the song sounded avant-garde, like the noises he had sought out for his high-wire, improvisational *Mwandishi* project. Hancock, legendary composer, jazz keyboard maestro, Buddhist, decided to use scratching on his next record, and said: 'I hoped it would sound as innovative as what Malcolm McLaren was doing.' Recruiting Material founder, producer and bassist Bill Laswell, Herbie Hancock made his own version of a hip-hop song, with scratching by Grandmixer D ST to the fore, and called it 'Rockit'.

He was delighted with the result but his colleagues felt differently. When he played it to his manager and bandmates they all hated it and told him his fans would feel the same and desert him in droves. He followed his instincts and ignored them. 'Rockit' became the biggest hit of Herbie Hancock's entire career.

Malcolm McLaren was a visionary chancer. When he put together a support bill for his artist Bow Wow Wow's debut New York show at The Ritz, he was in full curatorial flight and ensured that the line-up represented the four pillars of hip-hop. While Fab 5 Freddy MCed, breakdancing was represented by the Rock Steady Crew, Futura 2000 sprayed graffiti live onstage and both Afrika Bambaataa and Jazzy Jay DJed. Was McLaren actually an artist? Not in the traditional sense. But he would influence the creation of a lot of art.

A few streets away, four Jewish teenagers calling themselves the Beastie Boys made their first ever 12", 'Cookie Puss'. It was a pastiche of Malcolm McLaren's British novelty hip-hop song. Having liberated something within Herbie Hancock, 'Buffalo Gals' was working its magic again. Adam Yauch, Michael Diamond and Adam Horovitz were not yet known individually as MCA, Mike D and Ad-Rock, and their friend Kate Schellenbach was still in the band. They were in their post-punk hardcore infancy and had not quite started rapping yet. They had fallen in love with 'Buffalo Gals', which had become an unlikely anthem in New York's downtown nightlife scene. Like McLaren they were refugees from punk, finding a new energy in hip-hop.

Unknown to any of them, yet another Jewish fan of punk and hardcore was falling in love with rap music at this time. Rick Rubin, formerly guitarist in The Pricks, had pressed the first record by his new band Hose in a sleeve referencing Mondrian and created a name and logo for what was at this stage his fantasy of a record label: Def Jam. His partner was an ambitious Queens-bred promoter called Russell Simmons, also known as Russell Rush, whose brother Joseph Simmons aka Run was one half of Run-DMC.

It was apparent to Simmons that the Beastie Boys could rap, and that their punk value system made them anti-establishment outsiders, opposed to The Man. All this would help them succeed with the legitimate hip-hop crowd.

But there was another factor that excited Russell Simmons. In the Beasties' whiteness he saw the type of commercial potential he could build a corporate empire on. They were white insiders who were Jewish outsiders. Punk outsiders who rapped like insiders. Like millions of other teenagers, I would have my mind blown by their debut album.

In 1985 Mike D, just out of his teens, purchased two copies of a 12-inch single from a record store in Manhattan, an establishment on Carmine Street in the West Village called Vinylmania. Back in Edgware, I was turning fourteen. Five years later I would be serving customers from behind the counter in this same New York record store. Mike had never purchased 'doubles' before. This record justified the outlay. It was Schoolly D's self-released, reverb-heavy, proto-gangsta monster, 'P.S.K.', with another classic on the flip, 'Gucci Time'.

The original pressing of this record is to this day a perfect artefact, representing a special moment in the history of music. The song is incredible, and so is the physical object.

Mike D, on 'P.S.K.': 'It was the record we wanted to make. We couldn't believe someone had made it, and we wished we had made it. Because it was *the most* punk rock rap record ever. How loud can you make something by being really minimal? At the time I was like: how do you do that?' Rick Rubin knew.

As a child Rick had been interested in magic. The wizardry was somehow present in his production. He had already completed work on the debut album by LL Cool J, *Radio*. It would be a platinum success and it consisted of virtually nothing other than LL's rhymes and Rick's skeletally programmed drum machines. It was a spartan triumph, thrillingly bare.

I purchased 12-inches of Schoolly D's 'P.S.K.' and Def Jam's early Rick Rubin-produced minimalist masterpieces, LL Cool J's 'Rock The Bells' and the Beastie Boys' 'Hold It Now, Hit It'. Seeing Rick's name on these records and learning about who he was, he was immediately a hero to me.

Later I would ask Rick why these records were so astonishingly bare: 'The more sounds we use, the harder it is for each to be seen in its best light. The silence between each note is what allows us to notice the change of condition [silence vs sound]. The work has always been about getting to the essential and removing everything else. I thought the title of producer implied building things up. My interest was in breaking them down.'

My connection to these tough, noisy but minimal independent record label 12-inch singles in striking and distinctive house bags, made by maverick and uncompromising producers and entrepreneurs, was immediate and permanent. Somehow, I was going to have a go at this. Or something like it.

WELCOME TO THE CHURCH OF WHAT'S HAPPENING NOW

ADS (01-261

HARVEY GOLDSMITH in conjunction with THE DAILY EXPRESS presents

CLUB FANTASTIC DISCO EVENINGS

LIVE ON STAGE

WHAM!

with D.J.
GARY CROWLEY

Special Guests
Each Evening

THE LYCEUM
Strand London W.C. 2

SUN 13, MON 14, TUES 15, WED 16 & THURS 17 NOVEMBER 7.30 pm

TICKETS 5.00 FROM BOX OFFICE LONDON THEATRE BOOKINGS
PREMIER BOX OFFICE KEITH PROWSE ALBEMARLE STAR GREEN & USUAL AGENTS

At the dawn of the 1980s Jimmy Jam and Terry Lewis picked up on something Sly Stone had started ten years earlier. In the songs they made for artists including Change, SOS Band and that native of Natchez, Mississippi, Alexander O'Neal, they used drum machines to create a syncopated, repetitive rhythm track under very musical playing. Sly had used a Rhythm King Maestro, which he christened his 'Funkbox', and apparently only deployed in order to upset his drummer. It would have been the ultimate insult to a musician, at that time, to replace them with a plastic box.

Prince was also in on the future funk action. He favoured the LM-1 Drum Computer, designed by Roger Linn, who would go on to invent the MPC for Akai. Jam and Lewis's weapon of choice was the same as Rick Rubin's – the Roland TR-808 Rhythm Composer, the most bassy of these plastic beasts.

Costing $1,000 when they first went on sale in 1980, the 808 was discontinued after three years, during which time only 12,000 machines were built. A decent original model purchased on eBay now will set the keen producer back at least five times its original price.

A clash between the coldness of machine-driven rhythms and the warmth of human instrumental and vocal performance became the blueprint for a lot of the music which has most excited me.

While Jam and Lewis honed their production skills I was getting on fine at our local all-Jewish primary school, but towards my tenth birthday I became very specific in my view that not only did I not want to go to Jewish secondary school, but I did not want to attend the local comprehensive that my sister went to either, despite the fact that all my friends would be doing one or the other of these. It said in *NME* that a band whose records I'd never heard but who sounded cool, 23 Skidoo, formed at a school in Hampstead. I had seen Hampstead on the map of the London Underground; it was only six stops away, and apparently people went there and formed bands. To me, the idea of going to a secular school in Hampstead represented some sort of escape. To my mum, there was academic potential in the scheme. Perhaps this was a step on the journey that would lead to a mythical temple of higher education like Oxford or Cambridge.

She asked the headmaster of my primary school what she should do. He responded that not only was the school in question an unaffordable fee-paying establishment but that admission was dependent on a challenging entrance exam, and his primary school did not prepare its pupils for this type of exam. The solution he proposed was to let me sit the exam, and fail. Instead I passed and was offered a place.

Having twisted everyone's arm to make the whole caper occur, as soon as I arrived at the school I hated every single thing about it and could not have been more miserable. Institutions like this still existed in an old-fashioned world of rugby and strict uniform and stricter discipline. Teachers addressed pupils by surname only. Pupils had to address teacher as 'sir'. The 'masters', as they were also called, were always keen to enforce their superiority via rules that were petty and pointless at best. Why we were not allowed to wear underwear to play rugby, and why a member of the teaching staff had to sit in the changing room with us while we got changed was never explained, and it would not be allowed now. I made three friends there, and we stuck together.

I was an obedient enough pupil for the first couple of years but me and education, of the scholastic type anyway, soon started to lose interest in each other. School made me feel bad. Music made me feel good, and I had decided I was going to spend my life in music, somehow.

My parents could see no possibility of this working. Their dream was for me to get a law degree. Their feeling was that many teenagers liked music but that didn't make it a viable career option. They say now that I pursued music in spite of them, not because of them. Somehow I had faith in what I believed to be the right path for me. Perhaps I had inherited faith itself from them. Due to their own conservative upbringing, and the expectations they had of me, my parents made our relationship harder than it needed to be. I wasn't really doing anything wrong. But to them I was 'off the rails'.

My father had navigated successfully through the working world, being employed first as a store manager for Marks and Spencer and then becoming self-employed as a life insurance salesman, which offered him an autonomy he preferred.

His brother Phillip was a fine artist who undertook graphic design work in order to pay the bills. Phillip's daughters, my older cousins Lucy and Sally, gave me an early insight into how the line between musical fantasies involving my heroes and our humdrum reality could be blurred.

Visiting our house for Passover dinner, Lucy told me that she'd seen Adam and the Ants in concert the night before. I didn't know what she meant when she said she'd 'seen' them. How? On TV? No, she said, live. The shocking reality of this started to dawn on me. I asked her, incredulous, if she was saying she had been in THE SAME ROOM as Adam and the Ants? How did she achieve this? She explained that she had bought tickets. I was baffled. She was just an ordinary person. She was like me. And she was telling me that anyone could go to a concert.

This revelation was huge. I recovered my composure for long enough to consult the adverts in *NME*, as Lucy advised, and struck gold: an advert for the 'Club Fantastic Disco Evening' at The Lyceum, the Strand, London WC2, featuring Wham! live, with Gary Crowley DJing. I lobbied my parents to get me a ticket and eventually they could take it no longer. This would be the first show I would attend. Although this was before George Michael had fully tapped into his songwriting, arranging and producing genius, and he was dressed in a tight-fitting tennis outfit and hitting shuttlecocks into the crowd that he had first put down his shorts, it was a start.

Time Out, in its guide to London property, refers to Edgware as an 'unloved suburb with nothing in the way of nightlife – houses are cheap and if you've a spare decade there's a chance gentrification will have caught on by the time the kids start secondary school'. But people were saying that forty years ago.

However, Edgware had two portals to other worlds. One was the tube station, the final and most northerly stop on the Northern line, also known as 'the misery line'. Edgware station presented opportunities for socialising with the dressed-up mostly Jewish teenagers who used to congregate on its forecourt, members of an undocumented youth subculture known as 'Becks'. The moniker was an abbreviation of the popular Jewish girl's name 'Rebecca'. This was a maligned and derided niche suburban youth tribe, based in Edgware, Golders Green, Southgate, Gants Hill and Enfield. Becks made low-rent attempts at glamour and were in thrall to materialism and lightweight culture. They liked eighties pop and hair gel.

Everyone hated Becks: other Jewish kids who weren't part of this self-appointed 'in-crowd', the cooler and more sophisticated kids at my school from Hampstead and Camden, and the skinheads who terrorised them.

Outside of Becks' own culture, they were social lepers. 'Beck' was perhaps more of an insult than the name of a youth movement, but at age thirteen I liked the idea of being part of a scene, and made eventually successful efforts to infiltrate it.

I attended the Saturday-night discos at Edgware synagogue (starting after the Sabbath ended) and the Sunday-night events at Busby's on Charing Cross Road. I loitered outside the Coffee Cup on Hampstead High Street on a Thursday evening, until I got rumbled by a fellow pupil from my school who announced to everyone the next day: 'Russell is an Edgware Beck.' I was defiant in the face of this mockery. Being a Beck, I protested, was a good way to meet girls. But it was dawning on me that this was the only upside. Once I had been allowed to enter the movement, I decided it was rubbish, continuing a lifelong pattern of disowning my goals once they were achieved. The equivalent scene today would likely have a significant worldwide social media presence, but back in the early eighties such movements flew under the radar.

The spiritual home of a tribe called Becks, Edgware station, was a ten-minute walk from our house. Then it was a mere nine stops on the tube to Camden Town, another five stops to Tottenham Court Road. These were intensely alive destinations. Most significantly, Edgware High Street had a musical portal; a record shop with lurid green frontage and carrier bags to match. This was Loppylugs, less than five minutes from our house. I had been a loyal customer from the age of seven, and this was where I found treasures like The Beatles' *1967–70* compilation, aka 'The Blue Album', and Adam Ant's *Friend Or Foe*. I wanted in, and I had a weekend job there by 1986, when I was fifteen. Fellow Edgware native Trevor Jackson was already ensconced behind the counter. A couple of years older than me, he had a similar level of musical enthusiasm, and was a talented visual artist to boot. He made sure that I, the junior employee, was the one who hung the heavy and often wet metal grilles along the shopfront at the end of each day.

Records by Wham! were among the most popular in the shop. George Michael had himself until recently been serving customers in Edgware, working in his father's restaurant, Mr Jacks, at the other end of the high street.

I'd had my first taste of entrepreneurial activity just before this, working in Wembley market at the age of fourteen, on a stall run by my then girlfriend's mum. She sold belts and handbags, and while, outside of the 5am wake-up, the Wembley market experience was tolerable, I realised that the non-musical working world held no interest for me. I have always liked to work but never enough to do it in a way that doesn't involve music.

Both education and any type of 'real' job were unfeasible. Equally I knew that to have the independence I craved, the freedom from the restrictions that seemed to affect everyone in the area where I grew up, I would need to have money of my own. Using my dad's hi-fi, I was making pause tapes on cassette as soon as I worked out it was possible to do such a thing, stringing together snippets from other records to make something new. I called this series 'Def Sounds'.

I would soon be able to get a small amount of work at friends' birthday parties, hiring a twin-deck mobile console and a modest sound system from Youngs in Kentish Town, coming out as much as £100 ahead once I had paid the hire fees, which seemed like a miraculous feat of musical and economic alchemy. I used the mobile-disco name 'Bionic Boogie', creating a business card featuring a hand-drawn logo of a bionic man at the decks, the telephone number of our family home in Edgware listed.

But mobile DJing was not a role for someone with strong personal musical beliefs. The mobile jock is there to provide a service and give the people what they want. I only wanted to play records I loved.

The next step was to hire-purchase the console from Youngs and set about teaching myself to DJ properly. Countless hours would be spent in my bedroom in Edgware, attempting to emulate the techniques perfected by home-grown DJ superheroes like Cutmaster Swift, Pogo and Biznizz, all utilising techniques pioneered in New York by DJ Kool Herc not long before.

It was difficult to achieve seamless mixes using mobile DJ equipment that was not built for this purpose. The infinitely more suitable Technics SL1200 turntables were nowhere near affordable, not yet, costing £399 each.

A record called 'Beats + Pieces', the work of London DJs Matt Black and Jonathan More, aka Coldcut, released on their own aptly named Ahead Of Our Time label, was the first 12-inch record I had doubles of. 'Beats + Pieces' was based on John Bonham's drum intro to Led Zeppelin's 'When The Levee Breaks'.

Alternating between turntable one and turntable two, I attempted to create a seamless loop, precarious though the set-up of these decks was. I did not know I was actually accessing Led Zeppelin, via Coldcut. I never considered where they had got the drums from.

The bizarre racket I created in my quest for the elusive break-beat merry-go-round would have been an irritating mystery to my family, who were surprisingly understanding of this aspect of my activities. It was challenging to achieve the desired effect using inadequate equipment. But I got to know every one of my records back to front, their song structures imprinted in my mind. I would later learn that these structures, which I needed to memorise in order to be fully prepared for my DJ sets, were also known as arrangements.

My DJing activities and weekend job at Loppylugs were infinitely more important to me than school. Trevor and I were keen to educate our customers, whose tastes often ran more to Dire Straits and Meat Loaf than Mantronix. But records by all these artists were in stock, because this was a neighbourhood record shop, offering a community service (albeit one not motivated by altruism of any sort) and catering to all tastes. At this time there was at least one independent record shop on every high street. May they rest in peace.

Loppylugs was a suburban portal to exotic musical climes; a direct source of vinyl, just as a transformative period for both hip-hop and house music would dawn. As the 12-inches arrived, we vinyl acolytes were there to receive them.

Despite our lobbying to expand its range, Loppylugs stocked domestic vinyl only: UK-originated releases, including licensed versions of American records. The really high-grade product was shrink-wrapped US 12-inch singles and albums imported direct from New York. To obtain these treasures I travelled fourteen stops on the tube to Tottenham Court Road, and entered the tiny, thrilling Groove Records store at 52 Greek Street. It was owned and operated by a quiet Londoner called Tim Palmer, along with his brother Chris and an unlikely musical expert in the shape of his mum Jean.

Tim, also the founder of a label called Citybeat Records, would go on to play a significant part in my future endeavours.

My neighbour Daniel and his elder brother Paul were observant

47

orthodox Jews and kept their heads covered at all times. They also had another belief: the power of eighties soul music. They particularly loved Luther Vandross, who was always referred to familiarly, on a first-name basis, as just 'Luther'. Eighties soul, along with eighties pop, was big in Edgware. It was one of many suburban pockets of appreciation for this kind of music, which was touching on the mainstream anyway.

In 1985 we were listening to Robbie Vincent on GLR and Tony Blackburn on Radio London, playing Bernard Wright's 'Who Do You Love', SOS Band's 'Weekend Girl' and Steve Arrington's 'Dancin' In The Key Of Life'. The following year we would hear Meli'sa Morgan's 'Fool's Paradise', Zapp's 'Computer Love' and Nu Shooz's 'I Can't Wait'. Alexander O'Neal would release a series of classic singles through this period. We were awash in great soul tunes.

I wanted to possess all these records but the cost of vinyl was prohibitive. The *Street Sounds* series of soul compilation albums eased the pain a bit. These albums, and subsequently the *Street Sounds Electro* companion series that would do an equally good curatorial job with hip-hop, were lovingly compiled, and introduced me to gems I would not have got hold of otherwise.

(The compilation series that would have the most impact on me was the work of a livery driver from the Bronx named Lenny Roberts, who saw a gap in the market for a series of official-ish vinyl compilations pulling together the songs most sought-after by hip-hop DJs and producers - the Breaks. The purchase of the original pressings of the records these albums included would have been way beyond my knowledge or resources. *Ultimate Breaks And Beats*, available on import vinyl only, never stocked in Loppylugs, were themselves a mystical portal, pulling together some of the most exciting and often obscure music of the sixties, seventies and early eighties. Working with an editor and fellow sample hound called Lou Flores, between 1986 and 1991 Lenny Roberts would compile and release twenty-five volumes, on his label Street Beat, of well-mastered, unlicensed killer tunes housed in graffiti sleeves that provided me and many others with a crucial part of our musical education and formed the foundation of much of the best music made since.)

Much as I loved soul music, hearing hip-hop was to encounter something less polite, more honest and consequently even more exciting, and, along with many other like-minded rap fans I've met over the years, it spoke to me as soon as I heard it.

I was in love with the UK 12-inch pressing of 'The Message' by Grandmaster Flash and the Furious Five that I'd purchased from Loppylugs, having seen the group perform on *The Tube*. They would soon get lost in a transition between the old school, with its garish, shiny costumes, and the grittier new era that Run-DMC would usher in. But the song was a timeless worldwide hit, and this was their moment. And regardless of their outfits, lyrically Melle Mel and his cohorts were dealing with the harsh subject matter that would become the norm in rap.

I would sit transfixed by the song and its stories of street life, playing it on repeat on Dad's hi-fi. I recall him coming in and asking me what I was doing. I said I was listening. Dad sat down and took the music in, and asked me what a 'sacroiliac' was. I didn't know what he was talking about, but he had picked up on a lyric: 'Neon King Kong standin' on my back / Can't stop to turn around, broke my sacroiliac'. I hadn't caught that. I wouldn't have understood the oddly technical anatomical reference, and so I skipped over it.

'But I thought you were listening,' he said.

For shame. This was supposed to be my music; why did he have to say anything about it? It was a humiliating but instructive moment. The listener has to concentrate.

I'M WILLING AS A
A1 GENERAL

TEACHINGS
FROM THE
BHAGAVAD GITA

HARI PRASAD SHASTRI

Just as British rock musicians in the 1960s heard American blues records, related deeply to them and were gradually inspired to make their own version, I was one of many suburban eighties teenage bedroom-dwellers initially hearing artists like Grandmaster Flash and the Furious Five, and not long after that another wave of artists like Eric B. & Rakim, and finding myself transported. I had never heard anything like this before. Surely, I felt, no one had ever heard anything like this before.

When Eric B. & Rakim's first single 'Eric B. Is President' was released in 1986, we somehow had exactly the same reaction that the whole of the nascent New York hip-hop scene was experiencing some 3,000 miles away: this is it.

The power of music to do this, to create similarly powerful responses in people of all different backgrounds, to stimulate chemicals in the brain and free the listeners, is astonishing. Less-than-ideal recording scenarios can still lead to magical results and dramatic impact. 'Eric B. Is President' is a case in point.

Eric Barrier worked in promotions at WBLS, and he and his roommate, a DJ on the station, the up-and-coming producer Marlon Williams – aka Marley Marl – decided to make a rap single together in Marley's studio, which was actually his sister's living room in the Queensbridge housing project in the Long Island City neighbourhood of Queens, New York. Rakim was not Eric B.'s first choice of rapper for the project. When his preferred MC, Freddie Foxxx, failed to show for a recording session, Eric B. grudgingly accepted Rakim as a stand-in, and suggested that they utilise the bassline from Fonda Rae's Bob Blank-produced disco classic 'Over Like A Fat Rat'. It could not be sampled from the record, so Marley recreated it, using a Casio CZ 101 synthesiser.

Rakim suggested that they use the drums from James Brown's

'Funky President'. Marley emulated the 'Funky President' rhythm on an Akai SP1200 sampling drum machine, using the kick and snare sounds from The Honeydrippers' 'Impeach The President' and laid an 808 kick underneath. DJ Eric B. chopped in snippets of three classic breaks: The Mohawks' 'The Champ', James Brown's 'Get Up, Get Into It, Get Involved' and Mountain's 'Long Red (Live)'. Rakim surprised everyone in the room with the quality of his verses, written in two hours the night before in the basement of Rakim's parents' house. Freddie Foxxx later said, 'I did hip-hop a favour by not showing up.'

Everything was captured on a four-track recorder there and then, in the living room. Marley Marl said, 'Our limitations made us what we were.' He received no production credit on the record.

Rakim, aka the God MC, eighteen years old and until just recently known as Wise Intelligent, prior to that Kid Wizard, turned out to have the most poetic and mystical style hip-hop had yet seen, perhaps has ever seen. There was something indefinably different about his rhymes, a complexity, a subtlety, and yet a total relevance. Rakim was simultaneously on street level and on a completely different plane, and he readied the rap audience for the unprecedented wave that would now engulf it.

The next five years saw a series of artists emerge from New York who were able to reinvent the form in their own image again and again. I could not believe what I was hearing. My mind was blown. By 1988 I was seventeen and completely in love with rap. Every word of songs like Audio Two's 'Top Billin'' and EPMD's 'It's My Thing' is stored, forever, in my episodic memory system.

One group stood out among all others. Much like Jimi Hendrix some two decades before them, an immediately warm embrace greeted Public Enemy in the UK, compared to the initially confused US response they received. The more experimental ends of the black music spectrum have always found a hospitable welcome in the UK, and the British taste for sonic aggression has informed the home-grown genres that I would go on to be involved with. These have typically been based around a formula of taking influences from genres like soul and reggae and emphasising the harsher elements. Public Enemy's production wing, led by Hank Shocklee, named itself 'the Bomb Squad'.

Shocklee would later be described by Chuck D as 'the Phil Spector of hip-hop' and he had a grand vision. He wanted to make all of the music for the group's debut album, *Yo! Bum Rush The Show*, from samples. The $5,000 advance the group received from Def Jam did not put them in a position to use live musicians anyway. And he intended to utilise dissonance, saying that the music 'needed to be inharmonic – because harmony represented compliance'.

The British rap groups Hijack and Gunshot were never to achieve mainstream recognition but their fast, brittle records, released respectively on the Music Of Life and Vinyl Solution labels, joined dots between the Bomb Squad's progressive approach to abrasive sound and future UK garage, jungle and grime explorations. In terms of its frequency range, though, *Yo!* is more like a rock'n'roll record than it is anything else. It's only 'MPE' and the title track that rattled car systems with substantial sub bass, nothing in the album getting anywhere near the low-end assault of the Beastie Boys' 'Hold It Now, Hit It', and the other woofer troublers from their *Licensed To Ill* album, 'Posse In Effect', 'Slow Ride', 'Brass Monkey' and 'Slow And Low'.

Yo! was a sonic thrill ride, but it was actually a diversion from hip-hop's unfolding low-frequency narrative. The mid frequencies it occupied were more closely aligned to another 1987 album; The Cults' *Electric*, released on a south London-based independent record label called Beggars Banquet, and produced by none other than Rick Rubin.

Only a year earlier the architect of the Beasties' bass-heavy debut, while Public Enemy were recording for the label he was still involved with, Def Jam, Rick was now conjuring hard but polished, 808-free, rock radio-ready sounds echoing the music of AC/DC which he had loved as a child, in a successful attempt to help some Bradford goths break America.

Transatlantic appreciation was travelling in both directions.

Public Enemy's mutual love affair with the British audience was evident when I saw them support LL Cool J at Hammersmith Odeon in November 1987, and the introduction to the show would be captured and used to begin their next album, *It Takes A Nation Of Millions To Hold Us Back*, the masterpiece that perfected the group's approach.

Public Enemy were defiantly pro-black, and in their support of Louis Farrakhan there were controversies relating to anti-Semitism. This didn't bother me. Their cocktail of noise, funkiness and militancy spoke directly to a multi-racial UK audience who were ready for something as new as this, just as they had been ready for punk (with its swastikas) ten years before and would be ready for acid house a year or two later.

In juxtaposition to Public Enemy's sonic futurism, The Cult's *Electric* threw back to the rock music of a decade earlier and would make them beloved of US audiences. Public Enemy didn't do retro. By the time of the Hammersmith show they were already on to something new, having just released what would become one of their defining songs, 'Rebel Without A Pause'. We, their fans, were all obsessed with this track and its high-pitched, whining, screaming loop. I sat on a tube train full of PE loyalists en route to see them live and participated in a bizarre sample singalong to what was actually an alto saxophone glissando from JB's 'The Grunt'.

Over the course of three albums the Bomb Squad developed a technique for the layering of multiple samples into a cohesive wall of noise that no one would ever better. To me, no live instrumentation could have provided anything like as much excitement as this barrage of found sound, this beautiful, dense, multi-referential homage to all the music that had inspired the beatmakers. It was the product of a collaging process every bit as artistic as that of Robert Rauschenberg, much of whose work, including the 'combine paintings' he made in the fifties, saw him take a magpie approach similar to that of a sampling producer.

The hip-hop beatmaker might use a snatch of a James Brown record alongside a recording of a New York street, in itself perhaps lifted from a Stevie Wonder record, blurring the boundaries 'between art and everyday experience', just as Rauschenberg did. His pieces were sold initially for a few hundred dollars and are now worth tens of millions. When asked about his greatest fear Rauschenberg's response was that of a natural-born sample hunter: 'That I might run out of world.'

Eighties hip-hop production gave me an indelible musical education. From Rick Rubin's brutal minimalism (the sole credit on LL Cool J's *Radio* album back cover reads 'reduced by Rick Rubin') and Marley Marl's game-changing approach to sampling, to Prince Paul's light-fingered psychedelia, Ced-Gee's loping funk, Erick Sermon's smooth yet rugged productions for EPMD, the credible pop-rap Hurby 'Luv Bug' Azor made with Kid 'N Play and Salt-N-Pepa, or Kurtis Mantronik's continuation of what Kraftwerk started, these master curators and pioneering sonic architects delved into their (and their parents') record collections and shared whole worlds of sound with us. In programming their EMU SP12 drum machines they were also programming my musical taste, permanently.

The Bomb Squad, in their moment, were both the most avant-garde and the most aggressive, reflecting both punk and jazz, breaking any rules they could find. The first three Public Enemy albums are not just about production, of course, but the sonic adventurousness is incredible.

(And Public Enemy is far from the whole Bomb Squad story. Their other productions included excellent lesser-known cuts like Kings of Pressure's 'You Know How To Reach Us' and 'Give Me The Mic', and Son of Bazerk's reggae-tinged 'J-Dubs Theme', most of Slick Rick's *Great Adventures* album, Young Black Teenagers' 1991 and 1993 albums, and the solo debut album they produced for Ice Cube on his departure from NWA.)

To listen to a peak-era Bomb Squad production is to absorb a huge amount of sonic and cultural information, but this maximalism was entirely complementary to the more pared-down approaches to be heard on contemporaneous classic hip-hop albums by Boogie Down Productions and Eric B. & Rakim. The Bomb Squad were outside of everything else that was going on in hip-hop yet still part of it.

Three weeks after *Yo! Bum Rush The Show* arrived in stores on vinyl and cassette and two weeks before my sixteenth birthday, Boogie Down Productions released their debut 1987 album and minimalist masterclass, *Criminal Minded*. It is the rudimentary work of an artist with limited resources and a lot of hunger and integrity, making something for themselves, and the people around them, which would have an impact far greater than anyone imagined. KRS-One was born Lawrence Parker and his story is mystical. He has never seemingly referred to his childhood as being particularly deprived, but nonetheless by his mid-teens he found himself in a men's homeless shelter on East Bowery.

While living there, he not only developed his talent for writing and reciting poetry, but also pursued his interests in philosophy in a local public library. Hare Krishna devotees visiting the shelter gave him a copy of the Bhagavad Gita, the bible of Hinduism. KRS took to the book and was given the nickname Krishna by other residents of the shelter. He was not comfortable with this moniker, yet when the Bureau of Child Welfare found him to be too young to stay there, and reregistered him in order to move him to Covenant House for Children, he gave his name as Krishna Parker, which was subsequently abbreviated to Kris Parker. His graffiti tag and MC name KRS-One was based on this early example of crossover between hip-hop and eastern mysticism.

When Lawrence/Kris/KRS was moved to another shelter on 166th Street and Boston Road in the Bronx, he found himself arguing over subway tokens with a new social worker called Scott Sterling. Parker saw Sterling as a square, a tool of the system. Sterling, the authority figure in the relationship, saw Parker as a lazy good-for-nothing. But when Kris visited a hip-hop night at the Broadway Repertory Theater on 145th Street, he had an epiphany which he would compare to Moses and the burning bush. He thought the music was the best thing he'd ever heard, and was amazed to see that its source was the social worker Scott Sterling, behind the turntables in his other guise, as DJ Scott La Rock. Scott welcomed KRS into the DJ booth, and subsequently on to the stage where KRS demonstrated the MC skills he had been honing. A unit was born, initially known as the Boogie Down Crew.

KRS was supporting himself by mopping floors in a children's nursery in Brooklyn while recording what became his classic debut album with a fledgling producer called Cedric Miller. Professionally known as Ced-Gee, of a group calling themselves Ultramagnetic MCs, he was, according to KRS, the only person in the Bronx to own an SP1200 sampling drum machine at this time.

Boogie Down Productions' timeless masterpiece *Criminal Minded*, recorded in two weeks, all vocals done in one take, no samples cleared, was the first rap album to feature artists holding pistols on the cover. KRS was also sporting rounds of ammunition over his shoulder. Scott La Rock has a hand grenade by his side. The shoulder rounds and grenade were borrowed from an ex-marine friend of their label owners. The pistol was KRS's own.

The crime stories KRS tells on tracks like 'South Bronx' and 'P Is Free' made this the first New York gangsta rap album, but KRS would later say he was not proud of that, and while he may have owned a firearm for protection KRS-One was not a gangster. He says he wished to attract the thug audience in this way, so he could educate them later.

The album actually sounds curiously innocent by today's standards. It contains just one swear word, a single isolated 'fucking' used to denigrate Roxanne Shante on 'The Bridge Is Over'. But the cover imagery would prove tragically prescient. Shortly after the album's release, Scott travelled to the Bronx River Houses to try to clear up a misunderstanding involving BDP crew member D-Nice. Sterling was shot and killed in broad daylight. Criminality is caused by background and conditioning, not music. Rap music reflects reality, some of it violent. But KRS was on a spiritual journey and it's hard to avoid the karmic implications: shortly after the group posed with figurative firearms on their album cover, a real weapon took the life of DJ Scott La Rock.

The back cover of *Criminal Minded* reads: 'All cuts written and produced by KRS-One & Scott La Rock – special thanks to Ced-Gee.' As evidenced by Marley Marl's unlisted contribution to the creation of 'Eric B. Is President', eighties hip-hop production credits were an inexact science. While KRS and Scott La Rock undoubtedly played a part in the production of the album, the 'special thanks' nod seems to have underplayed the contribution Ced-Gee made. Either way, he had his own classic full-length in the works.

Ultramagnetic MCs formed in the Bronx in 1984, and by 1985 had released the little-known single 'To Give You Love' on the Diamond International label. The label was also little known but its owner was one of the best underground rap DJs on the airwaves: Hank Love, who, with his partner DNA, hosted a late-night show on WHBI 105.9 FM, broadcast from 2 to 4am, Saturday night/Sunday morning. Hank Love and DNA had two labels between them, and DNA's self-named imprint would launch duo Super Lover Cee & Casanova Rud with their 'Do The James' single. Ultramagnetic MCs' 'To Give You Love' did not connect, and they signed to a new independent called Next Plateau.

The label had been founded by Eddie O'Loughlin, a songwriter and song-plugger turned producer and label owner. He had previously discovered a young actor and singer called John Travolta and would also find a female rap duo, via producer Hurby Azor, aka Hurby Luv Bug, called Salt-N-Pepa. Ultramagnetic MCs released first the classic 'Ego Trippin'' for Next Plateau and then 'Travelling At The Speed Of Thought', and with this song the group's popularity grew beyond the New York metropolitan area.

The 12-inch would sell enough copies in my favourite record shop, London's Groove Records, that its owners, Tim and Chris Palmer and their mother Jean, would license the UK rights to the record from Next Plateau. They were able to do this because Tim had recently formed his own record label, in partnership with a softly spoken Oxford graduate called Martin Mills. Mills had formed Beggars Banquet, home to US stadium rockers The Cult, in 1973 as a record shop in Earl's Court. Four years later, at the height of the punk explosion, he decided to try launching a record label under the same name as the shop.

The venture Tim and Martin launched together was christened Citybeat Records, and was set up to reflect Groove Records' music policy: soul, dance and rap music. Customers would receive a yellow plastic shopping bag to transport vinyl home from the tiny and magical store on Greek Street.

The bag carried the Citybeat logo on its flipside and instant credibility. As Beggars parented Citybeat, Citybeat would later raise another independent dance label: XL Recordings.

The Ultramagnetic MCs' debut album *Critical Beatdown* showcased not just the production skills of Ced-Gee but the abilities of another group member: enter Kool Keith, rap's greatest eccentric, outsider incarnate. The man born Keith Matthew Thornton on 7 October 1963 was, for sheer otherworldliness, the Lee 'Scratch' Perry of hip-hop. His flow was not of this planet. He had arrived here from somewhere else. He was a wizard. As Gandalf said to Bilbo Baggins in *The Hobbit*, a wizard is neither early nor late. 'It seems weird your head is triangle / like a mango, somethin' I snack on', he said in the opening song 'Watch Me Now', and things only got stranger and better from there.

Ced-Gee had made leaps since the work he did with BDP, and now the drums were being chopped up with a different level of finesse. While never becoming a huge-selling artist, Ultramagnetic MCs were invariably acknowledged by initiates and will always be close to my heart. I am connected to this group in many small but cosmic ways. First, almost always first, as a fan. I purchased the UK Citybeat pressing of 'Travelling At The Speed Of Thought', from Groove Records. The second Ultramagnetics record I purchased was on the FFRR label, who I would sign to a few years later as an artist, for a brief and inglorious moment.

The first artist of genius signed to XL, fellow British suburban B-boy and hardcore producer Liam Howlett, would a few years later take a lyric from the album's title track, 'Critical Beatdown': 'I'll take your brain to another dimension / pay close attention', combine it with a substantial portion of Max Romeo's Lee 'Scratch' Perry-produced classic 'Chase The Devil' and create the evergreen banger that is The Prodigy's 'Out Of Space'. And some years after this, my favourite track on the Ultras debut, 'Give The Drummer Some', would provide the ill-advised source material for another sample-based classic by The Prodigy.

ALL THE YANKS SAY I SOUND AUSTRALIAN BUT HEAR ME NOW

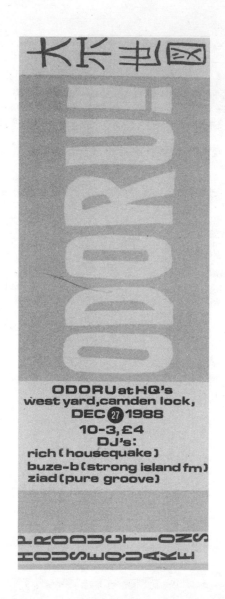

ODORU!

ODORU at HQ's
west yard, camden lock,
DEC 27 1988
10-3, £4
DJ's:
rich (housequake)
buze-b (strong island fm)
ziad (pure groove)

HOUSEQUAKE
AT THE
TABERNACLE
(POWIS SQ. WII)

SPECIAL GUEST DJ

SOUL II SOUL'S

AITCH B

HOUSEQUAKE CREW:

RICH

BIZ E B

+LIVE MC

-LORD JT

SATURDAY JULY 15

£6 9-LATE

EARLY ARRIVAL

ESSENTIAL

There were several potential next steps for the stunned and somehow lovestruck teenage rap fan in the UK; one idea was to try to make something with even a fraction of the grit and passion this music had. I was now DJ Rich, stringing breakbeats together in my Edgware bedroom for aspiring rapper and athlete Rafi Sigarney, in his guise as MC Lord JT, as my grandma brought us cups of tea.

It was inevitable that UK rappers would emerge, inspired as they were by what was going on across the Atlantic, and make their own attempts to capture the spirit and excitement of New York rap. Malcolm McLaren's attempt somehow resonated in New York, but at home it was a tiny part of the story. I was an enthusiastic fan of early UK hip-hop attempts from artists including Demon Boyz, Hijack and She Rockers, all on the Music Of Life label, and particularly reggae-influenced pairing Bionic and Rodney P, aka London Posse. This duo owned their Englishness better than any other artist of the period, and with their authentic subject matter and Jamaican-accented delivery had built a following since their first single releases in 1987, via Jazz Summers' Big Life and Tim Westwood's Justice labels, and would sign to Island subsidiary Mango and deliver *Gangster Chronicle*, now seen as a classic, the first truly great British rap album.

I made a friend at school called Marcus Domleo, who told me his dad worked at Island Records. Dave Domleo was the much-loved general manager of Island in one of its best periods, and in 1987 he gave me a summer job in the warehouse of the Island HQ in St Peter's Square in Hammersmith. This was an unpaid position where I was providing free manual labour, but I was more than aware that it was them doing me the favour. Everything about the place thrilled me, the people, the energy and the extraordinary smell.

Although my actual work consisted of duties like shrink-wrapping Force MDs' cassette singles to the 7-inch vinyl to form a value-for-money package that would move up the singles chart a bit faster, I felt energised by this alien environment. My formative experiences at Island planted the seed of an idea of what a record label should be; multi-cultural and forward-thinking, with music spanning different genres but all chosen with taste and integrity. Island had magic, and along with its then peers Virgin and A&M, all at this time still independent, was not wed to any particular style.

Although Island had started as a reggae label, it was by this time releasing records by artists as diverse as Run-DMC (licensed from New York rap label Profile), Tom Waits and Julian Cope. Its 4th And Broadway imprint released impeccably curated and packaged soul 12-inches. Sophisticated, cool and conceptual artists including Lizzy Mercier Descloux, Was Not Was and Kid Creole and the Coconuts were associated with Island via a deal with New York art/punk/dance label Ze.

Grace Jones had already been through two distinct musical phases, resulting first in three solid disco albums produced by Tom Moulton, and then under the guiding hand of producer and Island owner Chris Blackwell and his production partner Alex Sadkin, three astonishing albums incorporating styles from reggae to new wave and featuring Sly & Robbie as rhythm section.

She was now achieving a peak of pop success with the Trevor Horn-produced 'Slave To The Rhythm', issued via the Island-backed imprint ZTT.

Grace was life-size on my wall in Edgware, as a perk of my unpaid role was to have access to spare promotional items such as 60 x 40-inch posters. I was never sure what my grandma was thinking when she used to glance with uncertainty at the andro-gynous and provocative Jean-Baptiste Mondino-styled image of a near-naked Grace.

Grace Jones was at this time busily destroying barriers that existed for female artists, artists of colour and artists in general.

Chris Blackwell, as her producer and the proprietor of her label, was her enthusiastic collaborator and facilitator in this. The work they were doing together would provide inspiration for some of what I would go on to attempt.

In September 1986 I saw a line-up consisting of Run-DMC, LL Cool J and the Beastie Boys at Hammersmith Odeon, having seen Cameo at the same venue and Washington go-go outfit Trouble Funk at the Town & Country Club in Kentish Town earlier in the summer. In 1987 I saw not only the Def Jam tour featuring Public Enemy, LL Cool J and Eric B. & Rakim at Hammersmith, and Run-DMC and the Beastie Boys at Brixton Academy, but also shows by Luther Vandross, Atlantic Starr and Trouble Funk, all at the Hammersmith Odeon.

I didn't realise until long after the Luther show why the man next to me was shouting, 'Where's Marcus?' This would have been a soul and jazz buff disappointed that Marcus Miller, the bass maestro featured on Luther's records, was not part of Luther's onstage band.

I was enjoying myself at these soul and rap gigs rather than analysing anything, but I was seeing artists who were part of some very different traditions. The eighties soul acts were a direct continuation of a lineage going back decades. London clubbers of this era were fortunate, in terms of our musical education, that 'rare groove' had caught on as a genre for club DJs. The term was popularised via Norman Jay's *Original Rare Groove Show* on KISS FM to describe tunes he had been collecting when visiting his family in New York. We were hearing seventies soul records, learning about the roots of the new music that was being made, hearing retro sounds in the same context as the modern ones they had influenced. Like Northern soul, rare groove was entirely a curator's genre; you could not make a new rare groove record, though some tried.

Through this recontextualisation of older records, all of which featured live musicians rather than being technology-based, I would experience many of the artists whose work I had previously read about in *NME*, and would treasure for the rest of my life. Some of them I would even collaborate with and become close to. I would see Gil Scott-Heron live several times in this period.

Hip-hop leant on the music of the past, of course, but was still a radical new twist on black music. And in the clubs rather than live venues, house music from Chicago and Detroit was being seized upon by a small but growing UK audience. There were no house music vocalists who could sell out venues like the Hammersmith Odeon; it was a producer's genre, owned by the DJs who played it.

I attended Delirium! at Heaven, where Noel Watson pioneered the brand-new sound. He previously played hip-hop when the club was based at the Astoria on Charing Cross Road, a venue which no longer exists and without which I would not be here, it being the original meeting place of my maternal grandparents in 1935.

I wouldn't get to experience northern clubbing until I went to The Haçienda in 1989 while visiting my friend Dimitri at university in Manchester, but the north of England was particularly responsive to the earliest era of house music. Mike Pickering's 'Nude' night at the Haçienda, originally a live music venue, started to play the sounds emanating from Chicago as early as 1985, and Graeme Park adopted a similar music policy at The Garage in Nottingham, before joining forces with Pickering at The Haçienda.

In London, sound systems like Herbie Laidley's Mastermind Roadshow started to broaden their music policies to incorporate the new styles coming from Chicago and Detroit. Mastermind, founded in Kensal Rise W10, had originally been a reggae sound known as Conqueror, but in starting to incorporate soul and then hip-hop had gained a huge following, not least for their sets at the Notting Hill Carnival.

House music was rapidly becoming what many partygoers wanted to hear, and the arrival of ecstasy into the nightlife eco-system, which turned out to synthesise perfectly with the tempo and feeling of house, would provide the magical extra element, although the people controlling the supply of the highly lucrative illegal substances would bring a darker energy to the scene. It was inevitable, given my natural enthusiasm and barely tameable drive, that I would try to emulate the sound systems and DJs I worshipped at that time.

Alongside my friends Dimitri, Layo Paskin and Dan Williams, and later Nick Goldsmith and Barry Williams, aka Biz E B (who would subsequently make hardcore tunes as Code 071 for the Reinforced label), we had started to promote nights under the name Housequake Productions, at venues like Dingwalls and HQ's in Camden, then going on to attempt slightly larger-scale acid house parties, these led by Layo (who alongside Matthew 'Bushwacka' B would go on to success as DJ, producer and owner of The End nightclub) under the name Strawberry Sweatshop in east London.

A fledgling north London sound system called Pure Groove, consisting of Nick Worthington, brothers Tarik and Ziad Nashnush, and Jon Sexton, were already some way down the path we wanted to travel. Pure Groove were not quite on the professional level of a Family Funktion or Soul II Soul, but they were on the right tracks.

I began to sell my mixtapes on a stall in Camden Market. Nick Goldsmith would make the artwork and man the stall with me, and we'd split the proceeds. Pure Groove were already stationed in Camden Lock, selling records in an increasingly professional way, and were soon to open an actual record shop based at 679 Holloway Road, then becoming a record label and publishing company.

DJing would become the most exciting and important thing in my life at this time. Housequake Productions was our attempt, often inept, to emulate the London sound systems of that moment. While our intentions were good, and we hosted some exciting events, we were amateurish in sound system terms and didn't actually have our own system. The decks and mixer were ours, and we were able to upgrade from all-in-one DJ console, first to Citronic's cheaper imitations of Technics SL1200 turntables, then, finally, thrillingly, to the real things. We still had to rent the rest of the gear.

Dan was a talented graphic artist, and using Letraset and scalpel he would design our flyers, which I would get printed by a friendly local who had an after-hours arrangement with a print shop, and these leaflets used to come out looking hip and professional, comparing reasonably with those made by more established club runners.

We managed to take up a partial residency at a community centre called The Tabernacle in W11's Powis Square, and I met a local reggae MC called Dominic. Associated with a Ladbroke Grove crew called Mighty Ethnicz, there was nothing unusual about Dominic's broad Jamaican patois, gold tooth and swaggering delivery apart from the fact that he was not in fact ethnic but unmistakably Caucasian. Dominic told me that he was already a big figure on the reggae scenes in both Jamaica and New York; I wasn't quite sure if I believed him. There was no internet to check.

I loved DJing. Nothing could compare to the thrill of it; establishing a connection with the dancers using the decks and a box of 12-inch records I knew inside out. For many of the most successful DJs the most important aspect of all this was these dancers. Not for me. Crowd-pleasing was not my priority. I would not have dreamed of playing a record I didn't like, however great a response it might have received. This uncompromising approach lowered my chances of large-scale DJing success but it would inform my future work effectively. The music came first.

There were moments when the stars aligned. The intro from a 12-inch called 'Versatile Extension' by Supreme DJ Nyborn on a small New York indie called Payroll had exactly the effect I wanted at a sweaty and electric party Barry and I played in a low-ceilinged community centre in Swiss Cottage. The energy the packed dance floor generated when the tune dropped still feels tangible, and this moment thirty years ago may as well have been last night.

Promoting club nights, as opposed to just DJing at them, was a more complex affair. Sometimes the nights we organised would be rammed; there would be queues outside, the vibe would be great and we'd make several hundred pounds each. At these events we experienced the elation of entrepreneurial success. Doing things on your own terms, and winning.

At other times no one would turn up and not only would we be faced with small-scale financial disaster but also social embarrassment, the emptiness of the club announcing the lack of achievement in a way I found excruciating.

We booked a run of Saturday nights at a club called Flynns in Mayfair, out of our normal geographical comfort zone. Not only did this represent champagne aspirations on a beer budget, but Nick and I were attempting it without our other partners. There were lessons to be learned: break up a winning team at your peril. Never overlook the contributions of your collaborators.

We had booked Judge Jules to play on the first night at the new venue. He was yet to transition from the rare groove and hip-hop he championed as part of the Family Funktion sound system to the house music he became well known for. At the end of the night a grand total of about twenty paying punters had turned up. It was a disaster. Jules was incredibly gentlemanly about it, saying that he'd seen me out and about flyering and hustling so he knew I'd put the work in, and said it wasn't my fault. Generously, he said he would let me off his fee. But he also gave me a warning: 'Don't do this to Trouble. He won't be as understanding.'

The particular Trouble he referenced was Paul 'Trouble' Anderson. Jules had seen from our flyers that we had booked him to play the following week. Trouble was one of London's most respected selectors. He had served his apprenticeship in the seventies carrying records for other DJs. He went on to develop a reputation playing a wide selection of music, from disco, funk and jazz to Latin, samba and reggae. He became known as a pioneer first of 'boogie', dance-floor orientated soulful groove-based tunes, then the New Jersey-style garage and house that it spawned, hosting a hugely popular and influential Saturday-night mix show on KISS FM. He was also a great dancer.

And whereas Judge Jules was not just university-educated but a trained lawyer who would articulately and effectively debate with the Metropolitan Policemen who tried to shut down the parties he spun at, Trouble was street-educated.

While he claimed that he was named after Trouble Funk, his favourite band, I didn't want to take any chances. I heeded Jules's advice and some instinct for self-preservation kicked in. I realised that if we were to proceed with this venture, we would somehow have to pay Paul whether we earned the money on the night or not, borrowing the funds if necessary. In the end we bailed before the night, and Trouble had other gigs and required no cancellation fee.

One of Trouble's peers was a DJ at The Wag on Wardour Street, an east Londoner called Derek Boland, who became the A&R at fledgling UK rap label Music Of Life, and finding himself one track short for a compilation he was putting together, stepped in and made a song himself entitled 'Rock The Beat'. This led to him becoming the first UK rap artist to gain a degree of domestic commercial success and even some attention in the US, signing to New York indie and home to Run-DMC, Profile Records.

Derek B's music was criticised for its heavily US-indebted style and attempts at commerciality, but if nothing else he was lyrically an authentic documenter of the London scene at that moment. His song 'Get Down', while riding a cheesier than necessary Jackson 5 sample, listed the London sound systems that were the descendants of Anglo-Jamaican reggae sounds that sprang up in the seventies such as Saxon, Jah Shaka and Channel One: 'Family Funktion / Soul II Soul / Africa Centre on top of the world / Norman Jay with Shake and Fingerpop / Westwood with his fresh hip-hop'.

I was still more of a fan than an insider, but I was delirious with enthusiasm about DJing and nightlife and the different ways I could participate in it.

In 1988 I presented my first show on a pirate station called Obsession, which broadcast on 92.7 FM. It wasn't the best known of the pirates, but I wasn't a well-known DJ. I would turn up at a council block in Swiss Cottage with my records in washing bags. Record boxes would have given away the illicit nature of what we were doing and so the management of the station had banned them. The station bosses, armed with their brick phones, ran a tight ship, and their fleet occupied murky waters. The washing bags were awkward to lug but it seemed prudent to follow management instructions and not upset them.

Mum and Dad attended parents' evening at my school and the outlook was not good. I was mostly absent and looking unlikely to get any A-levels. The school were vaguely aware that I was involved with entrepreneurial out-of-school activities and said, 'Perhaps he will be a millionaire in his twenties, but he is going to fail his exams.' My mum was not impressed by this vague and unlikely-sounding promise of hope but my dad left the premises thrilled, which annoyed her no end.

In effect, though, I was gone.

My single-minded and obsessive approach to everything I was doing at this time was very teenage, but then I'm much the same now. When I'm working on an album, that album is the most important thing in the world at that time. Music demands this; you can love it, but without the do-or-die commitment it is unlikely to love you back. There are too many people who would give anything to make a living out of music for it to accommodate those who are not committed.

I was determined that I achieve independence through music at the earliest possible moment. I was obsessed with my record collection, DJing, making mixtapes, presenting my radio show and promoting parties.

As school life and my studies slipped ever further out of focus, it was an exciting time for me and a baffling one for my parents. Like all hard-working second-generation immigrants, education was of paramount importance to them. I would sleep all day and work at night, and on many nights make decent amounts of cash from DJing. Everything I was doing was positive but my mum thought I was selling drugs.

It seemed highly unlikely to them that academic failure would be followed by real-world success. They felt that I was simply continuing a pattern of reckless disobedience that would lead to my downfall. Via an advert in the back of *Music Week*, which we subscribed to at Loppylugs in order to see the Top 40 singles and albums sales charts, I landed a job at a vinyl wholesalers called Caroline Exports in west London, actually owned, it turned out, by Richard Branson. Unlike Island's Chris Blackwell, and despite the fact he started an enormously successful independent record label, Branson was not really a music person. His interest was empire-building, and for a while a record label was the best way of achieving that. He would invite me to lunch once in 2002, but I was busy.

In fact, I always have been busy. In 1989 I was in North Acton selling vinyl over the phone to various far-flung and exotic outlets, including a store called Vinylmania in New York. In one phone call with the owner, Charlie Grappone, he did not completely rule out the idea of giving me a job if I found myself in New York.

Finding myself in New York sounded about right to me.

PART 2

Part 2 Playlist

MFSB 'Love Is The Message' (Philadelphia International)

McFadden & Whitehead 'Ain't No Stopping Us Now' (Philadelphia International)

Grace Jones 'La Vie En Rose' (Island)

Manuel Göttsching 'E2-E4' (Inteam)

The Normal 'Warm Leatherette' (Mute)

The Clash 'The Magnificent Dance' (CBS)

Man Friday 'Love Honey, Love Heartache' (Vinylmania)

TW Funkmasters 'Love Money' (Tania)

Janet Kay 'Silly Games' (Scope)

Taana Gardner 'Heartbeat' (West End)

Sessomatto 'Sessomatto (Jimmy Stuard Mix)' (West End)

Nu Shooz 'I Can't Wait' (Atlantic)

Todd Terry 'Just Make That Move' (West End)

A Tribe Called Quest 'I Left My Wallet In El Segundo' (Jive)

LL Cool J 'The Boomin' System' (Def Jam)

En Vogue 'Hold On' (Atlantic)

SoHo 'Hot Music' (United States Of America)

Bobby Konders 'The Poem' (Nu Groove)

Joe Smooth 'Promised Land' (DJ International)

CeCe Rogers 'Someday' (Atlantic)

Rhythm is Rhythm 'Strings Of Life' (Transmat)

Lil Louis 'French Kiss' (Diamond Records)

Royal House 'Can You Party' (Idlers)

Raze 'Break 4 Love' (Grove St)

Royal House 'Yeah Buddy' (Idlers)

Longsy D 'This Is Ska' (Big One)

Looney Tunes 'Just As Long As I Got You' (XL Recordings)

Flowmasters 'Let It Take Control' (XL Recordings)

Moody Boys 'Jammin'' (XL Recordings)

Shut Up and Dance 'The Green Man' (Shut Up And Dance)

4hero 'Mr Kirk's Nightmare' (Reinforced)

Acen 'Trip To The Moon' (Production House)

Kicks Like a Mule 'The Bouncer' (Tribal Bass)

Awesome 3 'Don't Go (Kicks Like a Mule Remix)' (Citybeat)

Kicks Like a Mule 'Number One' (Tribal Bass)

Kicks Like a Mule 'DJ Talk' (Tribal Bass)

The Prodigy 'Charly' (XL Recordings)

SL2 'Way In My Brain' (XL Recordings)

SL2 'DJs Take Control' (XL Recordings)

Liquid 'Sweet Harmony' (XL Recordings)

Dance Conspiracy 'Dub War' (XL Recordings)

Aphex Twin 'Analogue Bubblebath' (Mighty Force)

House of Pain 'Jump Around' (Tommy Boy)

House of Pain 'Put Your Head Out' (Tommy Boy)

Eazy-E 'Only If You Want It' (Ruthless)

London Posse 'Pass The Rizla' (Ruffness/XL Recordings)

Geto Boys 'My Mind Is Playing Tricks On Me' (Rap-A-Lot)

Rage Against the Machine 'Killing In The Name Of' (Epic)

Beastie Boys 'So What'cha Want' (Capitol)

The Prodigy 'Voodoo People' (XL Recordings)

The Last Poets 'Shalimar' (Douglas)

Five Stairsteps 'Ooh Child' (Buddah)

Ultramagnetic MCs 'Give The Drummer Some' (Next Plateau)

Dr Dre 'Deep Cover' (Epic)

Nine Inch Nails 'Closer' (Nothing/TVT/Interscope)

The Prodigy 'Diesel Power' (XL Recordings)

AND YOU SAY
NEW YORK CITY

Larry Levan

BY MANNY
LEHMAN

VINYL MANIA
Interview

VM: How did your interest in being a DJ begin?

LL: I was never interested in being a DJ.

VM: So how did it happen?

LL: I was always interested in stereo equipment. I used to go to the Loft and the Gallery. I was drawn more to the party than playing records because I wanted to hangout, dance and do all the evils of the night time. I used to putz around the Gallery with Nicky Siano fooling around with records, then I started getting into it a little. I used to do the lights for Nicky while he played.

VM: So thats where your feel for working the lights while you're playing music came from

LL: Yea, I stopped doing lights at the Gallery and started doing lights at the Continental. The lights were more difficult to do there because it was a large open space. I had a good working relationship with the DJ Joey Buffigero. I worked there for a couple of months. One day Joey walked out, there was no one to play the records, the manager said "We got a new DJ" Oh yea, who? He said "You". Since then it's been non stop.

VM: What year was this?

LL: 1974. Oh my god ten years ago this May.

VM: Were you an instant success?

LL: I was a hit.

VM: After that, did you say to yourself, this is what want to make a career of?

LL: No, I said to myself after the first night, this is a very good job. I enjoy doing it. I just don't know what did, I really didn't. I had no idea what I did. At that time it was all mimicking of what I had heard from the Loft The Sanctuary and The Haven.

VM: How long did you play the Continental?

LL: Until the Fall of 74. Then Richard Long asked me to work with him. I worked with Richard in a club called the Soho Place.

VM: Had you developed your own style of playing by then?

LL: Oh yes.

VM: Who or what did you look to for direction o inspiration while you played music?

LL: I would watch certain people on the dance floor Since I always went out dancing, I would use that as my guide. I knew who went out, who used to dance what songs people liked. Thats what I used as an outline of choosing what to play. In those days DJ's were'nt too open to help each other. The communication between Jocks was very limited The only DJ's to have good rapore in those days, I think were David Mancuso and Mike Capello of the old Limelight.

VM: You worked at the Soho Place. What kind o atmosphere was it?

LL: It was a loft at 452 Broadway, with too much sound equipment. It was Richard Long's workshop as well. It was basically a black club and very energetic. Robert DeSilva worked with me, he did the lights. I worked there until the club was closed for overcrowding and all those things that used to close clubs in those days. So while the Soho was getting ready to close I got a call from a Michael Brody, I said "Who the hell is Michael Brody" I called him back and he asked me to come to his office. He told me he had a club downtown that I should come look at. I said "great, I could use the job." I went to see the club at 143 Reed Street. It reminded me alot of the old Loft. I worked at Reed Street until 1976 when that closed. Then I took off for a year. In that year Michael and I found a space where the Paradise Garage is now. In September of 1977 we had our first party and I've been working every weekend since.

VM: The rest is history. How did your studio work fit its way in?

LL: Oh I hate to tell the story. My first record was for Sesame Street.

VM: C is for Cookie. You mixed one side and Roy Thode mixed the other.

LL: Correct.

VM: "I Got My Mind Made Up" by Instant Funk, was that your first big record?

LL: Yes it was. David Rodriguez got me the job. The record went gold.

VM: Was there a sudden demand for Larry Levan after that?

LL: No, the next thing was the Salsoul consumption. Salsoul had a hit so they wanted me to stay in the studio and keep making hits out of other people's records, which is very strange. You read about the way companies devour artists, I mean you can see it, Billie Holliday for example. You see the way artists come and go. Record companies have a way of working you to death. That was the next thing in my career, the Salsoul period. I did have some small projects in the middle like "Bad For Me" by Dee Dee Bridgewater and the Westend products. I just kept going and going and going....

VM: One question that we are all dying to know the answer to. Is there a Larry Levan's greatest hits volume one?

LL: No, I was going to release Volume one after Volume two but we did'nt.

VM: So after mixing, producing was your next step.

LL: The Peech Boys was my first production. I was always asked to produce but I never wanted to. There were semi-productions like Serious Sirius Space Party, one side was done by Michal de Benedictus, Robert Casper and myself. That was sort of a test, a very expensive test. After working with Michael on "Sirius", "Heartbeat" and "Make It Last Forever",which never came out, I was ready to produce.

VM: The true Garagite would kill for the remix of "Make It Last Forever".

LL: The thing about it is that there is another mix, a real mix on it. The one I have is a rough mix, the other

mix is wonderful. In the one I have everything is going at one time, in the other there are some fierce breakdowns.

VM: How did "Don't Make Me Wait" come to be?

LL: It just happened, Brody Wiliams started writing it and we cut it. We cut "Don't" and "Life Is Something Special", which was called "City Fever" back then. Everybody said you need words for "City Fever" so Michael and I wrote lyrics for the song. Bernard Fowler came in and sang something completely different. He basically stuck to the same format. Singers have a way of custom tailoring things for themselves.

VM: Was "Don't Make Me Wait" the first song to have an Acapella?

LL: Yes, my idea.

VM: That must make you feel good when you hear all these songs with Acapellas now?

LL: It does, it also makes me feel good when I hear other songs with hand claps in them. No one had ever made rhythmic hand claps before. Now I want to destroy every drum machine with that clap.

VM: It seems now they use that to make the song, instead of making up a song then adding a clap track

LL: Yes, I love real instruments. I like the drum machine because its very hard to find a good drummer these days as sad as it may sound. Synthesizers I love, but they are getting out of hand.

VM: Will there be another Peech Boys album?

LL: Yes

VM: When can we expect it?

LL: This year.

CONTINUED ON PAGE 12

LARRY LEVAN AND
JEFFREY OSBORNE

Many significant cultural moments occurred in Charlie Grappone's Vinylmania record store on Carmine Street, like Mike D's purchase of two Schoolly D 12-inches and their subsequent impact on the Beastie Boys. But Vinylmania is best known for playing a crucial part in the history of dance music as the go-to vinyl outlet for DJ Larry Levan and his Paradise Garage crowd, who, having partied all night at 84 King Street, would head round the corner to Carmine Street, near Bleecker, to buy the tunes they'd been dancing to.

Charlie Grappone: 'Larry was very influential on what we sold. And gradually we started influencing what he was playing in return, particularly the imports. He could only have picked up a record like Nu Shooz from Vinylmania. He would break a record like that single-handed.'

These two master curators, one club DJ, one record store owner, helped each other with their work, using the same medium - vinyl - in different settings.

Though the Garage itself had been closed for nearly three years when I arrived in New York, its energy was still palpable. One of the birthplaces of house music and in effect club culture as we now know it, from its opening in 1977 until its closure ten years later, it was a sacred place where a mixed crowd danced until the next day to soul music of all genres, played on a legendarily great sound system. The owner, Michael Brody, had hired a sound designer called Richard Long to create the rig, which in the hands of Larry Levan was widely regarded as providing the greatest audio ever experienced in a club. Grace Jones, a Paradise Garage regular whose early tunes like 'La Vie En Rose' were anthems there, stated that watching Larry Levan mix records was like seeing Jimi Hendrix play guitar.

'Garage', as dance music genre, comes from Paradise Garage.

Levan's friend, a DJ called Frankie Knuckles, had moved from New York to Chicago and was blending disco, soul, funk, R&B and electro at an underground club called The Warehouse. 'House' was an abbreviation of the name of the club Knuckles spun at.

Frankie Knuckles referred to Levan as unbeatable because he was, in DJing terms, the purest. But that did not mean purist. Quite the opposite. Levan made room in his sets for dub reggae, The Clash, electro pop from the likes of Depeche Mode and obscure one-offs like Manuel Göttsching's proto-house experiment 'E2-E4'. These were spun among the Philly soul and disco which formed the basis of his sound, always emphasising drama and atmosphere. Levan was a cipher, embodying the dialogue between different musics and cultures.

The spark that inspired both Larry Levan and Frankie Knuckles, their primary influence, predecessor and guru, was a reluctant DJ, an orphan raised from birth in a children's home, called David Mancuso, founder of The Loft, which opened its doors at 647 Broadway, in the NoHo district of New York, in February 1970.

The flyers for his first party carried the acronymously significant slogan 'Love Saves the Day' and, aside from the care that went into the music, sound system, Buddhist shrine and buffet at this event, his alcohol-free venue, open from midnight to 6am, was unique in one crucial respect. It was Mancuso's home. He made the ultimate commitment to creating a sacred environment for people to feel comfortable in. From these beginnings grew a movement that would transform popular culture.

Just as Larry Levan and Frankie Knuckles were inspired by him, David Mancuso had in turn been heavily influenced by three main figures. The first was Sister Alicia, of the children's home where Mancuso was raised from when he was ten days old. In effect his adoptive mother, she would host a party with music, food and balloons whenever the opportunity presented itself and her ability to make the children feel safe and loved implanted itself in young David Mancuso's psyche.

There seems to have been something not just visionary but

Christlike about Mancuso. He had previously tried giving all of his belongings away and living as an ascetic. In a statement he gave to local residents keen to drive The Loft out of their neighbourhood, he said: 'We hurt no one. We have always acted decently. We did not have a happy childhood, but it has not soured us on life. To those who do not know us, do not be misled by gossip.'

The next major influence on Mancuso was an Italian DJ and dancer called Francis Grasso, who is regarded as the first person to use separate turntables to beat-mix two different records together for the dancers' benefit, cueing up the next song using headphones, first in the late sixties at a club called Salvation II, and then Sanctuary, a former church, significantly, on 43rd Street and 9th Avenue. To mix two records was a difficult and risky task. Not only did the Thorens turntables Grasso used have no pitch control, but this was the 7-inch era, the 'giant' 12-inch not yet having been invented.

Most records would only last two to three minutes and Grasso was in charge of lights as well as music. Nonetheless, he would take two records, such as Chicago's 'I'm A Man' and Led Zeppelin's 'Whole Lotta Love', and create his own custom blend.

A third influence on David Mancuso was the psychedelics guru Timothy Leary, whose house parties and lectures Mancuso had attended, and where he learned from Leary the importance of 'set and setting' – mindset and physical space, of great importance when experimenting psychedelically, or when setting up a place for people to transcend their consciousness through dance. Leary's *The Psychedelic Experience*, a manual for tripping based on *The Tibetan Book of the Dead*, would become Mancuso's guidebook.

Charlie Grappone, Loft regular: 'David was not just anti-establishment. He was anti-materialistic. The first time I went to The Loft I said to Debbie, "I've just had the most druggy music experience." The feeling I had when I went back on to the street . . . you didn't know what you'd just experienced. David was ahead of his time in every way.'

Both Sanctuary and The Loft had opened soon after an episode of civil unrest in the West Village. On 28 June 1969, when the

NYPD were routinely harassing the gay clientele of the Stonewall Inn on Christopher Street, the club's patrons decided they had had enough, and fought back, forcing the police to retreat and call for back-up. A full-scale, spontaneous riot ensued. The message was that gay people did not have to tolerate unfair treatment. That the gay community would protest against discrimination seems to have taken the authorities completely by surprise and marked the beginning of gay activism.

The following year the event would be celebrated on Christopher Street as Liberation Day. This was the foundation of the annual Gay Pride event.

The Loft was a singular location in music history, and without it there would have been no Paradise Garage, no Warehouse in Chicago and potentially none of the many temples to dance music worldwide that have been built since. By the time of The Loft's relocation to 99 Prince Street, Mancuso's impact was so significant that Charlie Grappone provided him with a service that no other DJ received: 'I would take the records to him. I would go to him, early in the evening, at The Loft, his home, and we would smoke weed and listen to records on that fantastic sound system. I would bring him the latest imports. I didn't even charge him. I just gave them to him. It seemed like the right thing to do. While we were listening, he would leave the doors open and people would wander in. I'd say, "You gotta shut the doors!" He'd say, "Why? They're my doors." And he would ask people who wandered in off the street why they had done that, and debate it with them.'

David Mancuso was not the only New York DJ who influenced Larry Levan and Frankie Knuckles. Other pioneers, including Steve D'Acquisto, Michael Cappello and particularly Nicky Siano, created a dialogue between DJ and dancers that had not existed before. This was the birth of club culture.

In 1990 Air India were selling tickets from London to New York for less than £200. You could smoke cigarettes on planes and they served curry and poppadoms, and I remember my first flight to New York as trippy and electric, a step into another world. I arrived on my nineteenth birthday. Charlie Grappone, charismatic and imposing Italian-American proprietor of Vinylmania, was not expecting me to just turn up on the doorstep of his store on Carmine Street, but he welcomed me.

Though the Garage itself had been closed for nearly three years when I arrived in New York, the scene continued and its audience were still avid customers at Vinylmania. All the city's key DJs frequented the store. It was a serious portal, and while they hadn't exactly offered me a job, sometimes it's best to just imagine you've been given an invitation and let the rest take care of itself. Without this lack of shame it is hard to achieve much in music. There are no established routes or fixed hierarchy.

Vinylmania was an up-to-the-minute treasure trove of nothing but vinyl, glorious, exciting black wax, mainly dance music, some hip-hop and R&B. New stock would arrive every day. There was always something fresh to hear. UK imports had their own place behind the counter, but much of the music was recorded, mastered and manufactured locally. As soon as I experienced the shop's atmosphere, and realised it was an important interface between producers, DJs and clubbers, Vinylmania was, as far as I was concerned, the centre of the universe. I'd had to travel 3,000 miles and yet I still had the feeling I'd sort of stumbled across the place and was meant to be there.

The store had formerly operated its own Vinylmania record label, releasing some beloved Paradise Garage classics including Man Friday's 'Love Honey, Love Heartache'. This record was the vision of Larry Levan himself, the group having been formed after the demise of Levan's first recording unit, the NYC Peech Boys, and he based it on an early eighties underground UK jazz-funk hit by south London reggae DJ Tony Williams called 'Love Money', released under the name TW Funkmasters. Charlie knew there were potential downsides to working with Larry Levan. He was not the most reliable character. According to Charlie, 'Larry was not the kind of guy to show up on time. He was eccentric. He only worked one night a week. He had so much freedom.' Nonetheless, recognising his creative power, Charlie gave Larry $16,000 in cash in the basement of Vinylmania for the rights to 'Love Honey'.

This song had been engineered by UK dub pioneer Mark Angelo Lusardi, formerly of reggae studio Gooseberry, where he would record artists including Dennis Bovell (himself a towering figure in the development of both dub and lovers rock in the UK), Creation Rebel and Prince Far I underneath a dental practice in London's Chinatown. Angelo had a prescient vision for incorporating reggae and dub effects into dance music production, which dovetailed both with Tony Williams' ideas for his debut production effort, and subsequently with the soundscape Larry Levan created at the Paradise Garage. They all sought to pull threads together, sensing perhaps that these threads were not really separate.

Vinylmania's original home at 52 Carmine Street had provided the location for disco label West End, owned by Mel Cheren, also a partner in the Paradise Garage, and Ed Kushins. One of Levan's favourite labels, some of West End's catalogue also became early hip-hop staples as breaks used by the first rappers, particularly Taana Gardner's 'Heartbeat' and Jimmy Stuard's remix of a track culled from an Italian movie score, 'Sessomatto'.

My arrival coincided with the West End label, which had been dormant for some years, being revived by Ed with a new release from Todd Terry called 'Just Make That Move'. I made sure I was available to help out, performing tasks including boxing up and delivering 12-inch singles. I was interested in any activity that connected me to the action. I was not to experience any type of significant success in the Big Apple, but I was working in one of the city's best record stores and helping out at an independent dance label with a legendary pedigree. I was also trying to get DJ gigs, to little avail.

Still, the seemingly small upsides of my job in the West Village were thrilling. A Tribe Called Quest's debut album, *People's Instinctive Travels And The Paths Of Rhythm*, had just been released, and a promotional item was sent to the store by Jive Records: a black, Velcro-fastening nylon wallet, with green A Tribe Called Quest logo, celebrating the group's breakout single 'I Left My Wallet In El Segundo'. No one else wanted it and I was allowed to keep the item. It became my favourite piece of swag until I was gifted a Stüssy-designed Carhartt 'Tommy Boy staff' jacket a couple of years later. Stüssy was my clothing label of choice at this time. I would wear drawstring trackpants and a white logo T-shirt by them, with a pair of blue suede Fila sneakers.

While I served DJ legends like Todd Terry and Clark Kent in the store, it began to dawn on me that I didn't have the slightest chance of getting any of the DJing work that belonged to them and their apprentices. For some reason I never made a cassette of my DJ set to play to any club promoters I met, a course of action that might have earned me the opportunities I sought.

I was away from my family and friends, and renting a room in an apartment at 56 South Elliott Place in Fort Greene, next to Brooklyn Tech school. I had found the room via a listing in the *Village Voice*. One night I went alone to see KRS-One perform at SOB's nightclub. Who should I see there but my reggae MC friend from London, Dominic, who told me that he was now an official member of the Boogie Down Productions crew, and would be performing with them later that week. It was all true.

I had no disposable income from my Vinylmania earnings, and was always on the edge of owing the store more than I earned there due to my vinyl-buying habit. Charlie gave me a fatherly warning at one point that I should make sure I had enough money for food and rent before I decided which records to buy.

But I was okay; I had a reserve of savings from my ceaseless small-time entrepreneurial hustles back in London, and I even dipped into them to go on a trip to the Jamaican resort of Negril. Kingston is an easy hop from JFK, and my arrival coincided with the holidays, so I got to see an incredible array of artists performing over a three-night period, including Shabba Ranks, Gregory Isaacs and Yellowman. On hearing my London accent one local I spoke to asked me if I had heard of the legendary London MC Dominic. Unreal.

My initial role at Vinylmania was mail-order vinyl sales. I was stationed in the basement of the store talking to working DJs across the US on a landline phone and taking their orders for the latest 12-inch vinyl. Between calls I would assemble the packages, to a musical accompaniment of mostly R&B courtesy of the then number one urban radio station, WBLS. I wanted to hear hip-hop but at this time urban radio lagged behind the tastes of its audience; a station called HOT 97 had just come on air but was at this point still playing rhythmic pop and dance music.

It would be another three years before the owners of HOT 97 saw the writing on the wall and committed to playing more heavyweight sounds all day, adopting the slogan 'where hip-hop lives', allowing DJs like Funkmaster Flex to give the audience what it wanted – all rap. In 1990 the US record industry was still in denial about the full commercial potential of hip-hop. US urban radio would play only the rap songs it considered programmable alongside the smoother R&B sounds that made up the bulk of its playlists.

The accompaniment to my morning activities was DJ Fred Buggs, and while I would rather have heard all rap all the time, it's relative scarcity perhaps added to the endorphin rush the right song would provide when a DJ like 'Buggsy' dropped it. One summer morning he took delivery, live on air, of a new Marley Marl-produced LL Cool J song called 'The Boomin' System', released on a by now post-Rick Rubin Def Jam, which sampled the recent R&B smash by girl group En Vogue 'Hold On', but had the Marley Marl knock. He played his test pressing three times in a row, creating more excitement with each play, his genuine enthusiasm for the track making a great record sound even greater. Real DJ power.

While stationed at Vinylmania I had also been given a role by a UK publication called *Rave*, to be their NY correspondent, and would fax them a monthly diary of my clubland experiences in New York which they published. The role gave me greater access to the people and places I was interested in.

Though the Paradise Garage by now existed only in hazy memories, echoes in the walls of 84 King Street, the soulful house sound of the Garage was kept alive in some of the clubs I visited, including The Shelter on Hubert Street. At the roving Wild Pitch nights, WBLS reggae DJ Bobby Konders explored club music, having just released his *House Rhythms* on the Nu Groove label. This six-track EP was huge in Vinylmania, mainly for its lead track, 'The Poem'. I was lucky to attend these places at this time, but people were already nostalgic for what had passed. Ghosts were everywhere.

New York's dance music nostalgia was poignant and intense because the scene had been ravaged by HIV and AIDS, and casualties would continue to occur throughout the next decade, including West End co-founder Mel Cheren and Paradise Garage owner Michael Brody. Larry Levan was unable to escape his demons, getting involved with PCP and heroin and dying from heart failure in 1992, at the age of thirty-eight.

I enjoyed the dance music scene but preferred hip-hop nights. Nothing could compare with the energy of hearing rap music in New York, the city of its birth. I was a wide-eyed acolyte at venues like The World, SOB's (now the only surviving venue from this era) and Irving Plaza.

I heard rap's DJ high priests, including the Bronx's Kid Capri at a Thursday-night event called The Powerhouse at The Building on West 26th Street. Through my day job at Vinylmania I had occasional access to record release parties and attended Tommy Boy's launch of Digital Underground's *Sex Packets* album. I had a toe in the door of the actual music industry.

On one memorable afternoon I visited WBLS to interview on-air personality Frankie Crocker for my *Rave* magazine column, a man whose career encompassed the invention of the term 'urban contemporary' and the breaking of not just classic, uplifting R&B anthems like MFSB's 'Love Is The Message' and McFadden & Whitehead's 'Ain't No Stopping Us Now', but the introduction of artists from Bob Marley to The Clash to US audiences. Crocker was an outsize persona, and his antics had included riding into Studio 54 on a white horse. He was friendly enough, and could tell I was genuinely curious and interested in his experiences.

Frankie Crocker, the self-styled 'Chief Rocker', had been keen to break through racial and economic barriers, carving out a sophisticated image and reputation for himself that was perhaps motivational for his audience but would be increasingly at odds with the less glamorous and more gritty feeling of hip-hop, which was now encroaching on the smoother R&B flavours that were his natural domain. He had been a champion of the Paradise Garage sound, and would give radio exposure to songs that were introduced there, name-checking the club on air. In communicating with him I was experiencing the tail end of several eras in American music and it was valuable experience.

The specialist record stores of this era were all part of an informal international network, and I bumped into Tim Palmer of the London-based Groove Records store and Citybeat label in Vinylmania one day, in town to attend the New Music Seminar, buy vinyl and do deals. He was excited about a new imprint he had just started: XL Recordings. We discussed our favourite music of that moment.

One of my co-workers was a teenager called Joey Longo; a former assistant engineer at the legendary Power Play studio in Queens, he produced under the name Pal Joey, and went on to make some of the most enduring and largely unsung underground dance music of all time, including 'Hot Music' under the name SoHo, an infectious groove cunningly built around a tiny Wynton Marsalis sample.

Almost all of the stock in Vinylmania was released on local independent labels such as Strictly Rhythm, Fourth Floor, Easy Street and Nu Groove (all specialising in house music), and labels like Wild Pitch, Profile, Sleeping Bag and Next Plateau, who provided homes to an incredible array of mostly hip-hop talent. The staff and owners of these labels would come in and sell their wares.

It was a thriving community, multi-cultural and diverse. A few years later, when riots had broken out in LA after the Rodney King verdict, some of Charlie's neighbouring stores boarded up their windows for fear of similar unrest. There was no need for this in Vinylmania. It was a melting pot. Charlie's employees and customers were black, or Italian, or Hispanic. Gay, or straight. It wasn't relevant to Charlie. They all loved the music the shop sold and were all treated with equal respect.

I'm not sure what I thought would happen when I went to New York. I found myself close to the heart of things at Vinylmania, and tapped into the reservoir of energy that exists in New York in a way that would inform my future endeavours. I had no career goals to speak of, more of an all-purpose enthusiasm for music, clubbing and escape. Freedom.

Some of my experiences were ill-advised. I found some unidentified speckled blue tablets in a plastic baggie on the floor of hip-hop club The Building one Thursday night, and elected to take one, in the interests of research. The tablets contained, I think, synthetic mescaline, and the powerful and lengthy psychotropic odyssey that followed had its enlightening moments, but also involved seeing a friend take a punch from a towering and muscle-bound Italian giant on 14th Street and put me off hallucinogenics for twenty years.

Vinylmania survived as an independent bricks-and-mortar record store until 2007, when it fell victim to a perfect storm of online shopping and rising rents. Charlie continued to sell records, mainly via the Discogs website.

In 2015 I visited the warehouse in Coney Island where he kept 300,000 pieces of vinyl. I was in New York with my son Sonny, having instigated the idea that a trip to New York with me would happen instead of a bar mitzvah as a coming-of-age ritual at thirteen, and Charlie took us to Coney Island to visit the funfair.

Charlie wouldn't let me spend long in his incredible vinyl cave, correctly pointing out in a grandfatherly manner that it was Sonny's day not mine; but when I mentioned that I was looking for a mint copy of Malcolm McLaren's *Duck Rock* LP, as I had somehow never owned it on vinyl, Charlie reached an arm behind and above his head and without looking pulled out the record I'd mentioned.

A vinyl wizard, pulling the wax from his cloak.

11PM TILL DAWN

Even prior to my New York adventure, London nightlife had changed my whole existence. I started going out at a time when there was a different venue to visit every night, and only a small total number of people attending all these places, so faces would soon become familiar. I was ridiculously young to start attending these clubs, and allowed entrance only because licensing laws were not enforced.

Nightlife leads social change, and London was being integrated one club night at a time. While the downtown New York scene had people from the art world and ghettos mixing, there was nowhere else in the world where such an extensive multi-cultural scene developed as London. Acid house, named for the burbling 'acid' sound made by the Roland 303 synthesiser, was itself synthesised in Chicago by pioneers such as DJ Pierre and Ron Hardy, and brought back to London via Ibiza by DJs like Paul Oakenfold, Trevor Fung and Johnny Walker, to then reach beyond the fairly exclusive London-centric club world it grew out of, and mutate into the wider rave movement.

Keith Flint, a raver from Braintree, Essex, before he was a member of The Prodigy, reminisced later about his fairly typical entry point to this world: 'Whereas acid house was exclusive and you had to know the right people and the right places, M25 parties made it more of a people's movement. My entry into rave culture was when I came back from travelling. I was a bit lost . . . my mate's girlfriend told me about rave parties with such enthusiasm and such passion that I thought I've got to be part of it. The next Friday we went down to The Barn [a club on Rayne Road in Braintree, Essex]. I took some acid, took some ecstasy and never looked back.'

The M25 had been completed in 1986 and it provided the physical connector from London to the home counties where many of the events took place. Shortly before my New York escapades I had attended outdoor events, including a Biology event in a field in Elstree. I spent the weekend before my A-levels raving there. I had done no revision anyway but this sealed my educational fate. I believe that subconsciously I wanted to fail my exams to ensure that I had no way back.

The rave scene had a less clearly defined stance than punk, but it was bigger, and belonged to the people. The parties were seen by the authorities as a social menace, presenting a threat to the existing order. As Keith Flint said: 'The government didn't know what it was. The police didn't know how to control it. The kids ran it.'

Laws were hurriedly passed to try to outlaw these gatherings, initially the Graham Bright Bill, also known as the Acid House Bill, resulting in the Entertainments (Increased Penalties) Act 1990, allowing the government to impose severe penalties on anyone organising rave events. Music has always been used as a scapegoat, something social problems can be blamed on by disingenuous politicians and commentators. By 1994 the Criminal Justice and Public Order Act would come into being, including Part V, which focused on raves specifically and included a definition of 'repetitive beats'.

It was not uncommon, in this pre-internet era, for several thousand ravers to be gathered in a field within hours of a pirate radio announcement of an event taking place. And while the large-scale raves were an amazing spectacle, the huge outdoor events did not provide the intimate experience and sensory overload of a small club night. I loved High on Hope, which took place every Thursday at Dingwalls in Camden Lock. Here, DJ Norman Jay, Ladbroke Grove native, rare groove pioneer and founder of the Good Times and Shake & Fingerpop sound systems, played soulful US house to a joyous dance floor that felt more like a congregation than a nightclub.

In concentrating on deep, vocal tunes in a London club setting, Norman Jay connected the acid house energy to a more soulful style of music. The music policy was informed and influenced by the Zanzibar club in New Jersey, hosted by Tony Humphries, which was a descendant of the Paradise Garage and thus a grand-child of The Loft. Norman Jay is now seen as an elder statesman of nightlife but even thirty years ago his High on Hope night was already fourth generation, a great-grandchild.

While in retrospect the scene was socially significant, the emphasis at these events was on hedonism, not fighting the powers that be, just as few Paradise Garage attendees were actually preoccupied by Stonewall. In the UK, music itself was highly politicised in the early eighties, via movements such as Red Wedge and artists like Billy Bragg and Paul Weller, both of whom were childhood heroes to me. I saw Weller hanging out at High on Hope. There was a connection between the more overtly political scene of the mid-eighties and the hedonistic acid house era, but a thread of ambivalence seems to connect scenes that were supposedly of a political nature.

The classic US soundtrack to the early UK events did not just sound outstanding at the time but resonates with great power today; some of the greatest gospel-tinged soul music of all time, rejected by the US mainstream, lovingly embraced in the UK. The nostalgic effect the biggest songs – Joe Smooth's 'Promised Land', CeCe Rogers' 'Someday', Phase II's 'Reachin'', Frankie Knuckles' 'Your Love' – still have on anyone who was present can be almost comical. On hearing these tunes, even in a domestic setting, I've seen grown people of my age group lose their composure, the structure of their grown-up, responsible lives dissolving as a moment of connection to pure rave essence occurs.

Rave had a power that impacted on the mainstream almost immediately. The biggest songs played at these events began to cross over to the UK pop charts, generally bypassing radio and all other media, the grassroots support being all that was necessary. A whole new record industry sector, geared towards these mostly one-off dance records, emerged.

It comprised three subsectors: existing labels such as Champion, owned by Mel Medalie; Desire, an offshoot of then indie Fiction; and Martin Heath and James Horrocks' Rhythm King label, all of whom had previously been focused on rap and more mainstream dance but saw the tremendous energy and opportunity in the new underground scene. Tim Palmer's Citybeat was another one of these.

There was a wave of new DIY independent labels, all with differing approaches, such as Neil Rushton's Birmingham-based Network label, who made licensing arrangements with the early Detroit pioneers Juan Atkins, Derrick May and Kevin Sanderson. Sheffield's Warp had an uncompromisingly artistic and tasteful approach which would remain their hallmark. There were also major-label subdivisions such as Polygram's FFRR imprint run by DJ Pete Tong, Paul Oakenfold's Warner-distributed Perfecto and DeConstruction, part of RCA.

My colleague from Loppylugs, Trevor Jackson, was by now an in-demand graphic designer and repackaging American house music for the UK's clubbing record buyers, creating memorable sleeves for many classics, including Raze's 'Break 4 Love' and Royal House's 'Yeah Buddy' for the Harlesden-based Champion label. Openings were created into a previously more conservative, conventional and older music business for a lot of colourful and entrepreneurial characters with an immense amount of youthful energy, and as small and nimble companies released one-off records by anonymous bedroom producers, there was room for real creativity on the part of the labels themselves. While there was money to be made, the spirit of early rave was defiantly anti-establishment and non-materialistic. It was a sub-cultural form of entrepreneurialism.

There was a gradual and at the time imperceptible shift in dress code. I had worn second-hand Levi 501s, Dr Martens shoes and, in the absence of the MA1 jacket I really desired, a black corduroy Levi's jacket with a Budweiser beer mat attached to the back for my early clubbing forays to Crazy Larry's off the Kings Road, Club MFI at Legends, Delirium at The Astoria and Philip Sallon's Opera House night. I quite fancied myself in this get-up but it was soon to receive an overhaul.

I had purchased a pair of white, red and blue Fila high-top trainers and wore these with white Champion jogging pants and a bright green hoodie. My flat top, achieved monthly for £5 at a barber's on the Finchley Road called Upper Cut, was grown out into the style often referred to as 'curtains', and I developed an adequate version of the look that took hold as clubbing (to rare groove and hip-hop) became raving (to acid house, and then hardcore).

The large number of disenfranchised UK B-boys attending and DJing at rave nights, where the atmosphere was more hospitable than at rap events, led to inevitable attempts to fuse the European synth sounds, cold Detroit electronics and Chicago-influenced pianos with rougher, more shuffly drums that reflected New York hip-hop and had their origin in funk, often with speeded-up snippets of disco a cappellas over the top. This was breakbeat hardcore. And over-the-top it was.

Speeded-up funk drums, it turned out, made a potent combination with the existing elements prominent in the dance music of the time. Hardcore rave was being born, and I was effortlessly connected to its different elements. As Keith recalled: 'The sound from Essex had beats from hip-hop. That's what sucked me in. It wasn't just a 303 and a 4/4.'

It was immediately exciting music that was also immediately unfashionable. Those of us who would choose to make this style of music didn't receive a warm welcome from arbiters of hip tastes at the time, such as *The Face* magazine. Perhaps it was too suburban. A purist's nightmare. It was also the birth of the first chapter in music to which I'd be able to make some real contribution, and effectively cross the line from fan to creator. In classical music, most musicians begin as students. In popular music we begin as fans, and to become a musician is to become a creator as well as a consumer of the music. But not instead of.

The sound we would create and popularise was utterly British, in its multi-cultural DNA and its DIY approach. Though it's difficult to identify the very first person to successfully pull these elements together, the most likely candidate to deserve the title of 'inventor of hardcore/breakbeat rave' was an Italian-American – Frankie Bones from Brooklyn, who had DJed with us at a Housequake night at The Tabernacle, W11. With his series of Bonesbreaks 12-inches, he laid some of the musical foundations for the breakbeat hardcore scene we subsequently built in the UK. The label for his 12-inches carried the slogan 'hard, raw and raunchy beats for DJs' and you could hear the hip-hop in there. Bones had been a graffiti artist in the days before rave, and had once nearly died hiding from the NYPD under a train which started to move.

It was easy and quick to craft a hardcore tune. No prior musical experience necessary. We were novices, enthusiastically banging out rudimentary work unhampered by knowledge of what key we might have been in, or whether our vocal samples were in any way in tune with our sub basslines. This amateurism helped us make something new and untamed.

While I've gone on to work with some highly trained and accomplished players, I continue to value the participation of non-musicians in the music-making process. If you have no musical training, but you have the desire to make music, and the confidence to not be hampered by your lack of formal education, you are in a good position. You are potentially freer than a musician with more knowledge, because you don't know the rules.

I had tried making tunes in a small studio in the back of that Ladbroke Grove community centre, The Tabernacle, the main room of which I still DJed in sometimes, with a helpful and patient local engineer called Jonny Colman, and had even taken my demos to brand-new rave label XL Recordings to see if they would release them as a 12-inch. The label had started as an offshoot of an offshoot. A grandchild. As Beggars had co-parented Citybeat, Citybeat birthed XL. Citybeat had been having some success with dance records it licensed from US labels but Tim Palmer and A&R man Nick Halkes felt that another imprint was necessary to better reflect the underground scene that was exciting them.

On a trip from Wandsworth to Soho, while discussing a suitable name for the new venture with Nick, Tim stopped for a burger, and grabbing his Filofax from the back seat of his car noticed the label in a promo T-shirt on the back seat: Size XL. The new label now had a name: XL Recordings.

A memorable logo and silver and black house bag was designed and XL began releasing 12-inches aimed at the burgeoning rave scene by an increasingly impressive transatlantic roster of pseudonymous producer/DJs, many of whom I had come across in Vinylmania, including Junior Vasquez (as Ellis Dee), Tommy Musto and Frankie Bones (as Flowmasters) and, from the UK, The KLF's Jimmy Cauty with reggae producer Tony Thorpe, as Moody Boys.

Nineteen-year-old native of Braintree, Essex, Liam Howlett, who four years earlier had indicated the extent of both his skill and his ambition by coming both first and third in a pause-tape-mix competition held by Mike Allen on Capital Radio, had hand-delivered a cassette of his first productions to the label. He used the name 'Prodigy'. Nick had immediately seen the potential of this intensely focused young man and offered him a deal. He accepted. The Prodigy were now signed to XL.

Conversely, Nick wasn't overly impressed by the demos I took him, but we got on well. I had also asked Tim about work behind the counter at Groove, and while there were no vacancies, Tim was able to offer me £50 a week to hang around in the basement offices of the label, helping out where I could alongside Tim, Nick, and a third XL team member Leah Riches. Soon I was turning up on most days, feeling like I sort of had a new job in the music industry. I liked the idea of that. It was indeed more of an idea than anything else, entailing no job description or salary. No matter; I was not going anywhere and had nothing to lose. I was still nineteen, back from New York, my educational career over. My parents were in full panic mode. In an attempt to calm them down I had applied to some universities, and been rejected by all of them except an outpost of a lowly north London polytechnic in Kentish Town, soon to close down and become a Pizza Express. I attended on one occasion only, for half a lecture. I now suspect I had some type of attention deficit condition that enabled me to focus with great intensity on my passions but made it impossible for me to concentrate on anything else. These things were not medicalised at the time. Either way I had no doubts about what I was doing.

EVERY FRIDAY THEREAFTER

Bouncer
Bounces
No.One
+1 Tronik
-1 Phog
-1 Sorg
+1 Sorg remix

+1 liquid
-5 Choci
+2 (liquid)
-1 Mon X } just one?

+4 Prod every
O Prod remix
+2 Tripper

+6 SUAD
-2 Acen
+4 You/Me
6 Chime
+½ Hardcore Heaven

Bounces
0 DJ s unity
-2 DJ s Jme
+8 Cutty
-1½ Tronik

+½ -1 Mad Ragga
-3 Rad Buoy
+2 Wayla Mix
+5 True d → -2 Blatant

WAY IN
330 ⅓
MY BRAIN

RICH

Many of my favourite tunes of 1991 contained one of the great noises of the rave era – a thick swirly racket that came out of the Roland Alpha Juno keyboard and became known as 'the hoover'. These kinds of sounds kept the generation gap alive and well in '91. I was rooted in hip-hop and that was my first love, but marrying hip-hop to the new scene felt powerful.

Nick seemed somehow risk-averse, oddly sensible given the times, but he was an astute talent-spotter as well as aspiring musician and DJ. He saw that I also might have an eye for talent, and made me feel at home at this new rave label, XL. It was fun, and we were highly motivated; to produce, to DJ and to attempt to operate a record company. These activities all fed into each other.

XL's peers, rave labels specialising in the UK-originated breakbeat hardcore sound such as Suburban Base, Reinforced, DJ SS's Formation, based in Leicester, and Hackney's mighty Shut Up And Dance were emerging. Production House, founded by former Galaxy soul star Phil Fearon, while seemingly more commercially orientated, counted gifted rave producer Acen Razvi among their roster.

Nick and I decided to make some music together. We managed to get some free studio time in the 'writing room' at MCA Music Publishing on the Fulham Palace Road, a small but highly successful publishing outfit housing a quick-witted A&R manager called Paul Connolly. Paul had first contacted me to find out how to get in touch with DJ duo SL2. This seemed nosy. When I asked him why he was asking, he told me what music publishing was. This was the first time I'd heard of it.

The night before we went into the MCA studio for the first time, we met at the tiny, dirty and unkempt flat I rented on Delancey Street in Camden Town for £50 per week, and discussed what we might do in the studio the next day. This would have been called a 'pre-production meeting' if we knew such a thing existed. I had two hip-hop records I was interested in sampling. One was produced by Marley Marl. I thought that his drums might provide a good rave rhythm track, once speeded up to 45rpm, by when they would be third-hand, Marley having heisted them himself. The other was an Ice-T a cappella that might make a good hook – the line in question being 'Bang! Nine automatic'.

Nick liked my idea for the drums but thought we could probably come up with a better vocal hook. My friend Sam Spivack began entertaining us by impersonating a local nightclub bouncer rejecting our attempts to gain free entry with a surprising degree of accuracy: 'Your name's not down, you're not coming in', which we duly recorded on to a TDK C90 cassette tape using a no-brand Walkman knock-off tape recorder.

'The Bouncer', which we chose to release under the name Kicks Like a Mule, was written, recorded and mixed in one day. Not that we knew we had performed three separate functions – we'd just strung the samples together until something new existed, something that we'd be happy to DJ with, adding a one-finger, two-note synth riff and equally monophonic bassline, keeping the lo-fi recording of Sam's vocal performance intact. With the help of Paul Connolly, now apparently our publisher, we took the tune to a few labels, thinking it might be better to keep some separation between the records we released on XL and our own efforts. None of them were interested.

Then Mike West, at that time aka Rebel MC, later known as Congo Natty after his conversion to Rastafarianism, showed up. Mike, who had started as part of the Mastermind Sound System and was one of the first British rappers to enjoy chart success through his collaborations with production duo Double Trouble, said he liked the tune and wanted to release it on his own Tribal Bass label. The label was being co-run by his manager Simon Goffe, an affable former soul DJ who had worked at the Desire label and also managed heroic rave duo Shut Up and Dance. Tribal Bass was also now home to UK hip-hop artists Demon Boyz, originally signed to Music Of Life. This all added up. We were in business.

'The Bouncer' by Nick and me, aka Kicks Like a Mule, was released on Tribal Bass and became a big tune in the raves and on the pirates, and ended up in the Top 10 of the national charts, as compiled by Gallup at that time. Our DJing diaries filled up, and we became busy on the PA circuit. When we performed at the Rage night at Heaven, I manned a pair of turntables onstage, and began the set by playing the 12-inch instrumental of Super Lover Cee & Casanova Rud's 'Do The James' speeded up from 33rpm to 45, the click of the Technics speed button immediately taking the record's tempo from a head-nodding 92bpm to a frantic, rave-friendly 136bpm, re-recontextualising the James Brown drums. Then from turntable two I mixed in our song, 'The Bouncer'. I was explaining how I got there. Hip-hop records played at the wrong speed were fundamental to the breakbeat hardcore sound, and I wanted to communicate that.

Back in the studio, we remixed a northern rave tune called 'Don't Go' by Awesome 3, chopping in various rap samples, and adding a satisfyingly rude amount of 808 bottom end, enough that the tune began to catch on in Miami, Florida, spiritual home of 808 bass. The production on this mix was the closest I'd got to the sound in my head. I wanted to make a rave sound so hip-hop that it wasn't rave any more. But I couldn't quite get there. My lack of studio chops had been no problem at first but it was starting to hinder my progression.

Simon was keen to manage me and proposed I give up the label work to concentrate full time on record-making, but the suggestion didn't stick.

Our agent Solomon Parker used to drive us to out-of-town gigs. On one early-hours trip home from the north-east, Nick, Solomon and I were seated in a rented Ford Granada alongside our MC Longsy D, himself a pioneer of underground genre fusion via his 1987 single with Cut Master MC 'Hip Hop Reggae' and his successful 1989 attempt at skanking rave 'This Is Ska'.

Solomon had an *A–Z* open on his lap and we were in either Redcar or Stockton-on-Tees. Speed, again, was an issue. As we hurtled south, Nick, the most sober among us, warned Solomon to slow down and check that the bridge above the stretch of water we were hurtling towards was not out. Idiotically I encouraged Solomon to ignore Nick's cautious suggestion and put his foot down. Except the bridge was indeed out, and had Nick not sounded his warning at the moment he did, and Solomon not chosen to ignore my reckless entreaty to ignore it, we would have lost the rave wars and met our watery Hardcore Valhalla that evening. Our car stopped inches from the edge of a steep plunge. Nick's risk-aversion had saved our lives.

We made a promo video for 'The Bouncer', enlisting luminaries including Paul 'Trouble' Anderson, Fabio and Demon Boyz to appear, and then got to fulfil a childhood ambition by performing on *Top of the Pops* on 30 January 1992. A *Top of the Pops* appearance was the dream of every aspiring pop star. My Edgware fantasy was real. Didn't this mean I'd made it? Not exactly. My childhood was over. This was an ending as much as a beginning.

My first *TOTP* appearance would be my last, and, while many extraordinary experiences lay ahead, it would be twenty years before I would play music on BBC TV again, performing with Bobby Womack on *Later . . . with Jools Holland*. *Top of the Pops* itself would by then no longer be in existence.

While we eagerly grabbed at the opportunity to be on national television, Liam Howlett was taking the visionary stance of refusing to allow The Prodigy to appear on TV shows, feeling that it compromised their credibility, and while we were having fun doing a lot of live work around the country and guesting as DJs on stations like the recently legalised KISS FM, unlike The Prodigy we weren't really building any sort of audience.

When we released a follow-up to 'The Bouncer' called 'Number One', with Longsy on vocals and a mix by our label boss Rebel MC on the flip, it didn't really connect with the scene we were in, and so it didn't really mean anything to anyone. Our artist career had just got started, but it was under threat. We had aimed 'The Bouncer' at our DJ boxes, and it was indeed an effective club tune for many DJs. But its hook ensured the song was bracketed alongside the novelty tunes of the time, putting us in a parlous position. To me this seemed unfair, as we had built the tune on a solid foundation of sub bass, breakbeats and synth noise, and the hook was in fact simply my friend talking into a cassette recorder. It was not exactly a calculated assault on the pop world. On the B-side of 'Number One' I had even crafted a cut-up sample-based hip-hop head-nodder called 'DJ Talk', which gained some traction among more adventurous hip-hop DJs.

But regardless of our intentions, what we were doing was perceived by some as a bit lightweight, and 'The Bouncer' hit just before a wave of TV theme-based novelty rave struck, including Smart E's 'Sesame's Treat' and Urban Hype's 'Trip To Trumpton'. And though our artistic focus and motivation may have been diluted, the releases on XL were increasingly successful. We were establishing the label as a real force.

Hardcore rave was a strange movement in that we were simultaneously pioneering some of the most innovative DIY music ever made in the UK, while skirting on the edge of commercial novelty. It was a precarious position, but we were infecting the mainstream nonetheless. It was bending towards us.

The Prodigy became XL's headline artist from the release of their second EP, which included a new version of 'Charly', the first of many huge hits they recorded for the label. Part of the joy of their success was that they were single-mindedly focused on the rave scene they came from, and uninterested in any type of commercial compromise. The ambivalence only fuelled the success. I absorbed this. There would be much more to learn from Liam.

Other signings of Nick's, such as SL2, aka hugely likeable Essex DJs Slipmatt & Lime and their MC Jay-J, were also proving to be winners. Their songs 'Way In My Brain', 'DJs Take Control' and the irresistible 'On A Ragga Tip' were initially underground and subsequently pop favourites. Despite their commercial success, in an ultimate gesture of underground DJ solidarity SL2 never made an album, as they felt it would have taken the music too long to get from the studio to the DJ boxes, and the whole point of the tunes would have been lost.

Nick signed a noisy Belgian techno record called 'Anasthasia' by T99. I thought we should add rap vocals to the song, and enlisted Flex, a member of original Ladbroke Grove crew Mighty Ethnicz, to deliver a verse. In a reflection of the ambivalent view of the rave world held by rap artists at this time, Flex was willing to undertake the gig only under a (second) pseudonym, regardless of the route into the mainstream it might provide him, rave records selling so much more than UK rap records at this time.

I signed rave producer Eamon Downes, aka Liquid, whose 'Sweet Harmony' borrowed the unforgettable piano hook from CeCe Rogers' Marshall Jefferson-produced Chicago classic 'Someday' and still puts a hazy smile on any ex-raver's face, and made deals for classic hardcore tunes like Dance Conspiracy's 'Dub War'.

Nick and I were focused solely on the music but Tim liked the idea of us promoting a large-scale event rather than being passive participants. XL duly became co-promoters of a huge rave called Vision at Popham airfield, which took place on 29 August 1992. It was understandable that Tim wanted us to be more involved in these parties, given the excitement around them. But I feared that running large-scale raves was best left to the experts.

The DJ line-up for the event was solid, including Grooverider and Jumping Jack Frost, but we were concerned when the flyers arrived. Rave promotion was all about hyperbole but this was madness. One side of the flyer showed a naked, Venus-type figure holding what appeared to be planet earth above her head. She was flanked by two XL logos. The text on the reverse made promises about an awaiting rave paradise that would be hard to keep. It turned out to be a messy night.

When Keith Flint reminisced about it two decades later, he smilingly said of Vision: 'We were really expecting huge things. The hype was massive. All I remember is that it was very wet and incredibly muddy. It was a little bit oversold and underdelivered. The *Blade Runner* set was actually just a few old cars.'

On the night, Nick and I found ourselves, soaking wet, trying to physically support a pillar which was about to collapse and appeared to be responsible for keeping the main tent erect. I recall with clarity this pillar and our comic attempt to support it. All else is hazy.

A short documentary on the event survives, though, in which one of the organisers can be witnessed taking to the main stage and announcing that there are 7,000 people too many in the tent. The crowd, by now well fuelled on a full tank of breakbeats and MDMA, respond to his dire warning with wildly enthusiastic grins, ecstasy-fuelled cheering and deafening whistle-blowing. Rather than continuing his attempts at potentially life-saving crowd control, he grins manically and, submitting to the rave energy, begins to pump his fist to the music.

Vision, amazing though it was in many ways ('A reflection of the past, a view to the future') was XL's first and last attempt at large-scale rave co-promotion, and Tim ended up embroiled in a lawsuit with the company responsible for the documentary. The evening's narrative was a microcosm of what would happen to the rave scene itself. Perhaps to all scenes.

As Keith Flint put it: 'The word is ethics. You don't sell out, don't rubbish your own thing, don't shit on your doorstep. There was ambition but [also] ethics. The rave scene was about being real. [But] towards the end of the rave era the money took it down. People putting DJs on the bill who weren't there. Charging too much for tickets, ripping people off. It became a big exercise to rinse people of their money. That's when the magic left. But there was a sweet spot. It was special.'

Large-scale event promotion was now thankfully off the agenda, and we weren't sure where Kicks Like a Mule was heading, but by releasing records on XL that worked well in our DJ sets, we had stumbled upon a seemingly foolproof A&R approach. We already knew that these tunes connected to the audience. But this approach also had a downside in that the most visionary music is not easily understood and might clear a dance floor rather than fill it. Our A&R policy was reliable but actually more conservative and limited than the one I would later develop.

The weakness of our 'road-test' approach was illustrated when I purchased Aphex Twin's self-released white label 'Analogue Bubblebath' from Zoom Records on Camden High Street. I took the 12-inch vinyl home to my flat around the corner on Delancey Street, and remember having some vague inkling that there was something special about it, but there was no way I could fit it in my DJ set, and I had a gig that night, so I exiled it to the high shelf. This was before Aphex Twin was affiliated to Warp Records, so I was in effect at that moment failing to recognise the then-unsigned most visionary experimental electronic musician of my lifetime.

Although Simon Goffe came from a club background and was deeply involved, as we all were, in the selling of 12-inch singles on the back of club play, he told me about the importance of music journalists, saying 'good press sells albums'. This was the first time I'd come across that concept, and it stuck, tucked away somehow for future reference. I contemplated that in making albums maybe you could experiment more than when recording 12-inches, because the music press might help promote the music even if it wasn't club or radio friendly.

But our way of working was largely about instinct so there was no right or wrong. As a small label in a niche musical scene, people knew what we stood for, so the demos we got sent were usually interesting. The bigger the label, the more demos you get, and the lower the overall quality of them. At this time, it took a certain amount of instinct and savvy just to send a demo to XL in the first place, and the artists who thrive tend to have these qualities.

Liam Howlett would have been unlikely to get anywhere sending his music to EMI or CBS in 1990. His instincts and decision-making were great from the word go, identifying tiny XL as the place most likely to understand his work because he liked the music released by the label, driving to Wandsworth from Braintree and delivering his tape. He was ambitious but he had perspective. His instincts told him not to approach a bigger company. That might have been too ambitious.

Every artist who achieves longevity does so not just through the making of music, but the making of decisions, eventually thousands of decisions, starting with what to call themselves and who to play their demos to, through whether to sack their friend and go with a professional manager, which live agent to work with, and then on to the lifelong navigation of an endless series of suggested compromises.

The artists who thrive are not just the most musically talented but the most dedicated to their core values. There is a toughness required for this kind of work, but given that artistry is delicate, a dichotomous nature is necessary. This is the thread that has linked the artists I have worked most closely with. Extraordinary strength coupled with a sensitivity that is so acute it is almost psychic.

In 1990 we had little by way of theory but our practice was good. I would cut dub plates, one-off lacquer-coated records that survive for about thirty plays, at a mastering studio called The Exchange in Camden, and take them to DJs to gauge the reactions. We could get music from the studio to the streets quickly. There was no friction. I would travel around the country in my white Renault 5, armed with a list of record stores and different DJs to look up.

And much as I was energised by rave, I got the opportunity to tip my hat towards the music I loved most, and also hint at the multi-genre future of XL, by striking a deal with New York independent rap label Tommy Boy to release the debut album by their new signing, the LA-based House of Pain, in the UK. The label we were licensing the group from was almost as much of a draw as the group themselves, Tommy Boy being the indie that had already introduced rap fans to an incredible roster of talent, including De La Soul and Digital Underground, two of my favourite groups of all time, in any genre. Tommy Boy had no UK operation of their own at this time and would license artists to different labels.

The label's Irish co-president Monica Lynch had received House of Pain's 'Jump Around' demo, and said of it, according to the band's producer Lawrence Muggerud, aka DJ Muggs: 'This reminds me of my brothers. After church, they go to bars and get in fights.'

The group's leader, Everlast, was an accomplished, gruff MC with a commanding presence. He had formerly been part of Ice-T's Rhyme Syndicate, and had formed this new group with Leor Dimont, aka DJ Lethal, and Daniel O'Connor, aka Danny Boy. They played on Everlast and Danny Boy's Irish heritage, and their liquor-drenched style struck a chord, their anthemic 'Jump Around' crossing over to become a US Top 5 pop hit, remaining one of the great classics of party-friendly hip-hop and utilising a mysterious yelp, the provenance of which remains hotly debated to this day by sample spotters.

House of Pain were part of the LA-based Soul Assassins crew alongside Cypress Hill and Funkdoobiest. The musical linchpin of the collective was DJ Muggs, formerly of 7A3, whose eerie yet playful soul-based beats were as great as those of his second-generation hip-hop production peers, Pete Rock and DJ Premier. I wanted to help make House of Pain as successful as possible in the UK, but I didn't necessarily make the best first impression on them.

On their first visit to the UK I gave them a lift to Tim Westwood's studio to guest on his Capital Radio show. The group were horrified by the state (and status) of my dirty white Renault 5. When they saw Westwood's gleaming black Jeep their leader Everlast questioned, with some concern, 'Westwood more paid than you?'

Their eponymous debut album, usually referred to as *Fine Malt Lyrics*, is tough throughout, courtesy of beats from Muggs as well as the band's own DJ Lethal. The entrance qualification for other rappers on the album seemed to be that they were possessed of a nasal whine which would contrast suitably with Everlast's gruff growl. Danny Boy, Funkdoobiest's Son Doobie, and especially Cypress Hill's B-Real all pass with flying colours. The album hints at a merging of rap and rock, which flowered in two other classic

1992 albums, Rage Against the Machine's debut and the Beastie Boys' extraordinary *Check Your Head*, and was embodied later in the more steroidal form of Limp Bizkit, the outfit DJ Lethal would go on to join.

The debut House of Pain album was a big success, one of the bestselling rap albums of all time in the UK at that point. We organised a celebratory promo visit to Ireland, taking the band and a bunch of UK DJs, writers and scenesters on a Guinness-drenched jolly, the band performing a rapturously received club show, the only time I have ever personally attempted the task of security, in order to beef up the lacklustre crowd control at the club we had been hastily booked into.

The second House of Pain album, *Same As It Ever Was*, contained no 'Jump Around'-size hit but was in fact superior to their debut, showcasing more of what the band was capable of. Everlast issues his trademark threats throughout, but his lyrics are never less than witty, as well as muscular. On tracks like 'It Ain't A Crime' he amply displays the ability that enabled him to have a successful solo career after the band, enjoying triple platinum sales of his album *Whitey Ford Sings The Blues*.

Despite the overall tone of aggression in *Same As It Ever Was*, Everlast is gracious in acknowledging the underground hip-hop artists that influenced him and paved the way for his crossover success. 'Over There Shit' quotes Audio Two's 'Top Billin'', and in 'Still Got A Lotta Love' Everlast gives a shout-out to Kool Keith and co.: 'And much love to the Ultramagnetic / 'Cause everybody knows you never got enough credit'.

I made another trip to Ireland with House of Pain around the release of the album, this time playing at the Féile Festival in County Tipperary alongside The Prodigy, both bands being rapturously received, other artists on the bill including Blur, Björk and Rage Against the Machine. XL, with these two artists, was suddenly feeling like an enterprise that was intensely alive in a world beyond rave.

I would interact further with the exotic world of West Coast rap.

Knowing I was going to make my first trip to LA around this time, I asked Paul Connolly if he had any ideas for what else I could do while I was out there. He asked me if I had heard of a label called Ruthless Records. Of course I had. This was the company owned by NWA founder Eazy-E and his manager Jerry Heller. It was the most notorious gangsta rap label in existence. Paul said that his boss had recently done a sub-publishing deal with Ruthless outside the US, and they were surprisingly friendly, and maybe I could meet up with them while I was in LA. Sounded good.

Security at the Ruthless HQ on a sketchy stretch of Santa Monica Boulevard was tight and not particularly polite. I greeted the first heavily armed guard I came across with a polite smile and cheery English 'hello'. He scowled at me. This was a tense time for Ruthless. NWA's best lyricist, Ice Cube, was long gone. Dr Dre had recently exited the organisation with the forceful help of ex-footballer and bodyguard turned music manager Suge Knight.

Ruthless boss Jerry Heller, one of the most controversial figures in the history of rap music, manager of NWA and with Eazy co-owner of Ruthless, formerly agent to seventies superstars such as The Who and Black Sabbath, was welcoming enough, though, in his way. Ushering me into his old-school exec-style office, he asked me a couple of questions about myself and XL and, idly, if I'd ever considered moving to America. He then showed me a framed picture on his desk of a blonde in a bikini and said, 'This is my girlfriend. You can have anything you want in this country if you have enough money.'

He then asked me if I drank, and told me that he was about to hit a sports bar before taking off for the Jewish holidays. He asked me if I knew what Jewish was. I told him of my heritage. He got very excited and said, 'Wait till Eazy gets a load of this! An English Jew!' I was taken aback by the idea that Compton's gangsta legend would be excited by the idea of English Jews. I didn't find English Jews very exciting, although I was one. But you never knew. Everything about the day was feeling unlikely.

Eazy arrived. He was diminutive but charismatic and looked

somehow padded. I think he may have been wearing a bullet-proof suit under his Carhartts. We headed off in a convoy, stopping to drop something off, I wasn't sure what, at an unfurnished mansion belonging to Eazy. As we wandered into the cavernous property, Jerry told me that Eazy mainly used the premises for the purposes of his sexual conquests and spoke with pride about Eazy's promiscuity. A prominent East Coast golden-age rapper would later tell a mutual friend of ours that his one regret was not attending more orgies with Eazy-E. His comment indicated that he attended at least one. I was not to receive any such invite, but the sports bar was fun.

There was a basketball game on the TVs, which I wasn't particularly interested in but everybody was very friendly, particularly Eazy. I told him I liked a song he had made recently with Naughty by Nature and he seemed surprised by my interest in it. I think the response to it had been lukewarm compared to the incredible reactions he had been used to receiving for music he had made with NWA.

Heller would continue to be publicly castigated by the departed members of NWA but always protested his innocence, offering detailed information to back his defence of his business practices. My visit to Ruthless was odd and otherworldly. Eazy would die from AIDS-related complications some three years later, and Jerry Heller passed away in 2016, wrapped up in fresh litigation with the surviving members of the group, and furious about how he had been portrayed in the *Straight Outta Compton* movie.

After my brief spell in Camden I was now living in Ladbroke Grove, where I would settle permanently. I was DJing, and continuing to pursue my artistic ambitions as rave producer but with ever-diminishing returns.

Nick and I signed to Pete Tong's FFRR label to make a rave record under the name Lifelike; this was a non-event for all concerned, and when I later heard the saying 'the music industry is worse than dog eats dog, it's dog doesn't return other dog's phone call', that kind of summed it up.

I continued to work in the studio on some rap music, including some British hip-hop I was proud of in 'Pass The Rizla' by London Posse, and two UK remixes Profile commissioned me to do for Run-DMC, but XL as a record label was increasingly the focus of my attention.

In 1993 Nick Halkes left XL to helm his own dance imprint at EMI, which he named Positiva. I was offered a role at the new label, but it didn't feel right to me to move. I had already established that my priority was to do things on my terms, and I was willing to go to great lengths to protect this.

And Liam Howlett was not just colleague but friend and role model, a constant reminder not to compromise. I felt connected to him. We were the same age, hip-hop obsessed, ambitious, and had a similar sense of humour. We were a formidable team, and we had work to do.

Soon after Nick's departure Tim Palmer, the always enthusiastic and supportive boss of XL, began to feel that he had achieved what he had set out to: building from scratch an independent label that would last with or without him, not to mention organising some legendary parties. Tim, approaching forty-five, wanted to experience a different life. He had found a natural environment at the full moon parties in Goa, and in 1994 asked to be bought out of the label, which Martin was able to facilitate, leaving him with equity he could pass on to me.

Stepping into Tim's shoes, I was a twenty-three-year-old with not much subtlety but a lot of enthusiasm and some big ideas. I was the boss. Now what?

RESPECT TO MY EQUIPMENT AND MY MIND

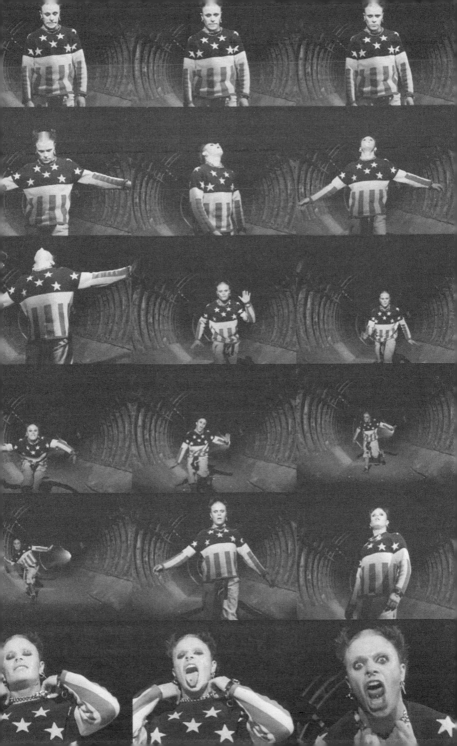

We moved XL from our windowless basement at 17 Alma Road to more adequate premises at number 25, and we were ready. Every interaction I had with Liam Howlett convinced me more of his potential, and this was as much to do with his uncompromising stance on absolutely everything as his musicality and technical wizardry.

Soon after he first delivered his demo to the label, he had assembled a group of fellow ravers from the Braintree area of Essex, comprising dancers Keith Flint and Leeroy Thornhill and MC Keith 'Keety' Palmer, aka Maxim Reality, and they had made their debut PAing in a sweaty club in Hackney formerly known as the Four Aces, once one of the UK's greatest reggae clubs, now reincarnated as hardcore rave haven Labrynth.

The Prodigy's signing to XL, small though the label was, represented an important endorsement, an authenticating of their aims. It would be significant for both parties. Tim had instigated the manufacturing, in New York, of the type of baseball jackets the US indie labels made as promo items. These became highly sought-after once they started appearing in rave videos. Keith later recalled: 'I remember when I got the XL jacket. I thought, "I've made it."'

While Liam was the leader of the band, and the musical visionary behind their sound, the three were able to communicate his vision when performing PAs in the clubs and raves, and made his music physical and real. They were a tangible, breathing manifestation of the sound. Without them Liam was just a producer, however brilliant. With them there was a flesh and blood rock'n'roll experience to be had, on and off stage. They were a gang, a bunch of mates, but it was a manifestation of Liam's ability to think completely differently that it even occurred to him to create a unit shaped this way. As Keith put it: 'What we always wanted was to have a great show. That came from rave PAs. Bringing something to the party sonically and visually. The buzz. That's what it was always about.'

When The Prodigy began they were managed by Ziggy Choudhury, aka Captain Naughty, a friend of Maxim's from Peterborough. He was shortly replaced by Mike Champion, brother of Nigel Champion from rave group N-Joi. Another local manager called Mike Barnett, who fittingly had enormous hair, took over for a while, mysteriously, but then Mike mark one took control back from Mike mark two. Whether Mikes one or two were qualified for this gig, with the responsibilities and prestige it brought, is debatable. But actually none of us were qualified to do anything.

Our lack of formal training in either music or business made us ideal for the music business. We did not know what the precedents were and that was our secret weapon. We were not scared of failure. Liam was different, though. Radical though he was, from his very first demos he was always employing a more melodic approach, creating an irresistible tension with the hardness of his beats. When he eventually took the rave sound further than anyone else it was, of course, not unrelated to his innate musicality.

I enjoyed working in an A&R capacity on Liam's records. I would drive down to his home studio in Essex and this clean break from London would help me to give clear feedback. I found that the countryside was good for concentration.

Liam trusted me; I had a deep understanding and admiration for his work and wanted to help him make it as strong as possible. Because we were coming from a scene where many artists including myself were from a DJ background and had little by way of musicality, his melodic abilities, songcraft and technical skill coupled with my quality control and overview made us formidable.

Liam suggested we record together, but, perhaps because I was beginning to lose confidence in my production work, I declined. My immaturity caused me to make a misinterpretation at this time; I had decided to stop making rave records because my rave records weren't as good as Liam's. Of course, what I was missing was that no one's rave records were as good as Liam's, and if everyone had let their insecurities hamper them in this way, there would have been no rave records apart from those by The Prodigy, and while he may have been the best, there were lots of great producers around.

Someone always has to lead, and astute creative types know to be inspired by the leaders in their field, rather than letting themselves be intimidated by the abilities of others. But for the time being I was to focus on other people's music, not my own, and on helping The Prodigy achieve their destiny.

A revolution had occurred in British culture by now. The *Hitman and Her* era of fighty discotheques with naff DJs talking on the mic and getting everyone to row on the floor while they played 'Oops Upside Your Head' was dying out, to be replaced by a dance music culture which (initially at least) had actual substance, as well as actual substances. Our colleagues at Beggars Banquet were part of neither the old wally disco world nor the dawning age of rave; as an indie rock label they existed in a different universe altogether. However, they were responsible for selling our records, and they had a head of marketing who was enthusiastic but culturally part of the soon-to-be-extinct Mecca ballroom world. The old world clashed with the new when he decided to offer a creative suggestion: a megamix of the first three Prodigy singles, to create a fourth hit.

His proposal was in itself a car crash, the opportunistic marketing-orientated outlook of the mainstream club world meeting the uncompromising youthful artistry of now. What seemed a commercially sound proposition to the person making it was in fact a supreme vibe-killer, funny in retrospect, but a threat to the integrity of what we were trying to build. It provided stark evidence of how important it was to be surrounded by people who had the same cultural value system. Otherwise in-fighting would consume the energy that would be needed for the real fight. I liked the head of marketing but he would not be long for his role.

I was hyperfocused. I wanted The Prodigy to become a huge worldwide artist, without any dilution of what they stood for. A big part of this had to be America. We had all grown up not just on Hollywood movies and hip-hop, but on the very idea that success in a big sense meant success in America.

While there had always been UK artists, such as Paul Weller, who took the position that US success entailed more aggravation than could possibly be worth it, for most British musicians succeeding in America had been the holy grail since The Beatles first pulled it off. In our minds there lay across the pond unimaginable riches and excitement, and a glamour that the UK could never offer.

The stench of fakery was never far off either, but we were not going to get hung up on that. I knew it would be an obstacle course but perhaps the obstacles would be entertaining. It's not like we had anything to lose. I thought strategically about the concept of breaking America, and studied the *Billboard* charts, seeing who was who. I suspected that we might need a big brother to help us win, in the form of a US licensee. A big record label who could help us achieve our ambitions without diluting our integrity.

One of my first interactions with a US major label would be with Rick Rubin's American Recordings, a good experience which was not to prove typical of what was to follow. Rick was very far from the typical label boss, being a childhood hero of mine. He was starting the second phase of his career, leaving Def Jam and moving to LA in 1990 as an act of personal and musical reinvention. He began to work in different musical areas, including metal and country, while predicting the rise of non-East Coast rap by signing the Geto Boys, from Houston, Texas, and Sir Mix-a-Lot, from Seattle. He also found rave music exciting and so offered XL a simple and inexpensive deal to release our efforts in the US.

Rick was encouraging and nurturing. A great listener. He had shrewdly employed a young DJ, christened Gary Richards and calling himself Destructo, who was a passionate advocate for the hardcore rave sound. Another employee was Lollapalooza co-founder Marc Geiger, and when I first visited the American Recordings offices in LA he offered to show me something that he said I would like. Leading me to his large and boxy desktop computer, he explained how in the future not only would most communication happen via one of these terminals; they would also be the main medium by which we consumed music. My response was a complete lack of interest. What he described just seemed boring, and the computer itself looked poxy.

While on the one hand I was failing to glimpse an accurate vision of the future, my lack of interest was valid. I was concerned with the music, not the means of delivery. That would never change. Marc's vision was startlingly prescient, and there was doubtless youthful arrogance in my total lack of interest in his predictions, but if I had fully embraced it there would not have been anything for me to do with it.

If I had known that in future music would be relegated to the status of 'content' in order to sell other products, I might have been dismayed, but it wouldn't have made any difference to my outlook. I knew then that my destiny lay in the music and in the music only. Rick Rubin affirmed this and encouraged me to be as open and creative as possible. He gave me some invaluable feedback on the nature of feedback. His advice had a spiritual quality. When you give people comments on their music, he said, if you are talking honestly about how it makes you feel you cannot be wrong. Do not think that you are right. Just know how you feel.

In beginning to explore the possibilities offered by US licence deals, and the route into the mainstream they might offer, I had in Martin a partner who had previously done deals for various Beggars-signed artists – Atlantic for Gary Numan, Sire for Modern English and Capitol for the Cocteau Twins. Martin was a pioneer but not the first to explore this type of split transatlantic arrangement. The Beatles were signed initially to Vee-Jay in the US, the biggest black-owned label prior to Motown, providing an authentically R&B-leaning outlet for a British group who were heavily influenced by R&B. The Beatles' US rights were available because EMI-owned Capitol had passed on them. The US labels had gradually woken up to the tremendous potential of UK artists after this.

Throughout the eighties, UK indies would license artist albums to US majors with great success. The Smiths were licensed from Rough Trade to Seymour Stein's Sire, and New Order from Factory to Quincy Jones's Qwest label, both Warners imprints. West Coast-based A&M would have success with records by Culture Club and Simple Minds, both licensed from Virgin. Island Records, having initially had a US distribution deal through Capitol, would take the ambitious route eventually followed by Beggars and XL of setting up their own US operation. Island US was based at 14 East 4th Street in Manhattan, and named its new imprint 4th And Broadway after the office's location.

The bigger American labels would typically be able to pay the UK indie an advance of somewhere between $75k and $150k per album. Beggars Banquet would have sunk without these substantial cash injections. Equally, these arrangements were often mired in difficulty.

Throughout the eighties it would prove hard for Beggars to get the US labels fully motivated; everything from properly packaging the records to providing decent radio promotion budgets was a battle. The A&R people at these labels would resent the outsourcing of talent acquisition that the deals with UK labels would represent. The power that a modern indie label or self-releasing artist now has to make music immediately available worldwide is an eighties fantasy made real. The existing US power structures of radio and retail were the only way to access the audience, and the major labels had much of their attention.

The first Prodigy album was called *Experience* and is the genre-defining rave album, a thrilling work of sample-based expression by Liam Howlett. Before we managed to get into business with Rick Rubin and release records through his newly West Coast-based American label, we had licensed *Experience* to Elektra in the US, part of Warner Brothers. Elektra were seen as a hip major, born out of the fifties folk explosion, coming of age in the psychedelic rock era, releasing classics like Love's 'Forever Changes', MC5's 'Kick Out The Jams' and The Stooges' 'Fun House'.

More pertinently to me they at this time had many of my

favourite rap artists signed, including Brand Nubian, Leaders of the New School, Pete Rock & CL Smooth, and KMD, all brought to the label by Tommy Boy alumnus, rap A&R legend Dante Ross (of 'Dante is a scrub' fame from a 3 Feet High and Rising interlude). They also had a personable and well-meaning A&R stationed in the UK called Harvey Eagle (whose brother used the DJ name DJ Ill Eagle) who genuinely liked The Prodigy, and managed to convince the powers that be in New York that this group, highly unorthodox in stateside terms, might have potential in the US.

Everything is wonderful when you work with a large American entertainment company. At the start. Corporations tend to have two modes of behaviour: if you are someone they wish to seduce, or who makes them a lot of money, they will treat you splendidly and nothing is too much to ask. Everyone else (including you when you are no longer in one of the categories above) is dispensable. None of this is to complain. We knew what we were getting into and what we wanted.

The Prodigy's *Experience* album proved to be a tough sell for Elektra, and they had been hoping for a hit. Having failed to deliver that success, we found ourselves no longer welcome in their Manhattan HQ.

As we exited our first corporate US home, visionary UK producer and label boss Daniel Miller of Mute Records turned up. As an artist in the early eighties, Daniel made the synth classic 'Warm Leatherette' under the name The Normal, later covered by Grace Jones. Rather than following through on the promise he showed as an artist, he devoted his energies to running a record label, founding Mute to release the electronic music he loved. This all seemed familiar.

He signed and produced Depeche Mode, and he and they had achieved a weirdly similar holy grail to the one we were pursuing; an Essex electronic band gaining mainstream US success. Depeche Mode's vocals and songcraft were more in the vein that mass US audiences were used to, but that wasn't to be dwelled on. I was starting to realise that a large part of the creation of success was about ignoring the reasons it might not happen. Blocking out reality and getting on with it. Focusing on what I wanted to happen and how to get there, not the reasons it was unlikely to work.

At this point, US industry insiders were certain that The Prodigy would not achieve mainstream success in America. My resolve was only strengthened. I became more convinced, not less.

Daniel Miller clearly saw an opportunity to repeat some alchemy and approached me via Martin, whom he knew from the formative days of the indie record scene in London, centred around the Rough Trade store. From the success of Depeche Mode, Daniel had built his own US operation, and suggested that we license the next Prodigy album to his label Mute in the US, rather than to a major. We were happy to accept his offer. No one else was interested.

The follow up to *Experience* was called *Music For The Jilted Generation*, and showed Liam honing his craft and making another classic long-player in a genre which was still dominated by singles. On *Jilted* Liam makes dance music, music from a scene, genre music. But he does it so well that it actually bears little relation to anyone else's work. His personality is expressed through the production: unshakable self-confidence in every note of every synth riff. It is the sound of someone working with a relaxed confidence: a flow. As with a great sportsperson, there is a tangible certainty to every move made.

In 'Voodoo People', Liam places the Last Poets in an electronic landscape they could not have predicted when they recorded the song he samples, 'Shalimar', some twenty-three years earlier. There was a clear progression in Liam's technique and ability since the *Experience* album. The rawness was intact but the production was more sophisticated and ambitious. He even slowed things down to a head-nodding hip-hop tempo on the songs 'Poison' (Maxim's first recorded vocal performance) and '3 Kilos', without losing any intensity.

By 1994 the 'golden age' of hip-hop was over and the platinum age had begun, when production values and record sales went up and up, and any innocence was lost. This was the year Wu-Tang

Clan became a phenomenon, of Nas's *Illmatic* and the Notorious B.I.G.'s *Ready To Die*, the year East Coast hip-hop peaked creatively. Meanwhile, Dr Dre's *The Chronic* (which was released at the end of 1992 but was still having a massive impact) and OutKast's debut *Southernplayalisticadillacmuzik* indicated where rap music was headed – away from New York, to the West Coast, and to Southern cities like Atlanta. These sounds were influencing what The Prodigy was doing, as were the Beastie Boys and Rage Against the Machine.

Needing an American voice to recreate the spoken word sample which we thought might provide an introduction to *Music For The Jilted Generation*, the first person who sprang to mind for me was an A&R at American called Dan Charnas, originally a writer at *The Source*, subsequently author of *The Big Payback*, the definitive book about the business of rap. Dan has the distinction of being the first vocal performer you hear on the album, despite having no previous (or I imagine subsequent) experience as a rave vocalist.

The album was a huge success in most of the world and The Prodigy were becoming one of the most thrilling live acts on the planet – a feat that would have been unthinkable for an electronic act a year or two previously. The only thing that continued to elude us was proper stateside success. There was always a healthy US audience to see the band perform, but we felt like we were still being kept in our 'dance music' niche there, and that was too safe.

Daniel Miller was a benevolent ally with excellent taste and Mute had kept all their promises. But we wanted more. Daniel understood that and we agreed to somehow bulk up our firepower going forward.

Other British electronic artists, including the Chemical Brothers and Underworld, were also receiving unprecedented levels of US interest. The music industry had decided that 'electronica' was going to be the next big thing. It was cringeworthy but I suspected it might be helpful nonetheless. We weren't going to dilute any aspect of what we did, so if the media wanted to group together disparate artists under a weak heading, that wasn't going to be our problem.

I was focused on helping Liam complete the third album, the record I thought would be The Prodigy's opportunity to reach the really wide audience to whom they were still unknown, and I didn't want him to over-labour the process. While the music has to be right and that is always the priority, getting the timing perfect is connected to that. Don't leave the cake in the oven too long.

We released the 'Firestarter' single on my twenty-fifth birthday in 1996, and it represented a successful attempt on Keith and Liam's part to merge their two main musical loves – hip-hop, particularly of the type made by the Bomb Squad, and punk – and the real triumph was that Keith, up to this point still a dancer, provided the snarly and Lydon-indebted vocal. The Prodigy had gone from conceptually being a band to actually being a band, in terms that the uninitiated might understand.

When the big-budget video we had commissioned for the song was delivered Liam hated it. We started again, this time with director Walter Stern, who had previously shot the 'No Good', 'Voodoo People' and 'Poison' videos. On the way to the shoot, Keith jumped out of Liam's car and into a second-hand clothes shop, returning with the stars and stripes jumper he wore to iconic effect in the video.

If Keith's spontaneous and unlikely adoption of American iconography would contribute subtly to the band's crossover success in the US, his performance in the remade 'Firestarter' video would make a seismic impact. Keith appeared unhinged and untethered and his performance spoke to people on some primal level. He was expressing something from deep within himself. Something dark.

It was one of the great music video performances of all time and the no-budget promo, shot in Aldwych tube station, crossed the band over worldwide. The single went in at number one on the UK pop charts, displacing Take That's cover of the Bee Gees' 'How Deep Is Your Love', and stayed there for a month.

The noise of both pop and Britpop was loud but The Prodigy and XL were remote from that, with a different set of influences and ideals to the more traditional-sounding bands of that moment.

The Britpop bands were heavily leaning on the music of British artists of the sixties; but because these sixties bands were themselves leaning heavily on the blues, much of this music felt like a copy of a copy, with the corresponding loss of quality that a second-generation facsimile possesses. The pop music of that moment was mostly worse still. But by identifying what we disliked we were able to define ourselves in opposition to it.

We were doing something original and there was much to celebrate, but I couldn't entirely let go, feeling like I was in charge of a speeding vehicle. While I was drinking a lot, I wasn't having that much fun. There were highs but the lows started getting increasingly gnarly.

Once 'Firestarter' lodged itself at number one the excitement around the band snowballed accordingly. We had chosen to release the single without having completed the album, a risky manoeuvre. To maintain the momentum, I wanted us to have another standalone number one hit single.

Seeing the band perform 'Breathe' for the first time, featuring vocals from both Keith and Maxim over a surf guitar riff, I had suggested that we make it the next single. The 'Breathe' video even managed to turn things up another notch. Liam had still looked young and innocent in the 'Firestarter' video but now the whole band looked like rock stars.

The single duly knocked early Simon Cowell protégés Robson and Jerome off the number one spot, and then kept Peter Andre at bay for a couple of weeks. We had advertised the fact that the forthcoming album, if completed in a timely fashion, was likely to be monstrously big, and this fact could not be missed or mistaken by anyone, including Madonna. And why would the fact that a British rave group were likely to have a very successful album be of interest to the still reigning queen of pop? Because Madonna was not only enjoying enormous success at this time as an artist, having consummately reinvented herself for her second decade on the pop throne, but also enjoying even greater success with her label imprint Maverick.

It had long been an age-old law of the music business that when an artist reached a certain level of mega-popularity, their fawning and supplicant record label did whatsoever they requested, and so along with the scented candles and floral arrangements, they received their own 'boutique' (the word itself is a giveaway) record label.

Why would an artist want such a thing, when they are already doing the most fun and creative part of working in the music industry themselves, i.e. making and performing the music, and making a fortune while they are at it?

If you are talented and driven enough to achieve enormous success as a recording artist, you will perhaps believe that the job of the record label is easy, because you yourself will have delivered such powerful music to your record company that they did indeed find it simple to sell it in huge quantities. So from the point of view of the successful artist, the job of the record company is easy. And, of course, the view is exactly the same in reverse from the label. It seems easy being a successful recording artist, when in truth it is anything but. In rap, though, all previous laws of the music business can be proved wrong, or applied in reverse.

From the time of rap music's first big commercial peak, almost all successful rap record labels were artist-run. From NWA on Eazy-E's Ruthless, to Eminem on Dr Dre's Aftermath, 50 Cent on Eminem's Shady, Kanye West on Jay-Z's label Roc-A-Fella before starting his own GOOD Music imprint, or Drake on Lil Wayne's label Young Money, rap artists being involved in an executive or ownership position became key to rap labels succeeding, culminating in Jay-Z's building his humongous Roc Nation empire. (This did not happen overnight: see Onyx's Armee, MC Hammer's Bust It or Prince Paul's Dew Doo Man for earlier examples of artist-owned hip-hop imprints that didn't make it.)

However, just as it is an age-old law of the music business that superstars get their own labels, if the superstar in question is not a rapper, the enterprise is usually not a resounding success. Historically, it did not seem to matter how talented the artist was. In fact, the more talented they were, the less likely the artist would eclipse their own success, and until they did that, the label is pure vanity.

When the corporate parent gives the artist the imprint, they know all of this. When they profess their tremendous enthusiasm for the venture, they are simply being less than truthful in order to keep their breadwinner happy.

The Beatles' Apple was perhaps the most famous artist-run disaster as record label. A fortune was lost, chaos descended, but we at least remember its name. Less impressive still was George Harrison's Dark Horse label. His partners in this ill-fated venture, LA-based A&M, were from the off disappointed by its roster, which consisted of Ravi Shankar, reasonably enough, but also several not-exactly-household names including Splinter, Jiva, Henry McCullough and Attitudes. Harrison signed a group called Five Stairsteps, consisting of the Burke brothers and sister from Chicago. Their dad was by day a detective with the Chicago Police Department but found time to be the group's manager, co-writer and bassist. Among the family was future bass maestro and 'Risin' To The Top' maker Keni Burke.

They had previously recorded the classic 'Ooh Child', one of the most truly uplifting soul songs of all time, when signed to the Buddah label, and in the wake of the Jackson 5 family soul groups were all the rage. But they were not to repeat the feat at their new Beatle-backed label home and would shortly depart Dark Horse.

Two years into a five-year deal, A&M surmised the venture was going nowhere fast and managed to weasel their way out by suing Harrison for $10 million for late delivery of his solo album. At this point Warner Brothers stepped in to offer an equally lucrative deal to Harrison and Dark Horse, which turned out to be similarly disastrous.

Led Zeppelin's ill-fated Swan Song label was referred to by their manager Peter Grant as 'a lube job for the ego'. The Beastie Boys were not only rappers but also had great taste in everything, but that wasn't enough to save their EMI-backed Grand Royal. Frank Sinatra's Reprise label would have been the exception to this rule, were it not for the fact that Sinatra sold his stake in the label to Warners two years after it started in 1963, so when the label was enjoying tremendous success with artists including Neil Young, Jimi Hendrix, Randy Newman and Fleetwood Mac, it was no longer an artist vanity label and hadn't been for more than a decade.

Madonna's Maverick, however, showed every sign of being the label that bucked this trend. She had not only her manager, former Michael Jackson consigliere Freddy DeMann running the show, but his protégé, a young and hungry Hollywood go-getter of Israeli descent called Guy Oseary. Freddy and Guy had a powerful com-bination of youth and experience. And with one of Guy's very first signings, a Canadian singer-songwriter called Alanis Morissette, they had the single biggest-selling worldwide artist of the nineties on their roster.

With every US label calling to ask if they could license the forthcoming Prodigy album for American release, I explained that we were already in a deal with Mute. That kind of information just doesn't slow an ambitious American record executive down.

'Fine,' one said to me over a landline, 'we'll pay you and we'll pay Mute. We don't care who we pay, we just want to be involved.' That sounded plausible to me. 'Because we love The Prodigy.' Still vaguely plausible. 'And we love XL.' Plausibility levels dropping . . . 'And we love you.' Plausibility levels through the floor. I was certain this person didn't actually love me.

No matter. There was a decision to be made. We went and did the meetings in New York and LA. Our joint delegation from XL and Mute met with Jimmy Iovine in his LA office at Interscope Records, the company he co-founded after engineering and pro-ducing albums for the likes of John Lennon and Patti Smith. Jimmy seemed the most musically intuitive person to operate a large US record label in the modern era, and when Interscope was releasing records by artists from Dr Dre to Nine Inch Nails, they were as good as any major had ever been.

One of Daniel Miller's staff mentioned how nice the bagels were, and asked Jimmy where he got them. The mogul looked unimpressed and the atmosphere in the room changed. 'Don't you get it?' Jimmy said. 'I don't get the bagels.'

The Mute employee looked crestfallen; it had been an innocent question, and as a New Yorker he was genuinely impressed by the quality of this particular, specifically Jewish, baked good, normally an East Coast delicacy. But Jimmy was right. The Mute employee didn't understand. Jimmy most certainly didn't get the bagels. It was like the scene in *Goodfellas* where Joe Pesci's character Tommy DeVito says, having been ribbed about his humble beginnings, 'I don't shine shoes no more.'

Of all the executives who pursued us, the most doggedly determined was Maverick's Guy Oseary, to the extent that, concerned that the deal wasn't going his way, and that I hadn't been proving receptive enough to his advances while on an exploratory US trip, he simply got on a Concorde, raced me back to London and turned up at the XL offices (then still in Wandsworth) unannounced, to ensure he got the audience he desired. It showed the kind of shamelessness that was the hallmark of a future mogul. We did the deal with Maverick, and Madonna attended some meetings and appeared interested in what we were doing.

While Liam strove to complete what would be his third and biggest album, one of the principals at our new US label home asked me who would be mixing the album, and started to reel off a few names of people he saw as the hottest mixers of the moment. I was puzzled. He wasn't talking about specialist dance remixes for clubs, that was something we were familiar with and would perhaps be exploring; a jungle mix from DJ Hype, say.

Mixing the original material was part of Liam's art form, and as far as I was aware the art form of any record producer. Liam had produced and mixed 'Firestarter' and 'Breathe' at home. He sometimes brought in producer, mixer and engineer Neil McLennan to help him achieve his final vision, but Neil was virtually part of the band, not a third party.

I pondered who had mixed the greatest albums of all time, *Songs In The Key Of Life*, say, or *Abbey Road*. I consulted the credits. No one. Because the producer had done it. Working with the engineer. There was no 'mixer'. To mix was not a separate process. The job simply didn't exist when these albums were made, yet the records sounded absolutely amazing. So what was going on?

In the eighties a new way of looking at commercial recordings had emerged. Certain mixers were perceived to have a radio-friendly sound, Bob Clearmountain being the first of these, and the A&R fraternity had started to see having the mixer du jour involved in a record as a route to more radio play. The idea of having a separate individual mix your record is not without its possible benefits. Just as an artist can get lost and a producer can help find the way, what if a producer gets lost? But from the eighties onwards, artists were being encouraged to have their records mixed by a third party as the standard position.

Many of the greatest recordings of all time have been lo-fi, have been 'wrong', and didn't sound like everything else going on around them at the time. That was a big part of their magic. We could not contemplate an outsider mixing a Prodigy record, because then it wouldn't sound like a Prodigy record.

As recording of the album was nearing completion, we got to collaborate directly with our Ultramagnetic hero Kool Keith, with the help of his DJ partner KutMasta Kurt. Keith was the only guest rapper on the album, featuring on the song 'Diesel Power', capturing some of the New York eighties hip-hop magic that had inspired both Liam in Essex and me in Edgware a decade earlier. As well as recording this new performance, Kool Keith was present in sample form, and this would prove more contentious.

Side two of that Ultramagnetics 1987 classic *Critical Beatdown* contained the song 'Give The Drummer Some'. When Kool Keith raps: 'Switch up / Change my pitch up / Smack my bitch up, like a pimp', he was tossing a violently misogynist line into his verse in a manner that was not unusual in hip-hop. It was not characteristic of Kool Keith, but neither was it the type of thing that anyone would have remarked on at the time. Liam sampled the line to create the main hook of the song 'Smack My Bitch Up', and with its extraordinarily powerful drum programming and synth riffs it had been a huge favourite in The Prodigy's live sets for a while, and was naturally going to be included on *The Fat Of The Land*.

I never considered its questionable nature. I did not even think about it. When we scheduled the song for single release, Martin Mills unusually made the short journey to my office at 25 Alma Road and questioned the validity of releasing this piece of music as a single. He approached the subject calmly and attempted to make me consider my actions. I ignored him. In the light of two decades-plus later, this says much about him. And about me. I wished to make my own mistakes.

The Sex Pistols had their swastika armbands. The Prodigy had this sample. Did anyone ever become a Nazi because of Sid Vicious? No. But were people entitled to be offended by the use of the armband, or the sample? Yes. Is it insensitive to victims of abuse? Yes. Were we thinking about that? No. Was that thoughtless? Yes. Should The Prodigy have been censored in any way? I don't think so. Is it pleasant? No. But is it art? Yes, just about, and a great deal of art is not pleasant. Was any woman ever abused because of The Prodigy? My instinct is no. But how can I be sure? So, do I regret releasing a single on XL with the title 'Smack My Bitch Up'? I doubt that I would do it again.

The Fat Of The Land was a global hit on release, number one everywhere, including America. On the night we got that news, Liam turned up for our celebration in Soho wearing a pair of socks a fan had made him with a portrait of himself on them. When I queried this surprising sartorial choice, he flashed a gold-toothed grin and said, 'No one can say shit to me now.'

He had a point. He had achieved globe-conquering success by making the type of aggressive noises he loved. We were succeeding on all fronts, including financially, but of our own volition we weren't making as much money as we could have been. We were choosing to sacrifice millions of pounds of income because we did not license the music to advertisers. We didn't want corporate money, we didn't want to help them sell their products, it wasn't why we were doing what we did. No compromise had occurred.

Equally, this wasn't Kansas any more, or Braintree, Essex. It certainly wasn't Edgware, Middlesex.

On the night of 12 November 1998 we found ourselves in Donatella Versace's mansion in Milan after the MTV Europe Music Awards, The Prodigy being winners that evening of Best Dance Act. The Prodigy never attended any shows of this nature, but for some reason we made an exception to our policy.

The party itself was a select affair but The Prodigy were by now of a level of renown, Keith particularly, that their presence was required, alongside megastar guests including George Michael, Madonna and various Spice Girls. I had somehow become part of a celebrity entourage. It felt uncomfortable.

A decade earlier I was engaged in wholly different activities to this. Whether I was shrink-wrapping vinyl in the basement of Island Records, lugging heavy speakers to sweaty parties (installing the sound at a series of events Trevor Jackson held in a fourth-floor studio in east London had required particularly heavy lifting), or stuffing 12-inch mailers in the basement of Alma Road, I was in it for the love of music and I was happy with my lot. Now things were different. I was on drugs – not the obvious ones – using the legally prescribed antidepressant Seroxat and tranquilliser lorazepam, and due, I think, to this, little memory of this evening and many other evenings of the era survive, memory impairment being a potential side effect of lorazepam usage.

While much of this period is hazy, what is unforgettable is that Liam, Keith, aka Keef, Keety, aka Maxim, Leeroy and their loyal and hard-working associate John Fairs were unfailingly great company, genuine people who could see through the glamorous surroundings, yet take things lightly enough to still enjoy themselves.

Many highlights were provided by Keith, who, despite his troubled and difficult background, I was finding to be one of the sweetest people I'd ever worked with. As the nineties had progressed, Keith had developed a powerful image for himself. When

The Prodigy started he had a classic hippie/traveller look with long, stringy hair, and in many ways this original style was the most authentic expression of his mostly gentle and slightly mystical (not to mention hilariously funny) personality.

But punk was a big influence on all of us. We had been too young to experience it first-hand but all related to the DIY ethic, and Keith had decided to borrow and adapt the hairstyle created and first worn by one of the most influential original punks, Soo Lucas, aka Soo Catwoman. The do in question consisted of two parallel shark fins, everything else shaved clean, the fins them-selves, in Keith's case, dyed bright green for good measure.

Soo Catwoman, a powerfully enigmatic figure who has always shunned publicity (her website says 'solicitation for interviews is futile') had achieved the look originally by asking an obliging barber in Ealing, west London, to shave the middle of her head. An old Myspace post of hers gives an insight into her views on punk style: 'It seems quite funny that what started out as anti-fashion became a fashion in itself. I'm sure for many people around at the time none of them (despite their claims) could have known the impact the whole thing would have, and still be having so many years on.'

Keith was adorned with tattoos and facial and body piercings before that was the norm, and he had fun shocking businesspeople and tourists in the somewhat posher hotels we were getting to stay in as the band's popularity increased. He used to enjoy bondage clothing and accoutrements, and would sometimes wander the hallways of a Marriott Marquis in barely-there outfits that would give the other hotel guests something to talk about over dinner.

Keith was not a poser. He was the real deal; constitutionally counter-cultural, marginalised and rebellious. As the pop main-stream embraced him, he actually had fewer hang-ups than artists who might not be sure of who they really are.

Keith knew who he was so he did not take himself too seriously. When he was discussed and satirised in the mainstream it amused him. It might have horrified someone less certain of their own credentials. The day after the 'Firestarter' video was shown on *Top of the Pops*, Keith's performance was discussed by one of the UK's most beloved light entertainers on his radio show. We then experienced Keith Flint impersonating Terry Wogan talking about Keith Flint, adopting his lilting Irish accent and saying, of himself, 'Did ya see him? Did ya see the little firestarter? He's a scary little fella.'

But I would witness dark disturbances. A member of the band's management team turned up to meet us on tour in Dallas brandishing something he somehow thought Keith would find amusing. It was a British tabloid containing a story about Keith that a close family member had sold to them. I recall an almost slow-motion sequence as I saw the newspaper being handed to Keith and knew that I was seeing a disaster unfold.

There was no need for him to see the newspaper. It had no possible upside for him. Keith's mood plummeted as a result of this public betrayal. I was fortunate to see a lot of Keith's most playful side, but his darkness and its causes were never far away. The newspaper incident was a glimpse of bleaker times to come, and perhaps of the root cause of them.

For now, though, Keith could escape his demons while becoming one of the world's greatest and most recognisable live performers. He was flanking Liam Howlett, a down-to-earth wizard who could routinely wring sonically unique material out of the same equipment everyone else was using, along with Keety Palmer, aka Maxim, the stable core of the group, a poised and self-confident family man and a naturally relaxed but incendiary live performer who held everything together. Original fourth member, dancer Leeroy Thornhill, would exit the band in 2000, but for now this was a group of friends on an epic journey together. Liam and his bandmates loved each other and their audience could detect and were able to connect to their bond.

But despite the joys of being around these characters, that night in Milan was not fun. I was working with one of the most exciting British artists of that era and we were enjoying incredible success together. This was my outer world.

My inner world was increasingly miserable. The evening after the MTV awards I was back in London, sinking pints of lager in The Bonaparte pub on Chepstow Road. I was telling some friends about the night before and trying to make it sound good. But not only was I suffering on the come-down, I hadn't even enjoyed the high point, and I could tell they were unimpressed.

Soon after The Prodigy's US success began in earnest I started receiving calls from the principals of Maverick saying that Guy and Freddy had fallen out and so it was going to be necessary to take sides. Freddy, every inch the suave Hollywood impresario, was culturally very different to us. Guy Oseary was also not really coming from where we were, but he triumphed and is Madonna's partner to this day.

The Prodigy's manager Mike Champion was something altogether different. No empire builder, he was an authentic Essex rock'n'roll party animal with little interest in the consequences of his actions. At the peak of the rave era few people would make much sense once it was past, say, midnight. But Mike's hedonistic behaviour was not restricted by any such quibbles as time of day. He would routinely arrive in Wandsworth for an early-morning meeting not of sound mind. I recall him beginning one of these meetings by issuing the incongruous statement, 'I am the coolest person Liam has ever met.'

From this puzzling opening he actually made less and less sense as the discussion progressed. While Mike's recklessness would cause issues for him long term, his disregard for anything that might get in the way of a good time was part of the magical alchemy surrounding the band. People were scared and shocked by him, and when we went to America he was exactly what the local industry types wanted in a British manager – a wild man. Mike and I had different approaches but we both liked to break rules and achieve things on our own terms. Mike, like myself, believed absolutely and unconditionally in Liam, and our utterly different approaches and personalities but equivalent commitment created a powerful energy.

In 1998 the worldwide success of The Prodigy really should have been enough to satisfy me. But I wanted more. I came across the demo of a band called Stroke. They comprised of a singer-songwriter from Manchester called Jason Kelly and a producer called Steve Hitchcock and were on the verge of signing a major deal. I took to both individuals immediately on meeting them, I could tell Jason particularly had a sweet nature, and heard the ambition in the songs. Their appeal, though, was intrinsically linked to the problematic flaw in what they were doing. The music was not just ambitious - there is nothing wrong with that - but over-ambitious. Some ambition is necessary for creative achievement. Too much ambition has a tendency to prove fatal to music, or at least to music that I should get involved with. It has an unappealing smell.

This music lacked a strong core, a foundation. I blinded myself to this. They sounded like an attempted hybrid of The Prodigy and Oasis, and I convinced myself that this unworkable fusion was a good idea, because I wanted the success that I was telling myself it would bring.

I was not alone in sensing their entirely theoretical potential. Once XL, flush with cash from Prodigy sales, had inked a costly deal with Stroke, the US majors came calling again, visualising huge and immediate success for the duo. That we had recently achieved mainstream US success with The Prodigy made the possibility seem all the more likely to them. We were a horse who had just won and was likely to be on a streak.

We were courted by every US label and eventually inked a lucrative deal with Interscope, covering all of our outlay and putting money in our pockets and the pockets of the group. One senior Interscope staffer told me that Stroke's first single would be the biggest hit the label had ever released. What could go wrong?

I was compromised from the start of this project. It's not that I didn't like the music at all, it was peak nineties and bombast was in, but my inner fan was not properly engaged. I was enjoying speed garage, and US rap and R&B records that were being made at this time by producers like The Neptunes and Timbaland. Thankfully, a few years later I would be able to play a meaningful role in the popularisation of music from the UK that echoed some of these sounds, working with artists like Wiley, Dizzee Rascal and MIA, at a time when XL had become a far more collaborative unit. But for now my ego and ambition were in charge, and the solid bed of musical integrity was missing.

While we were getting excited about the enormous commercial success that Stroke were theoretically about to enjoy, we were oblivious to the fact that the group itself was imploding. Steve, the talented producer responsible for a kind of proggy electronic feel that underpinned the songs, exited the duo. Jason and his advisers promptly decided that they were a rock'n'roll band with stadium ambitions . . . and didn't need Steve anyway. I was unnerved but went along with it.

In hyped artist signings that go wrong, the deal is the peak of the excitement. The energy gradually drains from there. Music fans were not interested in this group. The group's intentions, or perhaps the intentions of those around them including myself, had misguidedly become pop success rather than the creation of something interesting. There was nothing to fall back on when the expected pop success didn't materialise. It's a story that happens again and again, but it's an existentially miserable experience. With ego running the show and the desire to achieve commercial success taking precedence over creativity, it's not like anyone is going to feel sympathy when it blows up in your face.

The label in a situation like this does not have nearly as much at stake as the artist. Having said that, few independents could withstand many expensive misses like this without going out of business. While the artist was far from blameless, in this case he was misled, and I was part of the team that unwittingly did the misleading. This speaks to the true nature of what it takes to succeed as an artist. Every decision has to be the right one, and that includes not just the choices of who you surround yourself with, but which bits of their advice you choose to take. If you're being misled you have to call it, because you're the one who will suffer. It's a brutally difficult job in that regard.

There is something about the role of A&R, in so many ways a dream job for any music lover, that can bring out the worst in people who do it. It's a prestigious role yet its practitioners are considered with disdain. A&R and ego are closely intertwined. Perhaps it is the very idea that a person's taste is so good that they deserve to be paid for it. The lack of female A&R people worsens things. The music industry is deeply sexist. It has so long been an environment mainly controlled by men. And A&R in particular has always been an overwhelmingly male-dominated role. The songwriters and producers are perhaps mostly male because they are being hired by males.

Conversely, the music industry is not particularly anti-Semitic. While I felt like an outsider in Edgware, I experienced no friction as soon as I was in the music industry. I realise now that my face must have fitted. That was the nature of my privilege. Though I always would have maintained I didn't *want* to fit in, unnoticeably to me I would have been able to enter whichever doors I wanted to.

Even in the midst of the Stroke debacle I was blessed with some good luck. The universe would somehow not let me achieve any success with anything that was not of real quality. The absolute low point, my rock bottom after which a twelve-step approach to A&R rehabilitation was necessary, was when we resurrected XL's original parent label Citybeat to release a Dutch novelty dance record based on the Charleston called 'Doop'. We had a national number one pop hit, but it still ended in tears and a follow-up single which failed to chart altogether.

Credibility is hard-won and valuable, yet I seemingly spent parts of the nineties trying, for reasons unknown, to blow the hard-earned respect that XL had earned via The Prodigy. However hard I tried to achieve success with music I should not have gone anywhere near, I was never any good at it, and I crawled back to music I really loved with my tail between my legs, until I finally learned my lesson and stopped trying to occupy terrain I was unsuited to. Every time I've succeeded, it has been because the music was great. On other occasions I was lucky to fail.

I had attempted to steer Stroke's music in a more credible direction by having them work with my old colleague from Loppylugs, Trevor Jackson, by now an acclaimed DJ, remixer and producer as well as graphic designer. He was being managed by a west Londoner of Latvian descent called Marts Andrups. Trevor had also formed his own hip-hop label, Bite It, and was producing UK rap group The Brotherhood, who Marts also took on for management, signing the whole unit to Virgin. This was a competitive major-label deal that didn't work out, the desired commercial success not materialising, but all of the music and visuals were made with taste and integrity by those involved.

I had been keen to sign the band myself, but no one would have chosen XL over Virgin at this time. Virgin, based then in huge headquarters on the Harrow Road near Ladbroke Grove, was in the nineties enjoying unprecedented success via not just monster pop artists including the Spice Girls, but some of the most culturally influential musicians including Massive Attack and Daft Punk.

Outside of The Prodigy, XL had no artists making a significant impact either critically or commercially. Marts had not just a deep knowledge of music but a merciless sense of humour and a predilection for pointing out hard-to-hear truths. When we watched *Pulp Fiction* together, I said that I thought Tarantino was doing something totally different from anyone else, and that no one was doing that in music. Marts said, 'Maybe. You're definitely not doing anything very good.' I was shocked but realise in retrospect that no one else was pointing out the obvious to me – that I was not fulfilling my potential or being true to myself musically at this time. He said it to be helpful. Some rough healing.

I was compromised by my outsized ego and desire for success, and the most important thing, the music and the originality, was suffering. Exactly one person, Marts, said something along these lines to me. I didn't like hearing it at the time, but it takes courage for friends to point out these unwelcome and disturbing truths, and it's rare that anyone takes the risk. Mostly we are alone, working out who we are for ourselves.

ALL FALL DOWN

As I hit my late twenties, I had achieved something that I felt was important by making XL successful. Along the way I had developed a big ego and a lot of arrogance. These masked a lot of fear, and a lack of awareness of my own fragility. I'd stopped making music and DJing; I'd created an identity for myself as head of a record company, and The Prodigy's success was exactly what I thought I wanted, but what I discovered, inevitably in retrospect, was a void. While I was theoretically now in a more fortunate position than before, my outlook had changed in ways that were not healthy. I'd lost sight of my core values. I may have been unconsciously imitating some of the wealthy and powerful executives I'd met in the US.

I was thirty pounds heavier than I had been before. I had stopped wearing streetwear by Stüssy and my other favourite label Pervert, and was buying expensive clothes, mostly black, from French boutique Agnès B. For some reason I was trying really hard to be grown up. It was ridiculous. I was twenty-seven, often the age where if you haven't properly unpacked your emotional baggage, it starts to become a burden. Like most men I know, I did not grow up communicating with friends or family in any meaningful way about emotional issues. This lack of discussion and introspection meant I didn't really know who I was.

I recall hiding in an upstairs meeting room at the Beggars offices in Wandsworth, trying to pull myself together to the point where I could face another human being; and sitting in my empty flat frozen to the spot, not knowing what I was meant to be doing with myself. I found myself lying on my bedroom floor at 4am, hyperventilating and drenched in sweat, racked with an indescribable feeling of panic and thick with dread. I had to accept that my coping mechanisms had somehow been eroded. I felt desperate.

I thought that the fearful state I found myself in had come from nowhere but now I see that it had a long gestation period. I was clinically depressed.

It's hard for anyone who hasn't experienced it to understand this illness. The inability to carry out the simplest of tasks makes life next to impossible. I woke up every morning in severe physical pain, sharp aches all over my body which resembled some serious physical affliction but were, in fact, just a psychosomatic manifestation of my condition.

I'd always had a lot of ambition, some of which was useful. But my ambition had become toxic, and was threatening to damage me and the people around me. I needed help. The process of putting myself back together needed to begin. I had to find meaning.

Initially, I was resistant to psychotherapy because it felt like an admission of defeat, so I imagined, hopefully or lazily, that there would be some sort of chemical solution. I vaguely presumed that I would be able to get a prescription and that would be that. While a course of antidepressants, Seroxat initially, was indeed necessary, it did not begin to address the underlying causes.

Our past traumas - and everyone has them to greater or lesser extents - can weaken and compromise the already fragile underpinning of our psyches. Once medication is prescribed that seemingly strengthens these foundations, the need to explore one's history, habits and lifestyle, with the pain that entails, seems less pressing. But this exploration is the best way of attacking our anxieties. The drugs do not, in fact, work. Not on their own anyway. And not on any deep level.

I embarked on seven years of therapy where I explored my upbringing and relationships, and was thus able to examine my own behaviour and motivations. The therapeutic process, where I explored the childhood experiences that shaped me, felt like learning to walk. I began to keep a diary, and the emptying of my thoughts on to the page was cathartic. My constant internal dialogue lost some of its negative power when it was written down.

I saw the keeping of a diary not as any type of creative process but as a purge, like vomiting or a visit to the toilet. What is written in a diary is usually not art. It is of little interest once it's written; it tends to be much the same every day, like a bowel movement. But you've got to get it out. Keep it inside at your peril. Art and excrement do have similarities. It's art if you can find one person who is interested in it apart from you. Your shrink doesn't count.

While I'd never stopped being involved in music, I realised that I was no longer involved in it in the right way. I considered stopping the record company work altogether at that point. I wanted to survive the crisis I was experiencing, and success was suddenly not so important. Rather than giving up, though, I replaced my previously somewhat desperate, grasping type of ambition with something more detached. A bit of ambivalence would do wonders for my judgement.

Privately, I disintegrated. Part of my ego was destroyed, which left me vulnerable, but with the potential to transcend some of my limitations. Breakdowns and breakthroughs being closely related, the feeling of not having much to lose would be productive. And in the turmoil, it hit me that quality and originality might matter more than success.

It was a bewildering time. To everyone else I was the same as before, yet internally everything was shifting. It was painful but some part of me knew it needed to take its course. When my doctor first wanted to explore the nature of my relationship with my parents, I had a 'nothing to see here' type of response.

But my emotional baggage was weighing me down, and I had to find a way of looking at these cumbersome items and seeing how they were affecting my movement and my entire existence. Therapy enabled me to see the impediments and evaluate them.

My mum, in common with every stereotypical Jewish mother who has ever occupied a place in books, films or plays, was overprotective. Because she was scared. Of most things that could happen to me. Of course, this didn't mean that she didn't love me. Quite the opposite. It was a direct result of her love. The comic genius Garry Shandling said that he supported gay marriage with one caveat; no child should have two Jewish mothers.

I was a child of 1970s suburbia. My father was a man of his generation. He saw it as his duty to work, to provide. He was stoic and not prone to exposing his inner emotions. Having had an artistic brother in my uncle Phillip, my dad was the sensible McCartney to his sibling's less reliable and more mercurial Lennon. He carried this sense of responsibility into all aspects of his life and was a stable figure who prized that stability. My parents were part of a community where a lot was expected of people in terms of obedience to protocol, and my opposition to that was discomforting to them from an early age. My mum used to say to me despairingly, 'We don't know where you came from', and that had been an unnerving thing to hear.

This is a common journey for creative people. In later life the refusal to do what is expected (and this contrariness is my default behaviour) became my most valuable trait in my work, and when I saw positive things start to occur as a result of my acting on instinct, it was gratifying, and I began to nurture it.

I also gradually came to understand why my parents had acted in the way they had. They had not wanted to deliberately undermine me. They loved me. They did not offer me encouragement to follow my dreams because these dreams seemed completely detached from reality. They had no framework by which to understand them.

Nothing makes us feel better than forgiving people we think may have wronged us, especially those closest to us. There is nothing to be gained by holding on to resentment. Understanding my past enabled me to shed baggage. To free myself. When I became aware of my fear there was the possibility to accept it, neutralise it, and even turn it into something useful. What I was frightened of was actually irrelevant. The fear itself is the thing. And once I saw that, it's not that the fear disappeared, it's that the possibility of catching it, and recognising it as spurious, began to exist. A passing demon. To be ignored and thus dispelled.

I embraced this idea of rebuilding myself as obsessively as I tend to embrace all my interests. My drive was useful as a tool of reconstruction. I read voraciously about philosophy and religion and began to learn about yoga and meditation. These have become fundamental parts of my life. I embarked on a self-education which is ongoing and feels like it goes beyond anything I got from school. The crisis created the necessity for change.

As a result of the ongoing process of reassembly I started to feel music deeply again, as deeply as the teenage me did, and that led naturally into my wanting to resume my music-making. In 2001 Swedish software developers Propellerhead had released a new product, a digital audio workstation called Reason. Liam was impressed, and thought it might suit my approach to writing, as he remembered it.

He suggested to me in 2002 that I install the software on a laptop and learn to use it. I was blown away by the possibilities, and music-making became my new addiction. By 2003 I was proficient. This was the reawakening of my musical side.

There had been nothing like this in my formative studio days. I had never had my own self-contained studio set-up. This felt like unfettered creative freedom. Headphones on, I began to make the first of many hundreds of beats. I had not been making music for nearly ten years at this stage, and found that this process was not just great in musical terms but was the perfect physical and mental accompaniment to the therapy I was doing. I could put myself more directly into the music via this software than I had ever done before.

THE SPIRITS ARE YOUR PARENTS AND THEIR PARENTS AND THEIR PARENTS AND THEIR PARENTS

Jack Kreitzman, my mother's father, was born in a small village called Lask, near the Polish city of Lodz, on or around 9 November 1911. Births were not registered. My grandparents said that their Poland was fairly accurately depicted in the movie *Fiddler on the Roof*; a primitive world where there was no indoor sanitation, water was fetched from a pump, horse and cart was the primary mode of transportation and a person's faith was their most important asset. Jack was the first of only three children born to his mother Ray and father Israel, a word meaning 'to struggle with God', and not at that time the name of a country.

There was a specific reason why he had so few siblings by the standards of the day. Soon after she followed his father to London in 1913, when Jack was two years old, my great-grandmother Ray in her words 'got modern'; meaning she worked out how to avoid ending up with eight or nine children – presumably by using some form of contraception.

Israel Kreitzman, my great-grandfather, had fled Poland to avoid conscription to the Russian Cossack army. Jewish males were conscripted for a mandatory period of some twenty-five years, a life sentence by any other name, with brutal maximum-security prison-type conditions. He thought he was fleeing to New York, not London. If you could secure unofficial passage on one of the vessels that would take you hopefully to safety, the destination was often not clear.

On arrival in London my great-grandfather, relieved, perhaps, but dislocated, thought he actually was in New York. He would never have seen any photographic evidence to provide any clues. These cities, and the hope for a new life that they embodied, were the stuff of myth and imagination. Until you got there. But whatever the confusion surrounding his arrival, and however tough the circumstances were, England provided safe haven in a manner that my family is grateful for to this day. Ray never spoke of the rest of her family, none of whom, except her sister, escaped Poland, all to subsequently perish in the Holocaust. This unimaginable trauma was the reality of her immigrant story.

Some five years before the Kreitzmans had arrived in London, another immigrant, an ambitious seventeen-year-old calling himself Jacob Ross, had arrived in the East End from Kiev, then part of Russia, now the capital of Ukraine. He lodged with his future wife Rebecca in a room at the bakery shop which belonged to her parents. Rebecca already had three children, her husband having died of rheumatic fever in his early thirties.

Jacob took on not just the roles of husband and father, but also the running and expansion of the family business, and despite his being unable to read or write, ended up running a chain of bakeries in east London. Grandma Marie was the first of three biological children born to Jacob and Rebecca, joining her three half-siblings. In 1938 Jack Kreitzman approached Jacob Ross to ask for Marie's hand in marriage, and was surprised when he found himself, as a first-generation immigrant, rebuffed by another first-generation immigrant – on the grounds of his immigration status.

Jacob thought it beneath his daughter to marry a non-naturalised foreigner, something Jacob himself had been until relatively recently. The determined and dutiful Jack duly became English, signing his Oath of Allegiance to His Majesty, King George VI on 29 March 1938. Jack and Marie were married and she was soon pregnant. This turned out to be just in time for the Second World War to break out. My grandfather, the recently naturalised and thus unfortunately eligible Jack, was promptly conscripted to the British Army, who stationed him in a bomb-making factory in Woolwich then unceremoniously posted him to Burma.

Jacob had effectively sealed his future son-in-law's fate by insisting, for reasons of his daughter's social status, that he become an English citizen. While Jacob apparently went on to regret his intransigence, that would have been of little comfort to my grandpa

Jack, who never discussed what he saw or did as part of what became known as a 'forgotten army' in Burma. He returned much diminished: traumatised and weighing less than eighty pounds. He would never again eat a banana or a grain of rice, which my mother believes were the only foods the English soldiers received for long stretches of their posting.

I had a close connection to my grandfather as a child. I still see glimpses of a kind and understanding man, a spiritual person, a believer in the afterlife and in things greater than ourselves. It was rare to hear him complain. His wife, my grandma Marie, had a more sheltered upbringing than him and a more demanding outlook on life, a greater need for the material comforts. He endured her demands with patience and, when necessary, a dark humour. Once, when my grandma was saying how her widowed friend Florrie had been bought an expensive coat by her new husband, my mum heard Grandpa respond with a simple suggestion for how she might herself find such happiness: 'Shoot me.'

By the time my parents moved to Edgware from Luton in the late 1960s there were close to eighty thousand residents, 40 per cent of whom were Jewish. Given that less than one half of 1 per cent of the UK population was Jewish at that time, this was a ghetto of sorts. The word 'ghetto' is Jewish in origin, first used to mean the place the Jews were banished to in Venice, but if Edgware was a ghetto it was a much more comfortable one than the part of London's East End that my grandparents had inhabited when first arriving from Eastern Europe.

The Edgware I grew up in was not the East End slums, the Lower West Side ghetto or a primitive Polish rural village. It was by comparison a materially comfortable and sheltered environment. It shared few characteristics with the harsher worlds my ancestors endured. There was a familiarity and warmth that came from such an insular community, not to mention a slightly grim sense of humour which has never left me. I had fun growing up in Edgware. Nevertheless, it always seemed like a place to leave.

Most people from my neighbourhood stuck to a tight-knit social group which they then started families within, and whose own children subsequently attended the same religious and educational establishments. Economic progress was the goal. The idea of 'sticking to your own' was deeply ingrained in my parents' thinking, the Holocaust having had a massive impact on their lives and their psyches. And while there may have been a great deal of ethnic and religious pride, it was tempered by a fear that created a need for camouflage. For one thing, we were not actually Russells. This noble English aristocratic surname dating back to 1066 and meaning 'Son of Red' has nothing to do with us. My grandpa sampled it. This required chutzpah – Yiddish for audacity – but it was born of necessity.

My father's father had surmised that his actual surname – Rosenthal – was too Jewish and would make him unemployable and potentially a target. In the face of a rising tide of anti-Semitism, he took cover under an English-sounding last name, and giving my father the first names Stanley Lionel anglicised the part of their ethnicity which was most visible, in order to more easily navigate an anti-Semitic society. We were not really expected to integrate meaningfully with non-Jews; we were indoctrinated as part of a tribe. One specific view of the world was supposed to be held by all. The Israeli national anthem was sung at school assembly. Something told me there were other ways of looking at things.

On the day I was born my dad was busy at work selling life insurance. In the early 1970s men did not take a day off to attend their son's birth. It wasn't seen as their responsibility. Childbirth, and to a considerable extent child-rearing, were considered women's work.

My family did not take my birth for granted. My mum, Rosalind Kreitzman, had been told she couldn't have children. This was a catastrophe for a woman intending to devote herself to motherhood. When she then proved the diagnosis wrong and got pregnant with my sister Caroline in 1967, she saw it as a miracle, and my birth some four years later, following a course of newly launched fertility drug Clomid, was a cause for celebration.

Our family home was spotlessly clean and tidy. All food was kosher and, in keeping with Jewish dietary laws, meat and milk were never mixed. My dad would be out seeing clients some evenings, and when at home had his own chair opposite the TV that no one else would even have considered sitting on.

My mum has never in her life drunk alcohol or smoked a cigarette. I have never seen my father drunk. In fact, the only alcohol I ever saw consumed in my house was sweet kosher wine on a Friday night. Friday nights were strictly about Shabbat dinner, and there would never have been any possibility of Dad working then. It was sacrosanct family time.

Nothing bad happened to me in my childhood, and I know how lucky I am to be able to say that. My parents were decent, hard-working people, keen to give me a good start in life. Nonetheless, I absorbed a sadness in my early years that was hard to pin down and has never left me. I grew up surrounded by ghosts. The spectres of whatever my parents had to deal with, vague half-memories of their childhoods, things never discussed. Some reserve of anguish is built over the generations, and sensitive children end up tapping into this vague melancholy ache.

The Holocaust had wiped out the majority of European Jews only twenty-five years before. It was the defining event in the lives of my parents and their parents before them, and there was a collective intergenerational pain which was palpable. There was never any suggestion that we should forgive the perpetrators of the atrocities. It would have been considered unthinkable, grossly offensive. Other spiritual practices suggest forgiveness is the only way to transcend this kind of trauma, but the tribe I was born into, taught to 'never forget', were locked in a cycle of fear and repressed anger about what had happened to them, and while there were by now many fairly comfortable Jewish families such as mine, everyone was tightly coiled. Disquiet was in the ether, the vague notion that danger lurked. At least our surname wouldn't give us away.

The pathos affects people in a multitude of ways. I felt like an

177

outsider and wanted to be free. I knew I was not destined for that area of London, or the life that was laid out for me, and wanted an escape route. My parents loved me and that was beyond doubt, but I confused them. I was confused too. I felt a sense of dislocation.

There had been great benefits to my childhood circumstances, though. The house where my parents lived had a busy main road to one side, meaning our only neighbour was Mrs Margolis, an elderly Jewish lady who was virtually deaf. I grew up able to play music at a volume that would have been unacceptable elsewhere, and the decibels helped deepen my love for what I was hearing. My mum says the kitchen used to shake. It was generous of my parents to tolerate it, despite receiving complaints from neighbours who lived on Broadfields Avenue, all the way across a main road.

That feeling of the senses being assaulted is integral to the excitement I have always got from music. Apart from her deafness, the thing I really loved about Mrs Margolis was that despite her innocent demeanour she was a keen shoplifter, and would take me with her, aged seven, to pilfer from Hamleys, letting me keep the proceeds. We never got caught; who would suspect a sweet, hearing-impaired little old lady and a seven-year-old boy?

Many Jewish people of my parents' generation (though not my parents, who I can now see were open-minded and worldly by the standards of some of their peers) referred to all non-Jews as 'goyim', and that Yiddish word, literally meaning 'nations', identified another tribe, who were perceived to pose a threat.

The far right and openly racist and anti-Semitic National Front were prominent; you'd see the NF logo graffitied on street signs, in public toilets, on walls and tube trains. The local pubs were considered inhospitable and potentially dangerous places. This made no sense to me until I visited a pub at the end of Edgware High Street. I was sixteen. While I tried to get served, a fellow customer at the bar told me that I was dead if my eyes 'crossed him' again. What was this all about? How dangerous actually was this pub?

The pub is still there, and googling it for the purposes of writing this, I did come across the following search results:

'pub raided by police'
'man stabbed in Edgware pub fight'
'BB gun shooting pub to remain open despite police warnings'
'two men slashed across the stomach after "petty argument" outside pub'

One city guide has only one comment regarding this pub: 'Worst place ever! Don't go there.' All of which made me feel less victimised. But still, why was the man in the pub in 1987 so upset by my presence? Was it anti-Semitism? Edgware's indigenous white population and Jewish immigrant community didn't communicate and thus didn't understand each other.

Equally, the lives of the people I was raised among had been so affected by anti-Semitism that they saw it everywhere. But the problem was not simply anti-Semitism. That was too specific. It was just hatred, based on ignorance, which can manifest as any form of prejudice.

When my mother has visited me in the old house I own in Dorset, where albums are recorded and which those in touch with such things always claim has a noticeably ethereal atmosphere, she feels my grandpa Jack's presence. At the moment my first son Sonny was born, I saw the face of my grandpa clearly imposed on that of the newborn baby. It frightened me at the time, but now I see it as one of the best experiences of my life, a moment of transmission and a link to what went before.

PART 3

Part 3 Playlist

Gil Scott-Heron 'The Revolution Will Not Be Televised (Original Live Version)' (Flying Dutchman)

Smog 'I'm New Here' (Drag City/Domino)

Robert Johnson 'Me And The Devil Blues' (Columbia)

Gil Scott-Heron 'New York Is Killing Me' (XL Recordings)

Gil Scott-Heron 'Home Is Where The Hatred Is' (Flying Dutchman)

Kanye West 'My Way Home feat. Common' (Def Jam)

Kanye West 'Flashing Lights' (Def Jam)

Gil Scott-Heron 'On Coming From A Broken Home (Part 1)' (XL Recordings)

Tonto's Expanding Head Band 'Riversong' (Embryo)

Jamie XX 'I'll Take Care Of You' (Young Turks)

Todd Edwards 'Saved My Life' (Locked On)

Sneaker Pimps 'Spin Spin Sugar (Armand's Dark Garage Mix)' (Clean Up)

Nu Birth 'Anytime' (Locked On)

The Streets 'Has It Come To This' (Locked On)

Ian Dury 'Spasticus Autisticus' (Polydor)

John Cooper Clarke 'Evidently Chickentown' (CBS)

Scritti Politti 'Asylums In Jerusalem' (Rough Trade)

The Avalanches 'Since I Left You' (Modular/XL Recordings)

The White Stripes 'Death Letter' (Third Man/XL Recordings)

Andrew Oldham Songbook 'Theme For A Rolling Stone' (London)

Aluminium 'Aluminum' (XL Recordings)

Heartless Crew 'Heartless Theme' (Heartless)

Pay As U Go Cartel 'Know We' (White Label)

Wiley 'Eskimo' (Wiley Kat)

Wiley 'Ice Rink' (Wiley Kat)

Cage and Weed 'Creeper' (Roll Deep)

Jon E Cash 'War' (Black Ops)

Jon E Cash 'Hoods Up' (Black Ops)

Dizzee Rascal 'I Luv U' (XL Recordings)

Dizzee Rascal 'Everywhere' (XL Recordings)

ESG 'UFO' (99)

Billy Squier 'The Big Beat' (Capitol)

Run-DMC 'Here We Go' (Profile)

T. Rex 'The Scenescof Dynasty' (Regal Zonophone)

Björk 'Where Is The Line' (One Little Indian)

Blackstreet 'Love's In Need Of Love Today' (Interscope)

Clipse 'Grindin'' (Star Trak)

Badly Drawn Boy 'Road Movie' (Twisted Nerve/XL Recordings)

Doves 'Cedar Room' (Heavenly)

Sub Sub 'Space Face' (10)

Neneh Cherry 'Buffalo Stance' (Virgin)

MIA 'Pull Up The People' (XL Recordings)

MIA 'Paper Planes' (XL Recordings)

The Clash 'Straight To Hell' (CBS)

T.I. and Jay-Z 'Swagger Like Us' (Grand Hustle)

Giggs 'Talkin' Da Hardest' (XL Recordings)

Giggs 'Cut-Up Bag' (SN1)

The Streets 'Slow Songs' (Locked On)

Stormzy 'Wicked Skengman' (Merky)

Dave 'Paper Cuts' (Neighbourhood)

Adele 'Daydreamer' (XL Recordings)

Amy Winehouse 'Back To Black' (Island)

Tobias Jesso Jr 'Hollywood' (True Panther)

Adele 'When We Were Young' (XL Recordings)

Thom Yorke 'Analyse' (XL Recordings)

Radiohead 'Jigsaw Falling Into Place' (XL Recordings)

ALL THE DREAMS YOU SHOW UP IN ARE NOT YOUR OWN

YO, RICH:

I TRIED TO CALL YOU BACK AFTER YOU RANG ON SATURDAY AFTERNOON. I HAVE SPENT A LOT OF TIME LISTENING TO OUR PROJECT FROM 1 THROUGH 14. I AM PRETTY WELL PLEASED BUT I HAVE LONG SINCE REALIZED THAT OUR INDEPENDENT GEOGRAPHY PROVIDES NO WAY TO "CO-PRODUCE" A CD. PERHAPS IF I HADN'T BEEN A JAIL BIRD FOR MOST OF THE PRODUCTION PERIOD WE COULD HAVE WORKED MORE EASILY; ESPECIALLY IF I HAD BEEN FREE TO COME TO THE U. K. BEFORE OCTOBER. THIS PUT A LOT MORE WEIGHT ON YOU. HOPEFULLY YOU HAVE EXACTLY WHAT YOU WERE LOOKING FOR. AS YOU PROGRESS YOU WILL SEE HOW RARE IT IS TO GET A PROJECT, IN FACT, TO GET ANYTHING IN LIFE "EXACTLY, ETC.".

I HONESTLY THINK WE WILL HAVE A SUCCESSFUL COMMERCIAL RELEASE IF WE PLAY THIS LIKE A POKER HAND. I SUGGEST THIS THIS BECAUSE I HAVE LEFT STUDIOS OFTEN WITH "EXACTLY, ETC.", AND FOR WHATEVER REASON I WAS NOT SUCCESSFUL. SO I WILL NOT TAKE IT FOR GRANTED, BUT SPEAK ON WHAT I KNOW WENT RIGHT AND WRONG:

(#1) KEEP "A. M." ON THE WEBSITE AS THE ONLY ACTIVE VIDEO. WE SHOULD ADD OUR BEST-LOOKING PHOTOS OF PEOPLE WORKING ON THE PROJECT IN VARIOUS CAPACITIES FOLKS IN THE STUDIO (KIM, THE GUITAR PLAYERS, THE VIDEO FOLKS, THE CHOIR, YOU AND LOFTON), FOLKS DOING THE OUTSIDE WORK. THERE WILL BE TOO MANY PICTURES OF ME SOON ENOUGH. THE ONLY ADDS COULD BE RECENT REVIEWS OF SHOWS OR PHOTOS OF POSTERS FOR SHOWS. (L. A. REVIEW, DENVER REVIEW, POSTERS FROM B'MORE, D. C., "BLUE NOTE" AND "B.B. KING'S"

(#2) I SUGGEST A BLUE FEELING AND ATMOSPHERE FOR THE WEB. LIKE THROUGH A BLUE LENS. A SCENE IN "BLACK WAX" TALKS ABOUT THE BLUES AND BLUESOLOGY THE OPENING LINES OF "H2OGATE BLUES" FROM "WINTER IN AMERICA" CD CAN LEAD TO "ME AND THE DEVIL" OR "I'LL TAKE CARE OF YOU".

(#3) WHY NOT ASK THE BBC FOLKS FOR THEIR COLLECTION OF PROGRAMS I HAVE DONE FOR THEM. THEY HAVE AN EXTENSIVE AMOUNT OF FILM ON ME THAT GOES BACK TO 1976 WHEN I DID "JO'BERG" AND "LOVELY DAY" WITH THE ORIGINAL MIDNIGHT BAND. IT'S ALWAYS GOOD TO GET SOMETHING FOR SOMETHING AND YOU CAN REMIND THEM THAT YOU ARE THE KEY TO THEIR FUTURE WITH ME.

THE FINAL ELEMENTS ARE THE QUOTES: THERE ARE A FEW THAT WILL BE
VALUABLE BETWEEN SONGS, BUT THERE MAY BE MORE VALUE BEFORE THE CD FOR
THE LONGER COMMENTS THAT DAMN NEAR DEVELOPE INTO SERMONS OR SPEECHES
AT A BONUS MINI-DISC, ONLY AVAILABLE INSIDE THE "SPECIAL BOX" THAT WE
SELL TO COLLECTORS. LET"S ALSO REMEMBER THAT WE HAVE THE POSSIBILITY
OF ANOTHER CD SOME DAY AND DON'T NEED TO SERVE IT ALL NOW JUST BECAUSE
WE HAVE IT.

BE SURE TO SPEAK WITH JAMIE BYNG IF YOU'RE PLANNING TO GET INTO THE
BOOK BUSINESS. ALSO REMEMBER THAT THE "PIECESOFAMAN. COM. U.K" WEBSITE
OF THEIRS HAS BEEN RUNNING MATERIAL SINCE APRIL AND WILL BE USING MORE
THINGS FROM "THE LAST HOLIDAY" AS IT GETS CLOSER TO PUBLICATIOM.

NOW, ABOUT THE $$:
1) ONE OF YOUR CKS. FOR $9,000.00 WAS RETURNED, NOT ACCEPTED BY MY
BANK. I AM NOT SURE WHAT THE PROBLEM WAS OR WHAT THE DIFFERENCE WAS
BETWEEN THAT ONE AND THE OTHER TWO, WHICH WERE ACCEPTED.
2) I SPOKE TO PATRICK AT SOME POINT ABOUT MY POCKET EXPENSES FOR KIM
AND BRADY SESSIONS AT "CLINTON" AND "LOOKING GLASS". THERE WAS $1400.0(
PAID OUT FOR THE SESSIONS AND $500.00 FOR TRANSPORTATION, WASHINGTON
TO NEW YORK TO WASHINGTON ROUND TRIPS.
3) THE REMAINDER, ABOUT 70 OR 80 GRAND, MIGHT BE BEST LEFT OVER THERE,
NOT DELIVERED YET. I'M SURE I DON'T WANT IT ALL IN MY ACCOUNTS, BUT
I MAY NEED $5,000.00 OR SO FROM TIME TO TIME.
4) REMEMBER THAT WE AGREED TO SPLIT THE $10,000.00 SENT TO LARRY GOLD
AFTER THE PROJECT WAS DONE.
5) THERE ARE ALSO DEDUCTIONS OF VARIOUS PAYMENTS TO CHE OR FOR HER THAT
I WOULD APPRECIATE HAVING ITEMIZED.

I'M GETTING A WHOLE LOT OF REQUESTS TO PLAY VARIOUS DATES IN EUROPE,
PARTICULARLY IN THE U. K.. I INTEND TO WORK WITH GLP, WALTER'S COMPANY
FOR MY MAJOR EUROPEAN EXCURSIONS, BUT DO NOT NEED TO INVOLVE HIM IN
THE SMALLER PRESS GIGS YOU WANT ME TO DO TO PROMOTE THE CD.

I TRIED TO SEND YOU A TEXT MESSAGE AROUND 4:00 A. M. ON SUNDAY BUT
I DIDN'T REACH YOU. I ONLY WANTED TO TELL YOU THAT I HAD A GREAT TIME
WITH THE PROJECT, TAKE CARE OF YOUR FAMILY, MAINTAIN YOUR CALM AND STAY
SAFE. EVERYTHING ELSE WILL BE ALL RIGHT. BLESS YOU.

In 2006 I approached Gil Scott-Heron to see if he wanted to record an album together. I'd never stopped listening to Gil since I first heard his music in my teens, but the idea of working with him actually came from hearing Kanye West sample 'Home Is Where The Hatred Is' in the track 'My Way Home', which reminded me how much I loved Gil's voice, and how connected I had felt to him since I'd first heard it.

I wanted to hear a whole new Gil Scott-Heron record. And if I wanted this music to exist, I suspected that I would have to make it happen, personally. Gil had not made a record for fifteen years. But somehow I thought it might just be possible. I realised that it would be difficult, though, not least because Gil was at that time incarcerated in New York's Rikers Island prison, for possession of cocaine.

Once I'd had the idea of approaching Gil to suggest we record together, as far as I was concerned things were in motion, and I immediately started not only drafting a letter to him but making playlists of songs to listen to with him. I acted as if my idea, which at that point existed only in my head, was reality. There is an element of magical thinking to all this, and in some respects it is a slightly deranged way of going about things; but it was the only approach likely to yield results.

There's a fine line between being a creative person, a generator of ideas who can make imaginary notions real, and a deluded wreck. If your idea feels a bit mad to you, that's a good sign, but it's definitely going to sound incomprehensible to others. This is where the concept comes from that if people understand what you're talking about too easily, you're not trying hard enough.

Kanye West was, unwittingly, a catalyst for the existence of the record I made with Gil and he has always been a magical thinker.

For some time, he occupied a Bowie-ish space in music, making seven consecutive albums of brilliantly original music of his own, together with countless productions for other artists.

Then he started acting strangely in public, adopting a political stance which seemed baffling at best, and saying some ill-advised things about slavery. These were an echo of Bowie's mid-seventies behaviour, when he claimed 'Britain could benefit from a fascist leader', said 'Hitler was one of the first rock stars' and had his photograph taken giving a Nazi salute first outside Hitler's bunker and then again from the back of an open-topped Mercedes limo at Victoria station. *NME* ran the photo with the headline 'Heil and Farewell'. It was all madness, and Bowie reversed his position soon after. But something akin to madness is necessary to be as relentlessly inventive as Bowie in the seventies and Kanye over the last decade. That madness, with all its destructive energy, is so near the magic.

Gil Scott-Heron was born in Chicago, and raised from the age of three by his grandmother Lily Scott in Jackson, Tennessee. His father, Gil Heron, was a professional soccer player, and on signing to Celtic in the fifties became one of the first black football players in Britain, later stating that if he hadn't scored in his first game they would have killed him.

Lily Scott died when Gil was twelve. Heartbroken, he moved back in with his mother in New York City. He first attended DeWitt Clinton High School in the Bronx, but was spotted for his remarkable literary gift and transferred to the prestigious Fieldston School on the Upper West Side. In his admission interview he was asked by a member of the teaching staff how he would feel, coming as he did from an economically deprived background, attending a school where other children were ferried to and from the gates in chauffeur-driven limousines. Gil responded that he would probably feel the same way as the teacher, because he couldn't afford a limo either, and asked him, 'How do you feel?'

Gil then attended Lincoln University in Pennsylvania, the alma mater of his hero, the poet Langston Hughes, and while there saw the Last Poets perform. A spark was ignited.

Gil's genius flowered and by the time he was twenty-one he had released two novels, a book of poetry and his first album. The album and the poetry book were called *Small Talk At 125th And Lenox*. The album contained a song called 'The Revolution Will Not Be Televised' in its original bare bones live form. Its title and hook has since been referenced so often that it has taken on the life of a Shakespearean quote.

The nine albums Gil Scott-Heron went on to release in the seventies are a treasure trove of deep, heartfelt expression and social commentary. He never made a bad album. His second offering, *Pieces Of A Man*, from 1971, included a fleshed-out reworking of 'The Revolution Will Not Be Televised'. Gil himself was dismissive of what became his most famous song, feeling it stopped people exploring the rest of the album, and pigeonholed him as a militant spoken-word artist when that was only a part of who he was. He avoided playing 'The Revolution' live and it was testament to the breadth of his catalogue that audiences never missed it.

After leaving the independent jazz label he had started with, Bob Thiele's Flying Dutchman, and becoming the first artist to sign to Clive Davis's Arista label, Gil toured with Stevie Wonder and successfully campaigned to have Martin Luther King's birthday recognised as a national holiday, in doing so changing the constitution of the United States.

Gil was deeply flawed and he accepted that. But he wasn't judgemental of others. And he was also never corny. For his whole career he avoided the clichéd lover-man lyrics more or less every seventies soul artist veered into at some point. Having had a long lay-off from recording, his catalogue remained unsullied. The break from studio work might not have benefited him personally, but it means there's no fat in his recorded output. There have been few artists more literate, and more capable of both authentic tenderness and righteous anger. He was a student of the human condition and had deep insights.

Gil had not released records through much of the 1980s, 90s and 2000s; but he had maintained an active live career, and he saw performing to audiences as his role. Having communicated by letter, I went to meet him for the first time in person in 2006, on Rikers Island, the world's largest penal colony where some 15,000 inmates were then incarcerated. When asked later about my visit to Rikers, Gil said, 'I don't think he wanted to stay.' But when I got there he said, 'I was wondering when you'd turn up', which could be interpreted in a cosmic fashion if you believe in that sort of thing, which I do.

We spoke without pause for more than two hours in our first meeting, as if we went way back together, and when I commented that he never seemed to complain, given his surroundings, he gave me the first of many poignant and subtle insights: 'If you complain, no one wants to hang out with you.'

He told me he had done some research on me, and it had led him to believe I was honourable: 'I've asked around about you and you don't do under-the-table shit,' he said, which felt like as hearty an encomium as I would receive from a man as committed to truth as he remained, despite his circumstances.

There was some connection between Gil and me which went beyond the surface, and it would crop up in unlikely ways. Gil suffered from a major debilitating neurological condition which left him temporarily paralysed when he was forty-two. An identical fate would befall me.

I was instinctively drawn to work with Gil, but I was also barely ready to become a proper record producer. I had a strong urge to create, and had taken seriously the learning of some modern production techniques, by now using the digital audio workstation Logic Pro. This software had unprecedented versatility; it was not just a way of capturing and editing vocal performances, but a tool for creative expression for electronic and sample-based music-makers. All on a laptop. I loved it.

But the success of XL as a record label made me feel less equipped to be a musician and producer rather than more, because as the label grew other people had been producing all the music. I only just had enough confidence to try to produce (and subsequently co-write and play with) Gil, and going into the project I felt like I was bluffing. Now, I know: everyone feels like this sometimes. And who would feel blithely confident trying to make a record with their favourite artist, now seemingly in diminished circumstances?

The life of the record executive is for the most part more stable and ordered than that of the full-time creative person. The process of songwriting and recording often involves wild oscillation between feeling immensely empowered - godlike is how some describe it - by one's own abilities to make something out of nothing, and feeling like an idiot who is wandering around naked while everyone laughs. These extreme swings can occur in very short spaces of time and when they do you are fairly close to madness. The uncertainty of the creative process feels to me at times like chewing tin foil.

The manager of one huge artist proudly told me that he insists to the musicians he works with that they behave functionally. He said that he doesn't buy into the idea that instability is intrinsically linked to creativity. Perhaps, I thought, he is just working with talent so mediocre that their behaviour is as mundane as their music. Whatever abilities I possess feel like they are simply the flipside of the least functional parts of me. Dysfunctionality comes with gifts as a consolation prize. Whether a person is able to tap into these gifts is another question.

But no one whose art is really good tends to feel all that good for much of the time. Blissful happiness is an unlikely condition in any event and would certainly be an unusual place for a gifted person to inhabit, at least for long. The best a great talent can hope for is to reach some sort of an accommodation with themselves. An appreciation that they at least have something to show for their alienation.

I don't profess to understand the nature of the load that Gil carried. It was heavy, though. As his bandmate Tony Duncanson said: 'He lived the blues. Most people just sing it.' Whatever Gil was going through, whatever his condition, and contrary to advice I was given by others, my natural instinct told me I should put myself on the line and fully commit to both him and my own creativity.

Before attempting to record anything, we spent time getting to know each other. I hung out with Gil at his apartment in Harlem, where he was always welcoming. We would meet at The Mercer hotel in SoHo where I stayed, and it was here that I played Gil songs like 'I'm New Here' by Bill Callahan, aka Smog, one of the greatest and most unsung musicians of our time, and where we listened to Robert Johnson's 'Me And The Devil Blues' together. This was a key part of the process, as Gil connected to both of these songs and we eventually used them as repertoire for the album, alongside reworked versions of Gil's poems, and a new song, 'New York Is Killing Me'.

We spent a lot of time together over a five-year period and he never got high in front of me. I wouldn't have minded but it was probably useful for us both that he created these boundaries. He had given up alcohol some years previously, clearly had control over his remaining habits and had maintained his free will. His wit was acute. 'Get me a lawyer and an ashtray,' he once said to me, taking the Marlboros from his pocket, 'I'm about to smoke a cigarette indoors.' Turning up one day at 7pm for a 2pm session, Gil announced himself: 'It's the late Gil Scott-Heron.'

When I arrived in New York for the first session with Gil I had a panic attack, and my friend Mischa Richter, who did the photography for the album, talked me down and told me I was good enough to work with Gil. There may not have been an album if I hadn't called Mischa at the moment I did. We all have an inner coward. I'm well aware of mine. I am weak in that I'm often afraid, but equally I'm strong in that I will ask for help, and people are surprisingly willing to assist you. If you ask. Shortly afterwards I received a message from Liam, encouraging me to make the album with Gil, affirming my faith.

When Gil began to see how committed I was to the processes involved in making the album - everything from discussions about the phrasing of particular lyrics to the writing and recording of electronic music which I started playing to him and which formed the musical basis of many of the songs on the album – he asked me the following question: 'So is this what you're doing now?' I took this to mean making music and producing records as opposed to running a record label. He was putting me on the line. I replied in the affirmative. 'Good,' he said. 'We can use more people like you in this environment.' Then he posed a thought-provoking question. 'You realise it's a demotion?'

Coming from his generation of musicians, the head of the record company was seen as the boss. But I had never seen myself as the boss of any musician, and in no way considered dedicating myself to the creative process to be part of any downward trajectory. Quite the opposite. I saw this as being back where I was meant to be. And if it led to less output, and less commercial success than I would be having as a full-time label boss, I was happy to accept that.

I had used the word 'spartan' early on in our correspondence, and Gil would bring us back to that word whenever he thought my production became cluttered. In this way he A&Red me as much as I did him, enabling us to include only elements that were essential and fulfilled the minimalist intentions of the project. Gil's first album, recorded forty years earlier, consisted largely of spoken word and drums alone, and on what turned out to be his last album we referenced those foundations and used them as a guide.

The process of working with Gil Scott-Heron, rough healer, was beautiful and profound, and fraught and frightening. We had some arguments which in retrospect I realise were often my fault and caused by my fears of failure. As Jo Bagenal, Gil's product manager at XL, said of her experiences with him: 'Gil didn't fall into your life softly. He shook you up.'

When I heard Nas wanted to rhyme on a version of the album track 'New York Is Killing Me', it felt like a fulfilling of dreams that stretched way back, and I was so excited for it to happen that I sent Nas the instrumental without mentioning it to Gil. Gil saw that as a betrayal and got angry with me. He was right. My actions were what Buddhists regard as classic grasping behaviour. I was too attached to the outcome I desired, and that caused me to not communicate properly with Gil. I didn't ask him because I was afraid he would say no. If I'd patiently communicated, and not feared the outcome, there would have been no problem.

The rhythm track for that particular song is a home recording of mine, as personal an expression for me as someone else's singing is for them. Good art is personal, but if you take it too personally you tend to mess up. Some of the rest of the instrumentation of that song is by Chris Cunningham, who is known for his visual work, but less recognised for his equally brilliant music. Chris has let very little of his music be heard. I had to coax and drag the eerie synths and toy guitar on 'New York Is Killing Me' out of him, but the recording is a testament to how worthwhile it was.

Dexter was born shortly before I began to contemplate working with Gil, and over the course of making the album Jada was born, meaning I now had three small children and was keen to make sure I was being a parent and not missing anything at home while also executing what was to me the most important creative project of my life thus far. There were bound to be some issues.

Some years later I read Gil discussing our working relationship. When journalist Matthew Schnipper from *Fader* magazine asked what it was like working with me, given my enthusiasm to bring the project to fruition, Gil had responded with his customarily philosophical and poetic aplomb:

How did it feel to have someone so gung-ho about making this happen?
It felt good. That's how I feel when I'm getting ready to do something and I have some place I want to go. I'm all right, especially in a one-man race. You always know you're going to win. It's not a competitive thing. It's not me against him. It's seeing if we can work together, and of course we can because we both like music and most of the material. I'm sorry to say that we didn't battle and fight.

It's better that you didn't.

It's a more interesting story - Russell against Heron, you know? It was a good idea. In the middle of this, his wife was pregnant and he's gotta do this, he's gotta do that, she's gonna murder him and I'm not that important. So things happen. Your life goes on at the same time, but overall in terms of the project, it felt good.

. . . I like Richard because Richard likes Richard. He's happy with what he's doing. You meet unhappy people and you get the blues. You meet Richard and you get on the lighter side.

It's a rare attitude to come across.

I have to remember I'm nothing special. I have earned the potential to be the way I want to be, and it's nothing to hide. I got no things to live up or down to. The thought of Richard just makes me smile because I had a good time with him - most of the time. We've been on opposite sides of different things, but we worked that out. I wanted this, he wanted that, we got somewhere in there. It's on the record.

Both of you are very blessed to have met each other.

We were. And you take advantage of your blessings, or you kick them down the street and see if you get another one. Most of the time you cannot get one again. You come to understand, like in America, we're capitalist, so you look at it as an opportunity, but I look at it as a blessing.

Are you going to work with him again?

I think so.

To produce a record is a deeply personal process for me. I have never accepted the 'executive producer' credit on an album. Either I'm producing an artist's album, or I'm not. I'm collaboratively making that album and living that process, working with the artist note by note, or I'm hands-off. I had never before put myself into an album in this fashion.

While I was working with Gil, I had seen Jamie Smith, aka Jamie xx, use the Akai MPC sampling drum machine as a live instrument at an early xx gig in east London. He was effectively the drummer for the group, hitting pads with his fingers, each of which triggered a drum sound he had sampled, rather than playing a traditional drum kit. This was a breakthrough moment for me as I realised that my MPC was an actual instrument I had always needed to treat as such.

I set about loading my own machine with the sounds I had been collecting, and then practising the playing of the machine. I didn't wish to tidy the sounds once they were recorded, but wanted to leave them loose, creating a tension between the sampled sounds and the live imperfection of non-quantised playing. Learning to do this gave me an instrument I could play confidently, live or in the studio, alongside any musician of any calibre, allowing me control over the sounds and the ability to improvise. I recorded cavernous-sounding drums from old machines which felt like they contain ghosts, and played them with a live feel.

Working with Gil, I was able to imagine samples into being by looking through his books of poetry and suggesting that he did readings of certain poems and passages. I intended to use only snippets of these, but some of the songs on what became *I'm New Here* are essentially whole readings that Gil gave which I then laid over music. To open the album, I asked Gil to read the poem 'On Coming From A Broken Home' from his first volume of poetry. I selected this piece because it seemed to me that his reminiscences of his childhood would be just as poignant now, perhaps more so, than when he wrote the piece aged twenty.

And thus the album opens with Gil saying, 'I want to make this a special tribute', and he goes on to talk in the most moving possible terms about his grandma, Lily Scott, who raised him, and how he was sent to live with her as a small child. 'I was moved in with her temporarily, just till this was patched and that was patched . . . and I loved her from the absolute marrow of my bones. And we was holding on.' At the end of the song we hear of her passing.

The first thing you hear in this opening track, 'On Coming From A Broken Home Part One', is a sampled loop from 'Flashing Lights' by Kanye, and this was my way of referencing his influence. When I suggested using the loop to Gil, he laughed and said, 'He owes me one', I suppose referring to the sample Kanye had used in 'My Way Home'.

I recorded the synth and breakbeat that open the next song, the cover of 'Me And The Devil', alone in my basement studio. The lack of daylight is somehow audible, and Gil's weathered voice is as heavy as lead. The guitarist Pat Sullivan played on the Smog cover 'I'm New Here', and having rehearsed the piece we made a one-take live recording, and this song provides a moment of levity in the overall dark terrain of the album. Once we had recorded this most unlikely of covers, I knew the whole album would pan out well. There is breathable air in our recording of this song in what is a mostly claustrophobic album.

'The Vulture' was another piece where I asked Gil to read one of my favourite poems of his, and I provided accompaniment from the MPC, as well as recording string overdubs with engineer Lawson White. I would piece it all together afterwards but it was clear to me that everything would fit, and was meant to sound like this, and I knew Gil would like the end result. These things are right or wrong.

On 'Where Did The Night Go' I employ the 'no music' technique of vocals and drums only. Glancing back at Gil's debut, nothing would be used that was unnecessary.

I had made the music for the song 'The Crutch' prior to starting the album with Gil. It became clear to me that some of the recordings I had been working on at home were meant for this project. There was something liberating about this. After I began to play the MPC to accompany Gil, I suggested to him that once we had completed our album, we should ask Jamie xx to remix the whole thing into a companion piece of work, which became *We're New Here*. Jamie was more or less unknown at that time, and the exposure and acclaim he received for this work was a good exchange for the idea of playing the MPC in the way that I got from him.

Gil told me that he was realising that he and I were embarking on a 'two men and some electronics mission', and that he had been here before: see the cover of his album *1980*. Gil and his then collaborator Brian Jackson are perched in front of a huge bank of keyboards and patch bays, and the word 'TONTO' is visible. Tonto's Expanding Head Band were a New York-based duo who had named themselves after the polyphonic synthesiser they had built. TONTO, an acronym for The Original New Timbral Orchestra, was no ordinary instrument.

Synthesisers up to now had been playable only one note at a time. In 1970 a British ex-pat engineer called Malcolm Cecil had modified a Moog Series 3 belonging to his record producer friend Robert Margouleff, and over a period of years added more modules to it until he possessed an instrument unlike any other. It was six feet tall and measured twenty feet in diameter, and was not just polyphonic, i.e. able to play more than one note at a time, but was fully multi-timbral, meaning the tone of each note would be affected by how it was struck.

Having given themselves a name the pair made an album using this instrument, and only this instrument. *Zero Time*, released just a few months apart from Gil's debut in 1970, was an early electronic masterpiece which sold next to nothing but had a deep impact on those who sought it out. One of these open-minded listeners was Stevie Wonder, who promptly hired the pair as co-producers on the album he was about to embark on, *Music Of My Mind*, took up residence in their studio and kept the two on board for the world-changing run of albums that followed.

The world Cecil and Margouleff created and inhabited, and the context Stevie Wonder then put it in, served, along with other contemporaneous experiments by artists including Sly Stone, to redirect the course of black music in America, and to an extent all popular music that came after.

Gil had enjoyed collaborating with Malcolm Cecil on the five albums they made together between 1978 and 1982, as well as 'Spirits' in 1994, and in 2009 he suggested cryptically that I contact the creator of TONTO and ask him to send me something called 'My Cloud'. I thought this might be some technological device, but what Malcolm actually sent me was an unreleased song of extraordinary beauty that they had made together at some point. Although we couldn't find a way of making it work sonically on our new album, we did include it as a bonus track on the original double vinyl pressing, and gave it to Jamie xx to remix for the *We're New Here* remix project.

I was familiar with Bobby 'Blue' Bland's 'I'll Take Care Of You' through Mark Lanegan's cover of it. After Gil covered it, Jamie re-reinterpreted it for *We're New Here*, and it was reincarnated yet again after being sampled by Drake and Rihanna for their song 'Take Care'. It was now a re-re-reinterpretation, a sample of a remix of a cover of a cover of a cover, and this version went on to be a massive crossover hit a few months after Gil's passing.

An endless thread.

Gil was an intensely spiritual person, and used to believe in astrology in a way that at that time I didn't. In order to show willing and compromise, at one point I went to the Astrology Shop in Covent Garden and had readings done for both me and Gil. Mine seemed spookily accurate. Gil's horoscope described his bullish Aries-type character as being far more comfortable with conflict than my somewhat more delicate Piscean nature. When I put this to him, he said, 'Sure, but I'm a ram, and you came up the mountain to find me, I was quite happy just grazing. So don't complain about what you got.'

Gil believed deeply in the spirits, and he shared some of his insights with me on this subject once while we were between takes. I recorded all the off-mic conversations that occurred during the making of the record. The conversational snippets heard on the album sound as naturalistic as they do because they were actual conversations, with my voice edited out. I kept recording at all times in order to capture Gils spontaneous monologues. An edited version of some of the deep words that were captured became the interlude 'Parents'. Gil said: 'I believe that the spirits are your parents and their parents and their parents and their parents and their parents. And they are in your bloodstream, and they run through your body constantly. They want you to live on because they want to live on, and they are trying to tell you shit, and if you just spend a few minutes with yourself you will hear them.'

I recorded Gil summing up his own behaviour with a candour few will ever be capable of: 'If I hadn't been as eccentric, as obnoxious, as arrogant, as aggressive, as introspective, as selfish, I wouldn't be me. I wouldn't be who I am.' It became the interlude 'I've Been Me'.

It was never spoken but Gil was deeply aware of the importance of the project to me, saying to a journalist who praised the album, 'This is Richard's CD . . . All the dreams you show up in are not your own.'

My grandpa Jack had passed away back in October 1983, and by now Grandma Marie had outlived him by nearly twenty-five years, but she was increasingly lost to Alzheimer's over the last ten years of her life, and she passed away while I was in New York working with Gil. Although her huge spirit was never fully diminished, eventually she was in a virtually vegetative state. To see her lose her everyday competence was painful. One day I had found her walking in the middle of a busy road near her flat in Hale Lane, Edgware, as I drove to see my parents. On receiving the news of Grandma's passing, my mum was keen to speak to me. We were both distraught but we were able to comfort each other. Right after this I spoke to Gil. He talked about how his grandma had raised him, and how deep and fundamental relationships with our grandparents can be.

Gil was not healthy during recording, but he couldn't have been any more giving, or created more profound experiences for the people around him. Gil had suggested that the album we recorded together was released under both of our names - as 'Gil Scott-Heron and Richard Russell'. He explained that this is what he had always done, releasing seven albums under the artist name 'Gil Scott-Heron and Brian Jackson', and so he saw no reason why this should be any different. But the suggestion filled me with dread. There was no way, at that time, that I was doing that.

The reason why? Same as the reason I had once turned Liam down when he suggested we make music together - at the time the suggestion was made, I lacked the necessary confidence in my own creativity to expose myself in this way. I was not ready for the kind of public attention that equal billing with Gil would have entailed, and I have no regrets about rejecting it. I would have deeply regretted not making the album, though.

When *I'm New Here* was released in 2010 it was recognised for being the deep work that it is, and has never stopped being discovered. Musicians continue to be influenced by the record and that is for me the ultimate accolade. Given the immense appreciation many music lovers felt for Gil, there was relief that we had made something worthy of his legacy. I wanted to make a record with him that could stand proudly alongside the rest of his catalogue, and we achieved that.

Gil told me to make sure I enjoyed it, saying, 'You've put your whole life into this.' It would never have occurred to me that this was the case but of course he was right, peering into my soul, seeing what was really going on.

Adopting the roles of producer, mixer, musician and co-writer when working with Gil healed a wound and allowed me to reimmerse myself fully in music-making. Gil liberated me to make the music I've made in the ten years since *I'm New Here* was released. The run of albums I have made since 2010 would not exist without Gil.

There is no ready acceptance of healers and prophets in the modern world, but my experiences of Gil led me to see him, for all his flaws, as both of these. There was a depth to his every utterance that was unlike any other person I've met. And his habits, particularly his drug use which he did not hide and was widely written about, were to me not entirely inconsistent with his spirituality. Deeply spiritual people are not perfect; they are usually the most deeply flawed and searching for a way to transcend their weaknesses.

The prescient things he said to me are still filtering through. When I asked him about new forms of activism that were emerging online, and felt to me to have great potential, his response took me aback. 'There is a difference,' he told me, 'between wanting to change things and wanting to be famous on the internet.' Hardly anyone was 'famous on the internet' at this time. Instagram was not to be launched for another few months. Gil saw clearly where we were headed.

Like many other prophetic poets, there was a thread of disdain running through Gil's philosophy. The insightful see that some things are worthy of contempt. There is much in the world that is worthy of scorn; why maintain a completely upbeat outlook at all times? There's power in negative thinking as well. Gil was aware that the social media age was upon us. There was not much that Gil liked, and no one he followed.

I only ever made one attempt to persuade Gil to promote the album we made together; to do some press interview I considered important. Gil gave me short shrift. He was not particularly interested in talking to the media, he considered us to be a team in our endeavour and didn't appreciate my trying to coerce him into what he considered salesmanship. I told him that the writer was very good; he suggested that if the journalist was so talented I should get him to interview me, or to interview Jamie Byng, his book publisher (who had facilitated my making contact with Gil in the first place), or that Jamie and I should interview each other. Then he told me I was talking like a record company person and letting myself down. And he was right.

When Gil did get round to doing some press he was surprised to be asked about the record company he was now working with, his association with XL perhaps seeming novel to journalists who interviewed him. He was asked his opinion about artists on the label he had never heard of: 'What's a vampire rear end?' he asked me, mischievously misnaming New York newcomers Vampire Weekend, an artist on the label who were starting to receive attention at the time.

I've unwittingly put different figures in the position of guru throughout my adult life. They've tended to be people who are wilder than me, and who are ferociously talented and completely uncompromising in their work. Often, I become preoccupied with them, we collaborate to great effect and then we both move on, although there tends to be a lasting bond. I become a raft for people, to help them get from someplace to someplace else, and at the same time they are a raft for me.

Once you get to the other side of the river, you may be grateful for the raft - you should be - but you don't always stay in close contact. Happily, and despite the sometimes turbulent nature of our relationship, I would never lose contact with Gil.

I received a call from him the morning after my fortieth birthday celebrations. Fittingly, given Gil's relationship to the written word, I was in Foyles on Charing Cross Road at the time he called, and stayed there for the duration of the lengthy call. Gil had something specific to say to me. He said he wanted me to be aware that a person should not change just because they could. This would be the last time we spoke and he would pass away soon after.

I had a connection with Gil which I still don't completely understand the nature of. Other people who encountered him in the same period say the same.

Diminished though he may have been in some ways, his spiritual depth was unmistakable. It is an ongoing relationship in that it is now nearly ten years since Gil died but I think about him frequently, have dreams in which I encounter a happy and free Gil, and find him a huge influence on all the work I do.

I feel duty-bound to help keep Gil's music and memory alive. Currently that's not difficult to do; you just have to listen to Kendrick Lamar, one of the most important voices in music right now, to hear Gil's indelible mark - in the political nature of the lyrics and the jazz-infused and intricate nature of the music. A direct through-line is evident from Gil through Public Enemy to Kendrick. Gil was one of the architects of hip-hop before it had a name – *Small Talk at 125th and Lenox* from 1971 was to my mind the first great rap album. Of course, Gil never claimed to have invented this music. When asked about whether he was the godfather of rap he said, playfully, 'Well, you can blame me for a lot of things . . .'

YOU'RE LOCKED IN

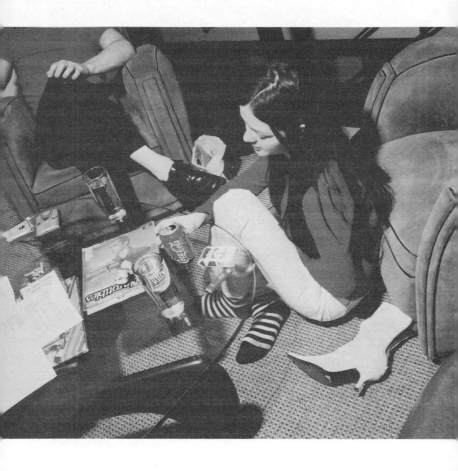

When Nick Halkes departed XL back in 1993, I had contacted another Nick, Nick Worthington, of north London record store and sound system Pure Groove, to see if he wished to join me at the label. We had collaborated on a number of events, and had moved heavy sound equipment around together. As well as this willingness to get his hands dirty, I recognised in Nick someone with a similarly obsessive musical outlook to me. He was not a DJ, but he was a rabid music fan.

Nick had an unusual habit. When I DJed, he would look through my record boxes and study the sleeves and labels of the tunes within. It was a bit presumptuous, but this combination of musical curiosity and chutzpah seemed appropriate for the A&R world. A good CV is one thing, but to be in the habit of mining DJ boxes for priceless intelligence spoke of more applicable qualifications. An obliviousness to certain societal boundaries could only help in this line of work.

Nick operated further behind the scenes than I did, and that reassured me of his musical commitment – he was in it for the right reasons, not to get attention. I was more of a mixture; it was not long since I had been miming on a synth on *Top of the Pops*. Nick was a reserved character, but with real self-assurance, and a bone-dry sense of humour. And he had a passion not just for dance music but hip-hop, R&B and anything else interesting.

Along with his colleagues, Nick had turned Pure Groove into an excellent specialist record shop based on the Holloway Road in Archway, not far from the then headquarters of pirate stalwarts, and recently turned legal dance station, KISS, now broadcasting on 100 FM. This was still a golden period for specialist dance record shops.

Groove Records, pioneering specialist retailer and birthplace of XL, was long shuttered and by now an X-rated video store, but Soho still housed vinyl meccas, including Release the Groove,

Black Market, Wyld Pitch, Mr Bongo's and Unity. A few short years later all of them would be gone. Pure Groove had started off as a relatively non-specialist type of specialist dance shop, carrying vinyl from all subgenres of dance music.

On Nick Worthington's arrival, while I continued to work closely with The Prodigy, XL would release a series of one-off dance records, often sourced from imports or white labels that were in demand at Pure Groove, aiming for short-term success with each release. It was a prosaic approach but something interesting was brewing. UK garage was emerging, a new strain of British club and pirate radio music. It was heavily influenced by the work of certain US house producers, including New Jersey's Todd Edwards, who was the main influence on the smoother and more melodic side of what was going on, and Bostonian DJ Armand van Helden, whose style was being borrowed by UK producers to create a sub-subgenre called 'speed garage', which had an extra-rough British edge, and was a step towards what would become grime.

American dance music, like American films, tends to be more polished than its UK counterparts. We don't do Hollywood production values. There was a rawness in this new sound that was distinctly British.

Pure Groove became closely identified with the music that was being championed by DJs including EZ, Spoony and Tuff Jam, and clubs such as Sunday-nighter Twice As Nice. As the shop became one of the main London portals for speed garage, they released a compilation mixed by Todd Edwards called *Locked On: Inside the Mix*, which served to crystallise the movement, gathering the tunes heard on stations like Freek FM and clarifying the connecting factors. *Locked On* morphed into a label releasing the best tunes from the genre. Nick's involvement with both entities meant that XL could seamlessly provide backing and help when necessary.

The imprint initially released underground classics like Nu Birth's 'Anytime' in 1997, Dem 2's 'Destiny' in 1998 and by the turn of the millennium was having huge crossover hits like Artful Dodger's 'Movin' Too Fast' and Doolally's 'Straight From The Heart'. The

Locked On/Pure Groove system echoed an earlier lifetime for XL, continuing the type of approach Tim Palmer had pioneered in the Citybeat/Groove Records days: independent dance label A&R done behind the record shop counter. Locked On became the leading label of the UK garage scene, trusted and respected by artists, DJs and record buyers.

On a train to Manchester in 2001, Nick played me a demo cassette that had been sent to the shop under the unpromising name 'The Streets'. As well as the role he played as part of the Pure Groove team, Nick had by now signed both Badly Drawn Boy and Basement Jaxx, two artists whose success with their debut albums would help XL to transition from singles-orientated dance imprint to trusted, album-orientated record label. He was cultivating a promising roster for XL, but I was less on the ball, still suffering from an A&R hangover related to The Prodigy's success. I was lucky to have Nick around at this time.

He said the shop staff weren't completely sure about this Streets demo but he could hear something in it and wanted to know what I thought. It was clear that there was something going on. I heard something different from the visceral but fleeting excitement of Locked On's 12-inch releases so far.

These garage records were manna for DJs and clubbers; they would cross over to the pop charts, and even had cultural depth, being part of a thread of music that went back to the Paradise Garage, but weaved in elements of homegrown sound system culture. UK garage was great London music, so timeless that the tunes still hold up today.

But the sounds on the tape a Birmingham-based twenty-two-year-old called Mike Skinner had sent to Locked On reverberated differently. To hear Mike was to hear Ray Davies, Ian Dury, John Cooper Clarke, Paul Weller. Working-class British poetry, simultaneously passionate and dry, full of pathos and humour. A lineage that extended back to the kitchen sink realism of the fifties and sixties. A couple of years later we would hear it in Alex Turner, another lyricist the equal of any of his predecessors.

Artists like this aren't less original because of their influences. They are part of a tradition. And they may not be aware of their influences; the nature of collective consciousness is that Mike Skinner and Alex Turner didn't need to know anything about each other, or about Paul Weller, or about kitchen sink dramatists like the writer John Osborne, author of *Look Back in Anger*, to be drawing from the same deep well. The invisible threads are endless.

In Weller we hear The Kinks and The Beatles but also Curtis Mayfield, who was in turn heavily influenced by Sam Cooke. Weller's band The Jam supported The Clash on their 'White Riot' tour, and while they were his peers they were also an influence on him. In The Clash we hear an endless variety of influences, from Bo Diddley and Gene Vincent to Prince Far I and Big Youth, via Mott the Hoople. Each wave infects and influences the next, and the strains mutate.

I was floored by the demo I heard on the train from Euston that day. Skinner was an outsider, but he had the insider combination of lyrical dexterity and honesty that all great MCs possess. I told Nick that with the greatest respect to the counter staff at the record shop, while they were a good barometer of authenticity, being 'real' was only so important. I did understand their reservations. This artist was not really from the streets. The music he made might not really reverberate on the actual streets. To compound matters, he was calling himself 'The Streets'. It was almost ridiculous. But the music was special. It might be hard for DJs to programme, but it benefited from its misfit quality, as I'd failed to recognise that Aphex Twin 12-inch had done a decade earlier. Rather than fitting any mould, these were artists who created new ones.

Mike Skinner was making music that was about the garage scene rather than of it, documenting something he was on the fringes of, and though that was risky, his music was all the better for it. He loved and understood the music he was influenced by and was making his own version of it. So it sounded like garage, but it mostly sounded like him. It was likely to be a bit controversial.

The Streets demo tape was incredible and I was greatly looking forward to Locked On and XL collaborating on what would be the first album-orientated artist the label had found. (The artist had actually found the label, Mike Skinner having had the insight to target Locked On with his demo in the first place, as Liam Howlett had targeted XL a decade earlier.) So I was shocked when Paul Connolly told me that he had heard that Nick Worthington was leaving XL to start his own Warners-backed label and taking The Streets with him.

When I confronted Nick with this, he confirmed that it was true; he had hoped to tell me face to face, but it is the nature of these situations that information leaks. The executive hiring Nick had leaked it himself, which said something about the environment Nick was headed for, and the different rules of engagement which applied. I had to grow up a lot at this point.

I was disappointed and my ego was bruised, but Nick was already a proven entrepreneur in his own right, with business interests outside XL, and having been offered an opportunity to steer his own ship it was understandable that he chose to take it. And in the conversation we had, he said something prescient; he pointed out that not only was this a great opportunity for him, but that I could be achieving more myself, and so maybe it was an opportunity for me as well. This was exactly right and provided me with just the wake-up call I needed at that time.

While I had been keen to give Nick space to develop his own A&R chops, and would go on to do similarly for a series of talented A&R people, I was struggling at this time and had lost direction. I needed to change my approach and Nick's departure proved to be exactly the spur I needed. A subtler balance was required; to give my colleagues space to pursue their interests, without losing my own voice. I had gone from having too much control over the musical output of the label to not enough, and it was time to try to balance that out somehow.

Nick was a more centred person than I was at the time we worked together. He has been involved, in his low-key way, in innumerable success stories, an unusual type of behind-the-scenes player. His exit was a moment of personal revelation, and these tend to be painful. But it was time for me to explore new directions.

After Nick's departure I found myself forced to clarify my idea of what the label should actually be about. My idea was not entirely new. It was a fusion of two seemingly contradictory things. I wanted to turn XL into a record label that did what independent labels did - put out music that they believed in, that was original and of high quality, not necessarily commercial. But I wanted to combine this with an important aspect of what major labels did - which was selling the music with a no-holds-barred approach.

I wanted to be liberated from the normal limitations of both independent and major labels. I wanted to merge what I saw as the best elements of indies - the taste and the integrity - with the best elements of major record companies - the ability to get the music to a huge audience. And, equally importantly, I intended to avoid the worst of both - the greed and snakiness of corporate entertainment companies, and the mediocrity and lack of ambition of some independent labels. It would be important that it was a collective effort. But what exactly was my role to be?

Stanley Kubrick described his job of director as being 'a kind of idea and taste machine. To make the right decisions as often as possible.' John Peel was an influential taste-maker, but I wanted to diverge from his approach as much as emulate it. He was probably the greatest champion of independent music ever because the way he chose which records to play was so ideologically powerful. His position was not that he would play good music, regardless. It was more political than that. If he perceived something as too pop, he would not play it.

So while John Peel was a supporter of Scritti Politti's early singles and debut album for Rough Trade, *Songs To Remember*, he never played anything from their masterpiece, and one of my all-time favourite albums, *Cupid & Psyche 85*. This music was even better than their previous output but he did not support it. Green and co. had decamped to New York and made the music they dreamed of, which was R&B, with storied soul producer and arranger Arif Mardin. But Peel stopped playing them because he considered what they were doing too pop.

I didn't wish to take this approach.

'Indie' to describe music was a term that was destined to become obsolete, and I didn't want this type of ghettoisation to happen to XL. I wanted to be able to back artists to be as ambitious as they saw fit. Equally, I wanted to discourage artists from being overly commercial if that meant their records would suffer. I wanted to work with the best artists and help them make the best music. I didn't want to be tied down to any ideology that would get in the way of that. I didn't want records to have to be commercial - like a major; equally, I didn't want them to have to not be - the way John Peel seemed to sometimes see it.

Rather than seeing majors as the enemy I wanted to use the lessons I had learned from them. Another aspect of the big labels that I saw as potentially instructive was the depth of executive talent that was sometimes apparent; many levels of good people, as opposed to what used to be the standard independent label approach of things being quite dependent on one key figure. A more communal approach needed to be taken. The success of XL would be based on the quality of the artists and their music, and this would be partly based on my taste and instincts, but the efforts of the staff of the label and the managers of the artists would be just as important.

Having managed to surround myself with some talented people, I took seriously the task of backing them, and encouraging their creativity. During his XL tenure Nick Worthington had hired an A&R scout called Leo Silverman. Leo was not from a DJing or production background but had boundless enthusiasm, and while he didn't have Nick's depth of musical knowledge, he was free-roaming in his tastes and approach, and he embraced the opportunity to fill Nick's shoes.

Leo enjoyed initial success at XL by licensing an Australian crew making playful, cut-and-paste sample-based music called The Avalanches from the independent label they were signed to, Steven 'Pav' Pavlovic's Sydney-based Modular. Their album *Since I Left You*, released by XL in the UK in 2000, is thought to have contained the highest number of samples ever used in any one album. Leo's next and greatest achievement at XL was to convince an act to join the label in 2001 who would not just become all-time favourites of John Peel, but one of the definitive acts of the decade.

Jack White and Meg White claimed to be a brother and sister duo, and were in fact an ex-husband and wife duo, from Detroit. They wore only red, white and black. All their artwork was rendered in these colours. Their music, up to now, had been made using only guitar, voice and drums. The White Stripes had already released three albums and built a solid fanbase. They possessed a perfect combination of artistic otherness and commercial savvy. Jack White was emerging as a ferocious live performer, classic songwriter, virtuosic musician and visionary record producer. It was an almost unprecedented skill set. He showed signs of being a Prince-level polymath. Meg, the drummer and occasional vocalist, balanced his guitar heroics with an opaque feminine strength.

They had an experienced LA lawyer called Ian Montone on board to help them navigate the murky industry waters; Jack convinced Ian to quit his legal career and become the band's manager. This was a great move. Being an artist requires insight in every conceivable area. If you can't find the manager you want, create one. Ian had a deep understanding of what Jack and Meg were doing and the ability to communicate clearly on their behalf. He would be an invaluable asset to them.

The White Stripes were poised for a worldwide breakthrough, and this was not lost on the record industry. Every label scrambled to sign them but XL was victorious. While these frenzied scenarios often lead to eventual disappointment, this was the start of what is now a twenty-year relationship.

It was Meg who made the decision regarding which label to sign to. XL's trumping of the majors (and other indies) was an unexpected outcome and bound to prompt resentment. Heavenly boss Jeff Barrett said that XL was unlikely to be a good home for the White Stripes. The reason he gave was that XL didn't know anything about the blues. This was accurate, but I was intensely interested in their music, and keen to learn where it came from, more than I would have been had I already considered myself an expert on what they were doing.

I was aware of my lack of knowledge and it proved to be an asset. At thirty years old, I was ready to pay attention and allow another stage of my own musical education to begin. Jack's blues-indebted style, and the White Stripes' covers of songs by artists including Robert Johnson, Son House and Blind Willie McTell ignited for me a love affair with the fundamental sound of the blues, it becoming a prism through which much of popular music has made more sense to me.

When the White Stripes' fourth album *Elephant* was released on XL, it became a worldwide hit. The album, recorded in London's Toe Rag Studios over a two-week period without the use of any computers or other modern studio technology, is invincible from its opening, 'Seven Nation Army', which has no chorus, except a guitar riff, a riff better and bigger, way bigger, than any number of supposedly commercial, crafted choruses. I did not recognise the potential of this song, but Jack was convinced of its appeal. This is the whole point of working with really great artists; you can make a terrible call and get away with it, because you're not in charge. The artist is. You can offer feedback but in effect they will A&R you as much as you will them.

Elephant is a high-octane tear-up aboard Jack and Meg's unorthodox blues-based vehicle. There had never been an outfit quite like them or a record quite like this. The ambition and scope are breathtaking. There are five-part harmonies over heavily distorted guitars. A hard-rocking Burt Bacharach cover. Detroit broadcaster Mort Crim reads a motivational tale in 'Little Acorns' and at the album's close there's an unexpected appearance from British singer-songwriter Holly Golightly. Meg's featherlight vocal in 'In The Cold, Cold Night' provides respite from the thunderous nature of Jack's vocal and guitar performances.

Michel Gondry's video for 'The Hardest Button To Button', in which Jack and Meg co-star alongside ever multiplying drumkits and guitar amps against a Manhattan backdrop, received perhaps the ultimate accolade of being pastiched in *The Simpsons*. Jack and Meg collide with Bart on a Springfield corner.

'Hey kid, why don't you watch where you're drumming?' says Jack.

'Sorry White Stripes! No hard feelings?' pleads Bart.

'Let's kick his ass!' snarls Meg, as they give chase.

The White Stripes were well on their way to worldwide household-name status, and seeing the duo perform at Tsongas Arena in Lowell, Massachusetts in November 2003, a mile from the birthplace of Jack Kerouac, two and a half from his grave, I was struck by how much the show seemed like an art experiment, a man and a woman playing primal, stripped-down blues to seven thousand people in a giant ice hockey dome, presenting high art to a Middle American audience under the guise of a mainstream rock show. Their projections were not working that evening, so it was just two people on a huge stage, and the minimalism was inspiring.

A lifelong Bob Dylan fan, Jack would receive the ultimate endorsement in 2004 when Dylan invited him onstage in Detroit, to perform the White Stripes' 'Ball And Biscuit'. Playing 'Seven Nation Army' on his *Theme Time Radio Hour* show, Dylan reeled off a list of seven things with white stripes, including Memphis Slim's hair. To be a Dylan fan is one thing. For him to become a fan of yours is quite another. I discussed it with Jack backstage in New Jersey, where Jack's other band, The Raconteurs, were now supporting Dylan on an arena tour. Jack wondered where else there was to go.

Shortly after this I was back in Dorset, doing the washing-up, my white iPod on random. Andrew Loog Oldham's *Rolling Stones Songbook* came on. It occurred to me to borrow his idea and make an orchestral album in tribute to the White Stripes. It would be an apt dichotomy, as most of the White Stripes' songs were rendered so minimally. To tease out musical elements using an orchestra would be an educational process for me. I would be participating in some obscure tradition, of industry figures recording orchestral versions of songs by blues-influenced rock acts. It also occurred to me that I shouldn't lumber Jack with the responsibility of approving it as an idea before it existed in any form. I had to make some reality of the project before asking permission to proceed.

Recruiting composer Joby Talbot to arrange, and setting up twenty-four musicians in Intimate Studios in Wapping, in the creepy shadow of Rupert Murdoch's News International HQ, we recorded three songs in the style I intended the album to embody. I flew to Ohio to play it to Jack, backstage at the Cincinnati Music Hall where the White Stripes were playing that night. He gave the project his blessing.

Joby and I made the rest of the tracks, releasing a limited edition of an album that we called *Aluminium*. It was a significant moment for me, deeply focusing on a studio-based project, taking main responsibility for its musical content and seeing it to fruition. It was a modest vehicle but I had placed myself in the driver's seat and re-engaged with music-making in a way that would help prepare me for my coming endeavours, and enable me to approach the orchestrating of material I made with Gil with confidence.

Not long afterwards I would be working with an ambitious young female artist named Adele Adkins, who was about to embark on recording her debut album and wished to better understand how pop songs could be orchestrated. Joby and I spent an afternoon with her in his garden studio going through some different approaches. She seemed to grasp the possibilities not just quickly, but deeply and instinctively.

In 2006 the choreographer Wayne McGregor based his one-act Royal Ballet performance *Chroma* on *Aluminium*, and the music we created was performed as the score for the piece. I attended the debut performance at the Royal Opera House on 17 November 2006. The following year *Chroma* won the Laurence Olivier Award for Best New Dance Production, and the Dance category at the South Bank Show Awards, subsequently being performed by numerous companies worldwide, including the Bolshoi Ballet. The music was heard in a context I could never have imagined.

There is an idiosyncrasy running through all of Jack White's endeavours, an indefinable aesthetic. He is one of the few all-time great rock musicians to have emerged in this millennium, and among his many achievements 'Seven Nation Army' has become an anthem of unprecedented popularity with supporters of sports teams worldwide. He always believed in the song but he could not have envisioned this.

There is at this point no guitar riff in recorded music history with greater recognisability and popularity. The 'Seven Nation Army' riff has overtaken longstanding pillars of guitar music such as Led Zepellin's 'Whole Lotta Love', Deep Purple's 'Smoke On The Water' and AC/DC's 'Back In Black' to become arguably the greatest axe riff of all time.

For XL, with its roots in suburban rave music, it's a remarkable song to have been involved with, a stadium anthem recorded by a duo who were on their way to becoming the most iconoclastic rock group of their era.

Meg White was always underestimated. She was one half of the group and a wonderfully minimal drummer, providing a rock-solid foundation during the duo's mind-boggling, set-list-free live performances. I used to drop everything to see them play any chance I got. They are still the best live band I've ever seen.

Meg had not expected their success, though. She suffered from crippling shyness and struggled increasingly with the White Stripes' growing fame. I was concerned when I witnessed her level of anxiety backstage before the duo's Madison Square Garden show in July 2007. Most people who end up playing to audiences of this size have at least something of the natural performer in them, some desire to communicate to an audience and maintain their attention that carries them through the nerves. Meg never had this, and her reticence may well have contributed to the band's onstage magic, but it made their increasing recognisability difficult for her to endure. When she inevitably decided to leave the duo and the music industry itself in 2011, it signalled the end of the White Stripes story. It was perhaps fitting and appropriate, even Beatles-esque, that the tale, only one of many Jack would tell, would come to such a sudden and final full stop.

IT'S YOUR MOVIE
SO DIRECT IT

However much energy and enthusiasm there had been in the first-generation eighties UK hip-hop scene, it was impossible at this stage to escape from the shadow of US rap. This wasn't down to any intrinsic UK weakness, although some artists betrayed a lack of confidence by employing American accents.

If the UK rap scene of the eighties was considered in isolation, it was as vibrant as any other local musical scene. The problem was of context and comparison.

US rap of this period was impossible to creatively compete with, by any other type of music, coming from anywhere. It was inevitable that UK rap would be directly compared to its more evolved US counterpart, and be found lacking. Even London Posse, considered by most to be the leading exponents of the genre at that time, did not make a second album. In 1992 Nick Halkes and I had recorded a song with London Posse called 'Pass The Rizla' for a compilation EP of UK artists I put together called *British Underground* on what was intended to be an XL hip-hop sub-label called Ruffness.

The EP was an attempt to maintain the interest that still existed in UK rap. I continued to be excited by homegrown efforts and considered the scene to have tremendous potential. Although I have never been particularly specific about any of my ambitions, nothing would have excited me more than to be involved with a really great and successful UK rap act.

There was a problem with my concept, though, and it was signposted in the name I gave the EP. No one in the UK rap scene wanted to be 'underground'. Most other musical scenes contain individuals who are happy with some sort of under-the-radar, sub-cultural existence. But in rap music almost everyone is hungry and ambitious, wants to be successful and will readily admit it.

(The indie rock scene grew increasingly disingenuous about

money and success over the years, so whereas John Lennon happily drove around in a psychedelic painted Rolls-Royce, outward signs of materialism became gradually less and less acceptable for rockers, who in reality tended to be just as materialistic as rappers.)

There didn't seem to be a way of competing with the ever-growing US rap scene, now no less creative but also increasingly commercially successful, juggernaut releases from the likes of Dr Dre starting to become the world's pop music. The gap between UK and US was wider than ever.

As the nineties progressed UK rap entered its trickiest phase, the hope and naivety of the eighties scene having dissipated, the mainstream doors not open. But UK rap never completely disappeared (though I allowed my Ruffness imprint to quietly die, RIP) and, as other wholly UK subgenres like drum and bass and garage blossomed and developed, new seeds were being planted. MCs in the jungle and garage scenes were there to hype the party and promote the DJ rather than show lyrical complexity, exactly like the first wave of New York MCs in the early eighties.

The natural terrain of these MCs was in the club, not the studio, and this was a new beginning. The raving audience loved hearing jungle MCs like Skibadee and the late, great Stevie Hyper D. Subsequently, the MCs who ruled the garage scene transitioned with some success into record-making, most notably Pay As U Go, So Solid Crew and Heartless Crew. These artists were also inspiring another, more musically abrasive wave.

Grime was garage's snotty little brother. Garage was a little embarrassed by its bratty sibling. Garage was aspirational, and people dressed to impress when attending events like Sunday-nighter Twice As Nice. Young hopefuls like Ruff Skwad and Wiley's Roll Deep Crew, emerging from pirates like Rinse and Deja Vu, were not dressed smartly in designer togs and shiny shoes. Something was stirring.

Grime instrumentals like Wiley's 'Eskimo', 'Ice Rink' and 'Igloo', Cage and Weed's 'Creeper' and Jon E Cash's 'War' and 'Hoods Up' were being pressed on white labels and introducing something new to the British bass ecosystem. While it was clearly influenced by garage, it was also a reaction to the smoother, slightly older sound, and the MCs who were about to emerge had something to say.

Two of these white labels, 'Ho' and 'Go', were the work of Dylan Mills, a teenage MC and producer from Bow calling himself Dizzee Rascal. When XL A&R man Nick Huggett, a graduate of the unofficial specialist record store A&R training system via Mr Bongo's vinyl shop in Soho, played me another Dizzee Rascal white label 12-inch, this one hand-scribed with the words 'I Luv U' and featuring Dizzee's vocals as well as his beats, only one thought occurred to me: 'Thank God'.

Everything about this piece of music felt new and somehow right. Dizzee did not use outside producers at this point. He made the brittle electronic beats himself. The sonic landscape he created blew me away. Everything about it was unapologetic. Dizzee was always underrated as a musician by everyone including himself. This is one of the downsides of being a star who is also a great producer - people tend to overlook the producer part as it becomes less noticeable. Prince, James Brown, Joni Mitchell, Kate Bush, all in different ways among the greatest record producers of all time, are rarely recognised as such. But just because others don't notice how good you are at something does not mean you yourself should undervalue it.

Dizzee's beats sounded unmistakably DIY. Rude. That was a big part of their appeal. And while they echoed garage, they also had something of the soulful quality of the Southern hip-hop sounds of artists like UGK, from Houston, Texas. But there was way more going on here than instrumental grime, as great as a lot of that was. Other MCs were loud, big and bassy, but Dizzee's vocals were higher, subtler and more expressive. He had the kind of voice that comes along rarely and sounded to me like an instrument he would be able to build a career on. It was that memorable and distinctive. Dizzee himself questioned his own voice, considering it squeaky. Those possessed of a truly special gift always doubt it.

It's hard to recall a first listen to any song having quite as dramatic an impact on me as this. 'I Luv U' was clearly a product of someone's gut instinct, and of their frustrations, and yet I knew that it had taken the UK more than twenty years to get to this moment. The icing on the cake was that Dizzee seemed to have included a girl's voice on the record and, wait a minute . . . did she just call him a prick? We were hearing realistic boy–girl dialogue, a window into a human relationship, in a way that I hadn't quite heard prior to this. Dizzee was creating what could clearly be an entirely new day for British music. The start of something.

In my first meeting with Dizzee he turned up wearing Nike ski gloves and accompanied by man-mountain manager Nick Detnon, aka Cage, who was not only an excellent producer in his own right but someone who could make sure his artists got paid by dodgy and potentially dangerous rave promoters.

Cage asked smart questions. Dizzee hardly spoke. He listened to my answers and it was clear to me that his bullshit detector was switched on to high. Dizzee was not a gangster but he was from the streets of Bow E3, and he was alert to lies and deception. He seemed to want to see if I was on the level. I felt like he was peering into my soul, and that was fine, because my belief in him was real and I was with him as soon as I heard 'I Luv U'.

He wasn't alone on his journey. Apart from Cage, Dizzee's spiritual big brother Wiley had been preparing him for this moment. Wiley was a second-generation soundman, his dad having owned a reggae system, and another producer of exceptional originality. Wiley and Riddles' sets on Deja Vu, when they started to veer away from standard garage lyrics and speak more about their lives, had provided boyhood inspiration to Dizzee. Wiley was the founder and ringleader of the Roll Deep crew and a magnet for all the talent that was just about to emerge from east London.

There was some heat building around Dizzee and Wiley, but the record industry as a whole had not quite cottoned on to the potential of what they were doing. They were performing in clubs and raves such as the infamously lively Sidewinder and had also managed to get booked to perform together as a support act for

Jay-Z at Wembley Arena. Nick Huggett and I went to see that performance and show our support. Afterwards we saw them in the backstage parking area. As Dizzee got into his Fiat Punto to leave after their slightly tentative performance, he flashed me an irresistible grin and said, 'Let's do some business.'

When I got home from Wembley that evening to find Esta tucked up in bed with the telly on and a pack of Revels on the go, I said that I was hopeful that we were going to sign Dizzee and Wiley, and how excited I was about that prospect. Perhaps sensing that I was setting myself up for disappointment if this didn't pan out, she said that presumably these things were unpredictable and I would have to be able to deal with it if they ended up signing to someone else.

The maturity of her response puzzled me. I remember thinking that no part of me would be all right with that. It was going to prove crucial for my own development as a person that I began to see things in the more accepting way that Esta did. I was going to have to realise that I was not in control of situations like this, and that things would unfold as was intended. But I was not there yet. For now, I just wanted to work with this exceptionally talented crew, and nothing else would do. Happily, they were up for that too.

XL unusually committed to not one but three albums initially, a 'three firm' deal: a Dizzee album, a Wiley album and a Roll Deep compilation. I recently mentioned to DJ Target, now one of the leading figures in British music as a DJ and A&R man, and at that time a member of Roll Deep himself, that it's a shame that this compilation album never came to exist. He said it was the first he'd ever heard of it. There was an element of chaos in the proceedings which contributed to the energy.

The first two fruits of the deal, Wiley's *Treddin' On Thin Ice* and Dizzee's *Boy In Da Corner*, were both classics. The potential of these two artists was obvious to those in the know, but on a wider level anything perceived as UK rap carried a lot of baggage, so there was more resistance to both and far less support from the wider music industry than I had imagined. No matter. We were all on a mission. We wanted the world, or at the very least the whole UK, to experience this music and take it to their hearts.

Wiley was the creator of the 'Eski' sound. The names of the instrumentals he made reflected, he said, the coldness in his heart at the time he made them. But there was warmth as well. He was always keen to promote his peers, not just himself. His album *Treddin' On Thin Ice* was unquestionably ahead of its time and the production still sounds current fifteen years on. The 'Eskimo', 'Ice Rink' and 'Avalanche' instrumentals are included as interludes and there is a permanent and intangible magic to these.

Treddin' On Thin Ice was a creditable reflection of what was going to be an important moment in music, but as the recording of *Boy In Da Corner* unfolded we were clearly on the cusp of a big breakthrough. On completion it was near-perfect.

Dizzee would swing between sounding justifiably angry, with the police, with his circumstances, and irresistibly cheeky in the space of a word or two, and his lyrics demonstrated the remarkable wisdom he had for his age. As a teenager he was already nostalgic about the loss of childhood innocence. He was using words like 'bait', to mean overly obvious or dodgy, which are now in every teenager's vocabulary but at this stage were not that widely used. What we thought of as simply slang but would become known as Multi-cultural London English was about to come into far more widespread use.

His lyrics touched on the gap between his inner and outer lives and there was a spooky prescience to many of Dizzee's words. I wanted Dizzee to make the best and most authentic record possible, which honoured his talent and the scene he came from.

The 'Fix Up, Look Sharp' instrumental, using Billy Squier's 'The Big Beat' breakbeat (first used on Run-DMC's 'Here We Go' nearly twenty years earlier) was made by Cage. He had wanted to illustrate to Dizzee and Target where the music in Memphis Bleek and Jay-Z's currently hot '1, 2 Y'All' came from, and played them ESG's 'UFO', track two on side one of *Ultimate Breaks And Beats* Volume 9.

The song ended, and the next track started. Side one, track three was Billy Squier's 'The Big Beat'. Dizzee thought this was a break he could flow on. 'Fix Up, Look Sharp' was the result of this. It was an accident but intention is key. Cage had wanted to play one fundamental breakbeat, and they had ended up making a song based on another. Dizzee and Cage had not intended to put 'Fix Up, Look Sharp' on the album, differing as it did from the rest of the record's more electronic palette of sounds. But if the quality and direction remain intact you can sonically stretch in all different directions within one album. I urged them to include this song.

From Dizzee's 'Oi!', which opens 'Fix Up, Look Sharp', it is irresistibly simple, becoming the biggest hit from the record and giving people a way into the rest of the work, without softening the message. Sparse, simple recordings that contain no sonic clutter can draw the listener in, making them turn up the music, and focus.

I have always loved records that contain only drums and vocals, dispensing with all but the most necessary ingredients, like 'Fix Up, Look Sharp'. Other favourite 'no music' songs of mine include T. Rex's 'Scenescof Dynasty', Björk's 'Where Is The Line' (actually not containing any drums at all, as all the rhythmic elements are made by human beatbox Rahzel), Blackstreet's Stevie Wonder cover 'Love's In Need Of Love Today' and in rap a host of examples including the incredible 'Grindin'' by Clipse. And while almost all long albums would be better if they were shorter, at a running time of nearly an hour *Boy In Da Corner* - streetwise, heartfelt and ruminative - never flags.

Two years before *Boy In Da Corner*, XL had enjoyed significant success with another idiosyncratic British debut album, Badly Drawn Boy's *The Hour Of Bewilderbeast*, after it had won the Mercury Music Prize. Badly Drawn Boy was Damon Gough, a singer-songwriter from Manchester, who, in working with a local DJ, graphic designer and label boss called Andy Votel, was marrying genuine songcraft to some audacious, highly listenable music. He was also collaborating with Doves, a Manchester band born out of rave act Sub Sub, who would themselves go on to make some of the most soulful British guitar music of the forthcoming era, and whose album *Lost Souls* would also be Mercury-shortlisted in 2000.

Nick Worthington had the vision to see Damon as a potentially good fit for XL despite (or because of) his lack of similarity to any other artist on the label.

Damon was picked up for representation by infamous UK manager Jazz Summers of Big Life, who had helped steer the careers of artists including Wham! and Lisa Stansfield in the eighties. A former jazz and blues drummer, he had been in the army, and subsequently the Workers Revolutionary Party, then forming a management partnership with Simon Napier-Bell.

Jazz had a mixed reputation but I'd liked a lot of records his label Big Life had released (including the very first London Posse single and De La Soul's immortal *3 Feet High And Rising* as a UK licence from Tommy Boy) and I saw him, with his experience and abilities, as a potential ally to achieve the type of success that I wanted for Badly Drawn Boy and thus XL. I also loved the fact that he had been expelled from the Workers Revolutionary Party for being too left wing. He was impossible but it was my kind of impossible.

Having seen the tremendous amount of attention that Badly Drawn Boy had received as a result of winning the Mercury Music Prize, I realised that the recognition this type of award could bring would be of unique benefit to Dizzee, starting as he was from a position so far outside of the music industry. And I thought he might have a chance. Perhaps the Mercury judges might be able to discern the originality of what Dizzee did in a way that mainstream radio programmers would not be likely to.

I encouraged Dizzee and Cage to complete the album in time for it to at least be submitted for Mercury consideration that year. Whether it actually would receive a nomination or not would be out of our control and utterly unpredictable, but if the album had been completed even a week later than it was, it would have not been eligible until the following year.

And I also felt that whatever happened with the Mercury Prize, timing was key to the success of this potentially landmark album, and no one should get the chance to overthink things. Creativity should not be rushed, but equally a deadline can be a powerful tool if used at the right time. As with *The Fat Of The Land*, this album felt to me like a cake not to be overbaked.

While we were focused on the launch of Dizzee's debut, and gearing up for the release of *Boy In Da Corner*, real-life circumstances kicked in and near-tragedy struck. Dizzee was attacked in the Cypriot resort of Ayia Napa and sustained six stab wounds. Although he was able to fully recover physically from the attack, he is a sensitive individual, all poets are, and an experience this traumatic cannot fail to have a dramatic effect on any person. The circumstances surrounding the attack had a far-reaching impact on the relationship between Dizzee and Wiley; they haven't spoken since the events of 2003.

On its release, *Boy In Da Corner* scraped into the Top 40 album chart, but a record this original often takes a moment to find its audience, and possibly needs some sort of catalyst; this did indeed turn out to be the Mercury Music Prize, and this victory opened doors not just for Dizzee but for grime and rap in the UK in general. I cannot think of a time a single award has had a more dramatic, positive and long-lasting effect on an album and subsequently the musical landscape. It wasn't immediate, though.

Seeing Dizzee support Sean Paul at Brighton Dome in October 2003, his album out and doing well, the Mercury win under his belt, but grime as a whole still flying largely under the radar, I felt strongly at the time that this was the most interesting music in existence but few people were aware of it. A couple of months after that, Dizzee supported Justin Timberlake on a run of UK arena shows. Watching Dizzee at Birmingham NIA (after we first went to the wrong arena, the Birmingham NEC, Dizzee nearly missing his set time), it was clear that he was still a completely unknown quantity to the mostly teenage and female audience. This would change.

We agreed that Dizzee should follow up *Boy In Da Corner*

quickly. Many artists get knocked off course by the distractions surrounding early success, and it seemed healthy for Dizzee both personally and professionally to keep his creative momentum going. The result was *Showtime*, which was released in September 2004, just fourteen months after his debut. It's a singular piece of work. There is barely a guest in sight and Dizzee has a lot to say. *Showtime* is a showcase for Dizzee's dazzling vocal ability and there are some heartfelt expressions of pain.

The album starts optimistically. On the title song he gives us a potted history of his life so far and nods to the genre that birthed him, prior to garage or grime, jungle. It is hard to overestimate how important jungle was to the majority of grime pioneers. One genre begets another. Hip-hop came from soul and funk. Rave, or the Essex breakbeat hardcore strain at least, came from both hip-hop and techno, and then itself evolved into jungle. Grime was the unwanted offspring of a coupling between jungle and garage, garage itself the product of house and reggae. Thus, grime is the grandchild of house, reggae, hip-hop and techno. But punk's grubby DNA was also in the mix.

Showtime showcased not just Dizzee but grime itself, this third-generation hybrid genre, in its most evolved form yet. 'Stand Up Tall' launched the album and became Dizzee's biggest hit to date, with a lo-fi but incredibly catchy beat sounding like it had been made on a PlayStation some years before, which it had, being partly based on Youngstar's instrumental 'Pulse X'. We get treated to a stunning display of Dizzee's skill on 'Everywhere', where he spits philosophically over hard drums, percussion and the most skeletal of sub basslines.

In the video for 'Graftin'', Dizzee delivers his bars in front of an east London tower block. This is 'the three flats' of Crossways Estate, original home to Rinse FM, near Belton Way E3, where Dylan Mills lived before he was Dizzee Rascal. In 2011 the Crossways Estate was sold off, privatised and rebranded as Bow Cross. In a short film shown at the 2003 Mercury Awards, Dizzee looked across from Crossways Estate and said: 'This is the estate

I grew up on. Over there . . . Canary Wharf. It's kinda like in-your-face. It takes the piss. On these sides people live in council estates . . . A lot of rich people moving in now, people who work in the City. You can tell they just ain't living the same way as us. It's all grimy round here. There wasn't a lot to do. You'd get into a lot of trouble. It was a lot of fun times as well, don't get me wrong.'

Earlier in the film Dizzee had truthfully articulated the basic and most fundamental thing that motivates him: 'My love for music more than anything. I just love music. I like creating it. I like making beats. I like writing lyrics. I love messing around with flows.' Then his expression changes as another galvanising force occurs to him, one he has heard a lot of talk about but had relatively little personal experience of so far: 'Money motivates me.' He repeats the word, more intensely this time: 'Money.'

Early grime had a freshness that made everything else seem boring and outdated, and would end up changing how British youth speak and dress. There were echoes of punk rock, abrasive, DIY music expressing deep discontent, upsetting the old order of things, capturing the imagination of a young audience, forcing an unwilling music industry to take notice. With *Boy In Da Corner* I was in my zone, thrilled to be able to support an artist and a movement that I knew could wake people up. It was waking me up.

Dizzee foresaw much that was coming, and when I mentioned to him how Sonny, just eighteen months old at the time, seemed weirdly drawn to my new iPod, Dizzee said to me that part of the souls of children born now would be digital. *Boy In Da Corner*, one of the greatest debut albums ever, maybe one of the greatest albums ever, still the best British rap album of all time, has never stopped influencing artists and being discovered by new listeners.

It was exactly fifteen years ahead of its time. *Boy In Da Corner* went platinum in the UK in 2018.

237

LONDON QUIETEN DOWN, I NEED TO MAKE A SOUND

In the relatively short time between Dizzee emerging from Bow and his becoming a fully fledged star, alongside his peers he created a new awareness of how people actually spoke. Dizzee's 'I Luv U' was far from the first time UK street dialogue had been used effectively on a record, though.

When Neneh Cherry asked the question, 'What is he like?' in her 1988 single 'Buffalo Stance' it was authentic, but the song was aimed squarely at the charts. The record was a UK creation but Neneh was a world citizen, born in Stockholm to a Swedish mum and Sierra Leonean father, raised by her mother and stepfather, American jazz trumpeter Don Cherry, in New York until she moved to London at the age of fourteen.

'Buffalo Stance' was radical for its time but it was not the uncut street product that 'I Luv U' would be. Its verses are delivered in an American accent, not unreasonably given Neneh Cherry's transatlantic upbringing, and the chorus is straight from the eighties mainstream pop playbook. This is due to the song's unusual DNA and ever-reincarnating form. It had been born three times.

Its cyclic existence began as 'Looking Good Diving', a Stock Aitken Waterman-produced pop single for the duo Morgan-McVey. It's a lightweight pop confection but it contains the synth riff that 'Buffalo Stance' would be based on.

Then model Neneh Cherry mimes guitar in the video.

Cameron McVey of Morgan-McVey, Cherry's collaborator and partner, asked his friend, Nellee Hooper of Bristol's Wild Bunch, to midwife the first rebirth, a remix for the B-side of the single. This time Cherry's involvement is more significant: she contributes rap and sung vocals to the new version, which was called 'Looking Good Diving With The Wild Bunch', and is basically a demo version of what would become 'Buffalo Stance'. The Wild Bunch contained a number of Bristol musicians of future significance, including Massive Attack's 3D and Mushroom.

For lifetime number three, DJ Tim Simenon, Saturday-night resident at The Wag, was brought in to give the song a more cutting-edge feel. Simenon was coming from clubland not the pop world, but he had already infiltrated the mainstream, having recently plundered his record box to make 'Beat Dis' under the name Bomb the Bass, a cut-and-paste collage which made it to number two in the national charts.

Engineer Mark Saunders programmed and co-produced with Simenon. He normally worked with grown-up producers Clive Langer and Alan Winstanley on recordings for artists like Madness and Elvis Costello. In an interview with writer Tom Doyle for *Sound on Sound* magazine, Saunders said of the 'Buffalo Stance' session: 'Working with Tim was really odd 'cause I'd averaged eighty hours a week for two years. He didn't come from a studio background, he was a DJ and really young. We got to six o'clock and he was like, "Okay, that's it then." And I'm thinking, "We've only just started . . . we've only done eight hours . . . what are you talking about? It's still really raw, there's hardly anything there." He said, "The track sounds fine, we'll get Neneh to come and sing tomorrow."'

As well as introducing this minimalist, results-orientated approach, Simenon's main task in this third rebirth would be to add samples and one of these would prove most significant. Once again, Malcolm McLaren's 'Buffalo Gals' worked its unlikely magic. This time McLaren's catalyst was used within an overall context of cutting-edge pop, taking his work into the mainstream again.

Cherry's approach to her performance on the record was consistent with Simenon's. Saunders recalled: 'She came in early afternoon and by four or five o'clock, she was done. Tim said, "Why would you change it? It sounds great." And we're only two days into the five-day recording budget. So we cancelled Wednesday, Thursday and Friday.'

After just half a day mixing the song, the engineer, versed in traditional approaches to record-making, had his doubts, but Mark

Saunders was to learn a valuable lesson: 'Until I heard it on the radio,' he says, 'I kept thinking, "It's still not finished, though, it can't be. It was two and a half days including a mix." I kept thinking, "It's gonna sound rubbish compared with everything else." But then the first time I heard it on the radio, it just sounded so fresh. It was a big eye-opener, like, "Oh, maybe if we don't work things to death they sound better."'

The follow-up to 'Buffalo Stance', 'Manchild', predicts the Bristol blueprint, melancholy soul over hard beats, and although Cherry berates the song's subject at one point – 'You'd sell your soul for a tacky song / like the ones you hear on the radio' – she is herself unquestionably making pop music, *Face*-approved though it might be. Equally she was breaking down barriers, in 1988 performing on *Top of the Pops* while heavily pregnant, at the time a radical statement of female empowerment that was frowned on by a male-dominated and misogynist music industry.

Examined now, the sleeve art of Cherry's debut *Raw Like Sushi* album is still powerful in terms of iconography, typography and design and looks perfect in a modern context, but much of the musical content is frothy and stands up less well. Still, Neneh Cherry's charm carries the day, and she would prove enduringly influential.

An artist calling herself MIA (Missing in Acton), real name Maya Arulpragasm, would arrive at XL in 2003 and say to me: 'I heard you were looking for me', which may have been true, though I wasn't aware of it. She was initially managed by the twitchy but charismatic Jonathan Dickins, who, having recently been let go from the Warners A&R department, had started his own label, Showbiz, and pressed and released the first MIA song, 'Galang'. He understood Maya's potential.

There were loud echoes of Neneh Cherry in her updated, global hip-hop-influenced vision. Maya said of Cherry: 'We were grateful that there was this person in England who was stylistically aspirational, how she looked, how she wore her hair. She represented a conscious ethos in pop.'

The non-musicality and rebellious energy of MIA was compelling, and the way she combined cultural influences and approached everything from a visual perspective was deeply ahead of its time, while also being familiar to me. She reminded me not just of Neneh Cherry, but of Malcolm McLaren.

Maya and I had common ground and we had both been in awe of the revolutionary energy of Public Enemy. She would end up in the crosshairs herself. Her approach owed something to punk, perhaps best summed up as: If it ain't broke, break it. She saw XL as a platform on which to communicate with the world. I knew a free-thinker when I met one, and working with her would help me to reprogramme my own patterns.

Maya was a refugee from Sri Lanka who had grown up on Mitcham's notoriously rough and racist Phipps Bridge Estate, and through self-motivation and willpower had got herself into Central St Martins. On completing her fine art degree, she met Justine Frischmann of Elastica, who she subsequently toured with and designed artwork for.

Maya could not afford an iPod when they first came out but her friend Justine could, and seeing its revolutionary potential Maya embraced the genre-less nature of the mp3. It was the format she had in mind when she began to make music. The arrival of MIA coincided with blogs, chat rooms and illegal downloading sites. The digitisation of the music industry.

Maya spoke like an art-school student rather than someone from a council estate (she was in reality both) and, partly because of this, in the UK her 'authenticity' was under question from day one, and there were many who didn't believe in her or wish her to succeed. I had no doubts about Maya.

I believed in the whole idea of MIA, and it struck me that if the UK was not ready for her, perhaps we could set our sights on a different horizon. I decided to visit some of the same US characters and institutions I'd explored on The Prodigy's behalf a decade ago. The person who seemed to understand what Maya was doing, and perhaps its connection to the new digital landscape, was Interscope boss Jimmy Iovine. In his office in LA I played him a CD with five tracks on it.

There were other US connections in place already. Maya was collaborating with Wes Pentz, aka Diplo, an up-and-coming DJ out of Philadelphia's Hollertronix crew with a mischievous and direct approach, and a writer for *Fader* magazine based in New York called Knox Robinson who was brimming with ideas. The first fruits of this collaboration came in the shape of the *Piracy Funds Terrorism* mixtape, where Maya and Diplo were able to throw every influence and reference into the mix with abandon. Maya had started to record her album proper at this time in a slightly more traditional way, and listening to a first draft of the mixtape it struck me that the mashup approach should be applied not just to the tape but more directly to the actual album.

Maya had a vision: 'I thought: everyone is going to listen to everything, at once, without a limitation based on a genre or an album or even the concept of an artist. My background helped. Refugee thinking. Not being rooted means you're more amenable to change. I wasn't precious about protecting a box, a category, because there wasn't one. Between 2002 and 2004 people were learning how to use the computer. It was the first time everyone had a computer in their house, not just academics and rich people. The web became accessible. It was a once-in-a-lifetime moment. Chat rooms were not sexy-looking, they looked basic and boring, but you could chuck anything at it, and that's how I saw the music. I wasn't deliberately provoking all the dissecting and analysing, but I couldn't sing and so I threw so much stuff at my music that it was perfect for this thing called the internet.'

Her debut for XL, *Arular*, would turn out to be a successfully executed attempt to mix a lot of things together that shouldn't have worked but absolutely did. That it was a glimpse of the future was evidenced by how few initially understood it, particularly in the UK.

'Pull Up The People' nodded simultaneously to dancehall and rave and still sounds current. MIA's global approach would be widely copied. 'Bucky Done Gun' aped Brazilian baile funk while chopping up the *Rocky* theme tune horns. There's a tangible eman-cipated sexuality in her work. Britain had never produced an artist quite like this.

It was a great moment for US rap and R&B production. And there's no question we were emulating what Timbaland and The Neptunes were doing, but *Arular* outstrips its influences: as an album it has more depth than much of the US R&B of the time, which was in a particularly glamorous phase and yet to re-politicise itself. As Maya says: 'We could never do the bling; there was no point in competing with that.'

The musical influences were truly global: America, India, South America and the Caribbean, courtesy of a Sri Lankan who was actually an archetypal Londoner, a citizen of the world. Pop music excites when the people making it are free, and rules are being broken. In *Arular*, Maya's liberation is audible.

Maya is not a good vocalist in any traditional sense. But she is infinitely more of an artist than any number of five-octave, trained and 'professional' singers. She makes her shortcomings into her advantages, and her lyrics are always audacious. In '10 Dollar' Maya talks of a girl from Sri Lanka who hooks up with a Yorkshire banker over a Miami freestyle rhythm courtesy of Richard X. Needing the visa she pays him 'with her knees up'.

Arular arrived in March 2005. Diplo and Maya were romantic and musical partners for a while. As two alphas it was unlikely to last but the results were seismic. A London DJ and producer called Dave Taylor, aka Switch, just as capable of generating banging club music with taste and humour as Diplo, would play a big part in the follow-up album, *Kala*.

Kala has its DIY roots intact. Like *Arular*, it provides any aspiring artists listening with some punk-style encouragement; it sounds like anyone could make it, despite the considerable cast of helpers Maya had assembled: 'Different artists emerge at different times to do different things. To use or misuse technology in different ways. Kool Herc putting two turntables together. The photocopier that was used for the flyers for those parties. Tower Records wanted to put me into the world music section and bury me. I wasn't going to make a record that fit any mould, any genre. It was for the internet. The birth of the internet was about communication and information and that was at the root of MIA. Talking about things people hadn't heard. It was like Wikipedia rap. People would listen and be, like, where is Jaffna? In fact, where is Sri Lanka? Or the samples I used . . . who the fuck are the Modern Lovers? You were beginning to be able to find that information out straight away.'

While there's many a good producer toiling away in the boiler room of this album, with feedback and encouragement being provided by Nick Huggett and me, Maya, ultimately, is the architect of *Kala*. Her vision is overarching and perfectly clear throughout. The initial trio of songs on the album, 'Bamboo Banga', 'Bird Flu' and 'Boyz', are a perfect realisation of this vision. And in 'Paper Planes', Diplo took The Clash's 'Straight To Hell' and gave MIA a bona fide US and subsequently worldwide hit, the first of many Diplo would go on to produce for an ever wider variety of artists.

By now Ian Montone was managing MIA, and though his tenure was brief, he helped convince Interscope of the song's commercial potential. In 2009 Esta and I found ourselves at Maya's then home in LA, where she was preparing to perform the next night at the Grammys, 'Paper Planes' being nominated for Record of the Year. I had never attended this event, and had no plans to, until I mentioned this to Jonathan and he said, 'But it's not about you, maybe other people might appreciate you being there to support them.'

In an overt echo of that culturally impactful Neneh Cherry *Top of the Pops* appearance from twenty years before, Maya would grace the stage heavily pregnant, and deliver the hook from 'Paper Planes' as part of a performance of another new hit song which sampled her already sample-heavy offering.

Kanye West had taken her line 'No one on the corner has swagger like us' and crafted a new tune around it, featuring not just his vocals but verses from other rap superstars Lil Wayne, T.I. and Jay-Z (the record eventually being billed to the latter two featuring the first two).

At the Grammys the four rappers decided to reference the Rat Pack and perform the song in tuxedos, all the while surrounding the heavily pregnant Maya, enhancing the already surreal nature of the performance.

Maya had always concerned herself with political issues; given her background it was hard for her not to. She would take a great deal of flak for her views. Whereas Public Enemy are referred to as politically revolutionary, MIA is described as pseudo-militant. I don't really understand why. They are all musicians who believe in the things they say. None of them are actual soldiers.

Maya: 'People didn't like me or believe I was revolutionary because I cared about fashion. But on the internet these things could combine. Neneh Cherry had to make a pop record to get on the shelf and in the magazines and get played on the radio, but I had the internet which wasn't about being mainstream or pop. And Neneh came from a musical family, whereas my family didn't believe in music. They saw music as frivolous, a hobby. Sri Lankans became doctors, not musicians. The internet gave me freedom.'

I saw the three albums I worked on with MIA as an opportunity to break some rules, and help her reach the audience I felt she deserved.

Back in the UK this level of rap glamour and success was still a dream. But something was stirring. Something raw. Giggs had been on the scene for a while making and self-releasing mixtapes, the latest of which was *Ard Bodied*. It contained the song 'Talkin' Da Hardest'. The authenticity of this felt like a reaction not just to the more polished and shiny UK crossover rap attempts of that moment, but also to the now glamorous and institutional-ised US scene. And 'Talkin' Da Hardest', with its witty and eerily real-sounding tales of street life, was becoming a bona fide club smash as well as early viral video hit.

Listening to Giggs it struck me that while we'd been hearing stories of street life from the US since the mid-eighties, I had never heard much real UK gangsta rap. It existed but had not yet transcended the scene it came from.

Giggs was unapologetic about where he came from, and ready to be seen and heard. On the follow-up to *Ard Bodied*, the *Walk In Da Park* album, on the song 'Cut-Up Bag', Giggs gave the audience some instructions over the outro: 'Trust me, you know what I want everyone to do right now? / Wind down all your windows, turn this up / Loud, let the bassline bang showing no respect / No respect for the law / Get me? Screaming out: "'caine in a cut-up bag / rags!"'. What he was saying was considered unacceptable in the UK. At this time Giggs relied only on the people around him. DIY. Self-reliant. What could be more punk rock?

Mike Skinner of The Streets, always astute and connected, had asked Giggs to guest on a song and video of his called 'Slow Songs', and this helped Giggs to start attracting attention beyond his core audience. And he brought Giggs to meet me at XL. I was barefoot. Giggs' reaction to this was, 'This is a bit deep for me.' Fair enough. Maybe I should have put some shoes on.

Giggs: 'I'd just left the EMI building. When you're from the streets the idea of getting signed is like going to paradise. And EMI was all new, all shiny glass. I didn't really understand what XL was. I was saying I don't know . . . I don't know if this is the place. I'm trying to get off the streets and this looks like a shed. I was just thinking . . . what the fuck. But then I saw all the new Macs, and that was an interesting contrast. The look of it just wasn't what I thought this world was gonna be. Now I realise how heavy it was. I don't wear shoes when people come to my yard.'

I saw us all as equal. We all had different strengths, and the ability to help each other. Giggs decided to sign to independent XL rather than the competing major-label option. The paperwork was ready to sign when things took an unexpected turn. Or at least it was surprising to me. Less so to Giggs.

I was staying at a friend's cottage in the Oxfordshire countryside when Ben Beardsworth, by now managing director of XL and in charge of day-to-day activities, called me to say that Operation Trident had been in touch with him at the label, and they had said that they did not want us to sign Giggs. This seemed like an odd call for them to make. The nature of Giggs' former activities was common knowledge, particularly given the revealing nature of his lyrics, and he had already paid the price for this.

XL saw his music as artistically valid and was looking to make records with him, so why would a division of the Metropolitan Police attempt to impede his progress into a legitimate and worthwhile career? To compound the bizarre nature of the conversation, the man from the Met advised Ben that we were not to mention this conversation to Giggs.

At that precise moment my children had a combination of three ailments: head lice, impetigo and teething. There were a lot of ointments, sheets to be kept clean and screaming going on. The Metropolitan Police attempting to involve themselves in our A&R decisions was more aggravation and I didn't really need it. Their actions seemed racially motivated. It was hard to imagine them trying to stop us signing a white artist. My diary entry at the time reads: 'Countryside fun apart lice, boils, teething, Trident'.

When we told Giggs what was going on he was sanguine. He informed us that due to the bad relationship he had with the police he was not surprised, and that he would understand if we no longer wished to enter into a deal with him. The deal went ahead, and Giggs became one of the most constructive and collaborative artists the label ever worked with, endearing himself to all staff members with his natural enthusiasm, sense of humour and powerful spirit, and from this base he went on to build a platform for himself as one of the most beloved artists the UK has ever produced.

He has helped open doors for a generation of other UK rappers who are now able to reach their audience either completely independently or with the help of record labels – as they choose. The power is in their hands. Artists such as Stormzy and Dave make their music and communicate their message without interference. Their connection to their audience is direct and powerful, and they cannot be pushed around by the music industry, the media or the police. Real progress has occurred. UK rap is currently healthier than ever, and the audience now sees homegrown artists and sounds as at least as important as rappers emerging from hip-hop's birthplace in the US.

And what of US success? Perhaps the UK rapper who breaks there will not at that point be the biggest artist in their home market, because he or she will be doing something too different from anyone else. MIA achieved great success in the US. The UK did not even consider her a rap artist and was painfully slow to embrace her. A misfit in one place can be a great fit in another. Equally, US success does not need to be any sort of holy grail for UK rap artists any more. A great career can be built without it, and it's easier to hit a target you can see.

The time that has to be dedicated to establishing US success is a gamble. There is no guaranteed return and the energy has to be taken away from the UK audience, and that can easily weaken an artist's foundation.

And, of course, the path to success at home is still littered with obstacles. Our UK rap audience has always been obsessed with credibility and authenticity. When I began attending rap concerts in the mid-eighties, the UK audience was unforgiving of not just homegrown talent, but of US stars who displeased them with any overt attempt at commercialism. The audience is still similarly tough in its judgements, though the views are now expressed differently. Despite or perhaps because of the lack of outlets for audience feedback in pre-internet times, criticisms would be expressed in visceral ways.

When I saw LL Cool J live in 1986 I was fifteen and he had just followed a run of minimal, hardcore street smashes including 'Rock The Bells' and 'I Can't Live Without My Radio' with 'I Need Love' – a slow jam aimed at R&B radio. When he attempted to play this song, he was pelted with coins, a trick the UK rap audience had borrowed from its football hooligan relatives, a tribe who were equally unforgiving of any protagonist whose integrity was in question.

One coin connected with the self-styled Ladies Love Legend in Leather, mid-flow. I couldn't believe what I was seeing.

LL halted his set. He was not best pleased. He informed the grumpy London B-boy who had just connected with his Kangol-and-gold-chain-wearing target that if another coin hit him, he would jump down from the stage and kick him in the face. The unimpressed fan with an accurate aim was nonplussed; he simply threw another coin. I suspect LL never had similar experiences in the US.

The UK audience is demanding and not to be underestimated. But we now have an optimistic reality. It is possible to achieve lasting long-term success as a rapper from this country without making any compromise whatsoever. This is the trail Giggs has blazed, and an artist such as Dave follows and extends.

Seeing Stormzy's headline Glastonbury performance in 2019 filled me with pride. He began the show with a clip of him and Jay-Z in conversation, both of them possessed of an effortless charm and a centred spirituality which has enabled them to transcend all expectations. In the space of the first three songs Stormzy referenced three other artists who had inspired him: Wiley, Dizzee and Giggs. MCs who have inspired countless others. The day is here.

SO REAL

ADELE: General Info

Member Since	12/31/2004
Band Website	**adele.tv**
Band Members	Adele - Vocals and Guitar Ben Thomas - Guitar Steve Holness - Keys Tom Driessler - Bass Louis Sharpe - Drums The Wired Strings - Strings
Influences	Etta James, Jill Scott, Karen Dalton, Bjork, Carole King, Ann Peebles, Dusty Springfield, Billy Bragg, Ella Fitzgerald, Roberta Flack, Cyndi Lauper, Paul Weller, The Beatles, Billie Holiday, Lauryn Hill, Jeff Buckley, Jamie T, Marvin Gaye, Noisettes, Camille, Erykah Badu, Martha Wainwright, The Cure, Amy Winehouse, Peggy Lee, D'Angelo, Eva Cassidy, Kings Of Leon, The Cranberries, Destiny's Child, The White Stripes, Suzanne Vega, Alicia Keys, Macy Gray, Amos Lee, Eurythmics, Johnny Cash, Kelis, The Police...
Record Label	XL Recordings
Type of Label	Indie

From Adele's Myspace biog, 2004

The seeds of success, like the seeds of failure, tend to be sown a long time before they manifest themselves. In the 1990s I would look at the upper reaches of the *Billboard* album chart and wonder how it was done. How did these records achieve such stratospheric levels of success, while others accomplished next to nothing commercially? How did albums sell 5 or even 10 million copies? And why did it happen so rarely for British artists?

By the time Adele Adkins signed to XL in 2006, despite the label still being small and independent, it was able to give an artist with her abilities and potential the resources she needed. As a teenager I felt music acutely, and emerging the other side of some personal struggles in my early thirties I was more able to feel the spirit and nature of music than ever before. My instincts felt strong.

I was sure of Adele's ability and having this kind of certainty is empowering. And it meant in turn that she found in XL an organisation that had her back 100 per cent. She was a teenager when we started working together, but her lack of age or experience could not have bothered me any less. I listened to what she had to say, as well as her music. This is not to say that I knew how successful she would be. I have never been able to predict the public's response to anything. All the more reason to concentrate on getting the work right.

Not everyone she came across took her as seriously as they should have done. While in the XL offices one day, a female member of another artist's management team asked Adele to make some teas, assuming her to be an intern.

I was taken aback by evidence of Adele's youthfulness only once. On meeting Penny, her mum, at the first Adele gig I saw, I had been expecting to meet someone old. Artists' parents were like my parents. Elderly. The petite, warm and enthusiastic woman

I was being introduced to looked younger than me, and was in fact the same age, meaning that at some point and without me noticing, a shift had occurred and XL was now working with a new generation of artists.

It was 2005. The *Billboard* Hot 100 was dominated by 50 Cent, Kanye West, Mariah Carey and Gwen Stefani. Sonny and Dexter were three and one. I had been through a breakdown and was engaged in the process of rebuilding myself. I was trying to adopt a less ego-based outlook, and stop seeing myself as the most important person in my life. There would be several stops on this journey. An epiphany would occur, inexplicably, while watching a QPR match at Loftus Road with Sonny, when I felt a great stillness, and became suddenly aware of my ego as a separate entity, like a half-brother who had been my constant companion until that point, controlling much of my behaviour, without my having been aware of his presence.

I became aware that the voice in my head was actually not me. I found myself witnessing the mental noise, and establishing some detachment from it. To become aware of this force was not to eliminate it but to suddenly understand the reasons for much of what was happening in my life, and to be more able to moderate my own actions. From this point on it would be a bit harder for the ego to control me, because I was more aware of it, and was determined to not be misled.

I would be grateful for the commercial success that would follow my seeing this seventeen-year-old singer perform at Cherry Jam on Porchester Road, near my house, and meeting her and her youthful mum. But this success wouldn't be the most important thing in my life at that time. It would have been, fifteen years earlier, and that would have made me less effective. But now I had some detachment. It was only success, an outer phenomenon, and I knew the dangers of identifying too closely with it.

Contrary to the mythology, no one person tends to 'discover' an artist. First the artist has to discover their own talent, and once they do, if it's significant it tends to become apparent to those around them. Tic Zogson, a young musician, producer and scout for XL, played Adele's Myspace demos to Nick Huggett. Tic needed something to offer in an A&R meeting, and was actually loath to play this promising vocalist from Tottenham via West Norwood, because she already had eleven thousand plays on Myspace, and so he was worried that he'd look late. But he couldn't find anything else that day.

That figure - eleven thousand plays - may not seem much given the billions of listens she has had since, but in fact it was a substantial number for the stage she was at, and in retrospect was evidence of the power of her music. Myspace offered the opportunity for artists or labels to upload songs and listeners to choose what to listen to, counting the plays as it went, clearly presaging streaming, a then little-used method of music consumption.

Nick was enthused by what he heard and in turn played the demos to me, and that's when I went to see the gig at Cherry Jam. Adele performed alone with an acoustic guitar and seemed to possess a singularity: vulnerability coupled with complete certainty. She had an intangible but unmistakable aura of originality. What she did may have appeared similar to what many other artists did, but it was actually unique, because there was so much of her in the songs and performance. It was pure and undiluted.

If an artist finds a way (and possesses the courage) to communicate who they really are in their music, it will be original. It will be theirs. Because each of us is unique; it's just a question of whether we have a way to own and express that. With Adele there was no apology.

She hired Jonathan Dickins to manage her, who had worked briefly but productively with MIA, and was now managing two other artists: Jamie T and Jack Peñate. Other record labels were showing interest in Adele but she made the decision to work with XL decisively, using her failsafe instincts. The desire to work together was mutual, but I had completely the wrong idea of the music Adele planned to make once she signed.

Because I'd seen her perform solo with guitar, I thought we

would be making a stripped-down acoustic, folky record. A Joni Mitchell for our time would have fit neatly with my vision of XL's roster. But when she explained that she wanted to work with pop-orientated producers, I had no objections. I would have spoken up if I felt that she was going to get it wrong, or that she had made that decision based on a lack of self-awareness, or fear. But instead I embraced her idea, because it appeared to be a way of Adele expressing herself authentically, despite it involving a process and personnel I was unfamiliar with. She didn't want to fit neatly. She would create a new mould.

Until this point I had only ever succeeded when working with artists who started out in an underground scene. Adele embodied the spirit that I was used to encountering in the most sonically adventurous of artists, while having an aesthetic that was closely aligned to that of the public, not of music specialists. It would have been churlish to suggest she become a bit more left so we could then help her infiltrate the centre. And by aligning herself with us, she would be starting from a credible position that she would benefit from. Otherwise the music snobs might have missed her quality.

One of the co-writers she suggested was called Eg White. I had never worked with this type of pop craftsman before. I thought I should visit Eg, formerly of nineties pop duo Eg and Alice, and learn about what he did, and after spending an hour in his home studio I could immediately see that he was in his own right a significant talent who could bring a lot to the process. Shortly after their first session, Eg used a word to describe Adele to me which was utterly apt but has rarely been used in reference to her. The word was 'genius'.

The reason that she is rarely described this way is sexism, and a touch of ageism. Any older male artist with the ability to write music and lyrics that touch people in the fundamental way that hers do would be widely considered a genius, but I've seldom come across the term being used in relation to Adele. She would turn out to be a crusader for pop music in the same way George

Michael had been, making pop which was not lightweight frippery but as meaningful and important to people's lives as any critically acclaimed 'serious' rock or soul masterpiece.

As Adele completed her debut album, music consumption was changing, and records were starting to be widely disseminated online. I felt that as long as she was heard she would succeed, so I suggested to her that we give her music away online as a free download, feeling that this (at the time) radical approach might open doors for her. She fixed a steely gaze on me and said, 'That idea makes me feel physically sick.' I liked this response. Her utter lack of deference left no room for uncertainty or miscommunication. She was only going to embrace an idea if she believed in it, nothing to do with who it had come from.

The team around her turned out to be highly capable. She made sure of that. Jonathan would go on to contribute a huge amount to Adele's success, helping her to formulate and execute her vision. She has always been quick to credit him with his contributions, which says much about her genuine confidence. As well as being her manager, he became her key A&R person. He required some managing himself at times, but he is possessed of a humour and charisma that helped to pull the project together and unify the people involved.

When Adele had attempted some recording with the successful XL-signed production duo Basement Jaxx for her album, I passed on a message to her from Simon Ratcliffe, one half of this talented outfit, that all of the sonic touches, the 'interesting noises' as he put it, were still to come. Her reply to me said much about her focus and desire to deliver something completely direct: 'I don't want any interesting noises.' It also confirmed to me that her aesthetic was different from mine, the interesting noises often being my favourite part of a record, and I made a mental note to ensure I did not try to impose my sensibilities on her.

Adele knew what she was doing, and just as it would be a clichéd record label manoeuvre to try to make an artist more commercial, it would be equally misguided to make an artist less so. The job of a label, or manager, is to help an artist be the absolute best version of themselves. Recognise strengths, nurture them and make sure they are utilised. Acknowledge weaknesses and marginalise them.

I was present in a meeting where Adele announced that she did not yet wish to perform at any festivals, because she did not consider herself ready for that environment. That willingness to delay short-term income and acclaim told me categorically that her potential was unlimited. She was not grasping. She knew that good things would come at the right moment.

I heard mutterings that XL was compromising its independent rave roots by working with her. This was not correct. From day one Adele was utterly uncompromising and thus a consistent part of a thread that was close to my heart. The default mode for any artist should be 'I'm not having it', and 'it' should refer to more or less everything. This, also, is my default mode.

I attempted to contextualise who she was by describing her as a 'punk Barbra Streisand'. And regardless of any mainstream or pop ambition, Adele's debut album *19* opens in traditional singer-songwriterly territory, as she accompanies herself on guitar to sing her song 'Daydreamer'. The song's subject is referred to as a 'jaw-dropper . . . feeling up his girl / Like he's never felt her figure before'. The 'h' of 'her' is dropped, unapologetically. She conjures images of London in a way that is somehow authentically romantic. There's dirt under her fingernails, and she captures the genuine romance of the city. It's when the strings kick in on the chorus of 'Chasing Pavements', and we find ourselves in the terrain occupied historically by singers such as Dusty Springfield and writers such as Burt Bacharach that her scope becomes apparent.

The work of the producers of *19* was important. Mark Ronson provides the type of hard, hip-hop-indebted drums he so expertly recorded for Amy Winehouse's 'Back To Black' on the song 'Cold Shoulder'. Jim Abbiss faithfully captures live performances. Eg White takes a Tin Pan Alley pop approach and pulls it off.

But the record remains unquestionably Adele's.

Male pop and R&B producers have often skirted on the edge of treating the (usually) female artists they produce as 'vehicles' for their ideas. Adele has been willing to work with any number of producers because she knows they can help her serve the song they collaborate on, and there is zero possibility of their manipulating her in any way whatsoever. She is too strong for that to happen. Every song she records is her song, and that includes when she covers Bob Dylan. On *19* she makes 'Make You Feel My Love' her own, as convincingly as Hendrix did with his version of 'All Along The Watchtower'.

It struck me that Adele's lyrics were unpretentious but often contained turns of phrase that hadn't been heard before, which sometimes became song titles, 'Chasing Pavements' being an early example of this. Anyone who's written words to go with music will know just how difficult it is to coin phrases for the first time; it was probably easier at the dawn of popular music but a lot of songs have now been written.

19 was a perfect opening salvo, achieving a number one UK album chart debut and a Best New Artist Grammy, but it left room for more spectacular feats to come. Ben Beardsworth was responsible, alongside Jonathan, for the marketing and selling of the album and it was evident to us all that this was really a set-up album, a prelude. We had people's attention but a different vista was beckoning.

I was edging into recording with Gil as Adele's career was starting to take flight. There was something about my working, simultaneously, in completely different roles with these two artists, at dramatically different stages of their lives and careers, that felt like it created some sort of equilibrium for me. Adele's career was a juggernaut, starting to build momentum. Gil's recording career had been stationary for more than a decade. But these were two special, strong yet delicate individuals who I was fortunate to be working with, and I needed to do whatever was required.

Adele and Jonathan played the first draft of the follow-up *21* to me and Ben in my basement studio at home on her return from

LA. Something was amiss. The sessions hadn't produced the feeling she wanted, and she was devastated. I told her that this was in fact no problem; she should simply continue the recording process until she reached the destination she had in mind. She seemed surprised at my response but I saw no reason why she should be. Although the sessions had been costly, it was common sense to me to speculate whatever was necessary to help achieve her goals. I knew everyone involved would eventually be happy we had.

To back Adele to the fullest was the easiest thing in the world. Just as it was to back Liam Howlett. I knew that we were all in the right place. Liam once said that I was in tune with The Prodigy because I was equally committed to risk-taking as they were, and this is a crucial component of any significant creative endeavour. Put yourself on the line. That is the essence of artistry.

Initially Adele had envisioned 21 being helmed by one producer, in the manner of many of her favourite classic albums, which hail from a period when there was only ever one producer per album. This would have been contrary to the modern method of pop, R&B and rap album production, where different songs are helmed by different people.

Rick Rubin had by now become perhaps the most significant mainstream record producer of the modern era, his work with artists from Johnny Cash to Jay-Z going beyond any genre limitations. Adele had been keen to work with him, and 21 started with Rick alone at the helm. Without his contributions the album would have been a very different entity, but gradually a roll call of the best producers of that moment stepped up and helped Adele execute her singular vision.

The producers of 21 all helped her create music that was distinctly Adele, a task, it turns out, better achieved by a range of people than just one. There was a massive amount of experience and ability between the producers of this record, and they were all utterly different personalities, and yet it's not that easy to discern who did what without referring to the credits.

The first single, the bluesy 'Rolling In The Deep', saw Adele again coin a phrase and title that had not existed before. And I was taken aback when I realised what the backing vocal lyrics were: 'You're gonna wish you never had met me'. The brutality was somehow shocking. The narrator has been wronged and is not taking it lying down. Clearly such raw emotion touched a nerve that cut across stylistic boundaries; no other song in history has topped so many of the different *Billboard* genre charts, including Rock, R&B, Latin and Dance. 'Rolling In The Deep' would become the biggest new crossover song of the last twenty-five years.

This book is not about sales figures or awards. Too many artists whose work is close to my heart have *not* achieved huge sales for me to think of units sold as what is important. Commercial success is a measure of something outer; not necessarily of anything deeper. The record industry's obsession with figures is limiting and stifles creativity. Music that reaches a lot of people but has no substance is of no interest. Music that has depth but only reaches a small audience is often the most important and long-lasting.

But Adele did achieve a holy grail. Music with genuine emotional resonance that transcended all modern commercial expectations. In the UK, *21* has now been outsold only by an album seen by many as the greatest of all time, the Beatles' *Sergeant Pepper's Lonely Hearts Club Band*. In an age of short attention spans, where many album releases are forgotten a week after they arrive, *21* stayed at number one in the UK for twenty-three weeks. For XL, initially trading in rave 12-inches, to release an album with this kind of reach was never really a likely outcome. In the US, the album stayed at number one for twenty-four weeks. It was the world's bestselling album not just of 2011, the year of its release, but of 2012 as well.

Somehow the reaching of the very limits of the worldwide music audience was always part of Adele's destiny. *21* connected with music fans to a degree that is generally perceived, in music industry terms, to be a lightning strike. But there is a type of archetypal female artist, perhaps first defined by Carole King, who is able to command a far greater level of loyalty from her audience than any male artist tends to be able to. That's not to say anyone can rest on their laurels.

So, while Paul Epworth and Ryan Tedder returned to play an important part in the production of 25, and Rick Rubin again gave invaluable feedback and shared insights that only he could have had, most of the production personnel had not worked on any previous music released by Adele. A new team was recruited.

Greg Kurstin, already hugely successful but working with Adele for the first time, co-wrote and produced two songs on the album, one of which would turn out to be the lead single, 'Hello', a stately ballad with a subtly modern production twist in the filtering of its drums, not the type of technique that had been used on an Adele record before. The long-reigning Swedish king of pop production, Max Martin, made a significant contribution to the album in 'Send My Love'. While the Adeleness was in no way diluted, the sound was current and also aimed at the hips, with a dusty guitar riff and syncopated kick drum that hinted at dancehall.

One of the best and most unusual albums of the last decade is *Goon* by Tobias Jesso Jr, on which this innately gifted singer-song-writer bares his feelings about the break-up he has recently experienced. It recalled mid-seventies Californian rock music without being cheesy or retro. I fell in love with it, and side one of the album contains as good a run of songs as anyone has written in recent years. Adele had particularly loved his song 'Hollywood', and in collaborating to write 'When We Were Young', Tobias Jesso Jr, Adele and producer Ariel Rechtshaid made a recording that is probably my favourite of hers to date. It has the type of emotional resonance that was more commonly found in seventies soul music. It's difficult to make complex pop music, and things can easily sound over-musical. In 'When We Were Young' balance is achieved. The production cast of the album all contribute much to the proceedings.

But even with its updated feel the album, once again, is strictly Adele. When thirty seconds of the album's first single, 'Hello', was broadcast to the UK TV audience, unannounced, on 18 October 2015 as an advert during ITV's *X Factor* talent show, the internet duly ignited and another juggernaut was set in motion. 'Hello' immediately lodged itself at number one but it was the performance of the album that followed it, *25*, that was truly astounding.

The album sold 800,000 copies in its first week on sale in the UK, the highest number ever achieved, more than Oasis's *(What's The Story) Morning Glory?*, going on to sell nearly 4 million copies in the UK alone.

In the US it sold 3.5 million copies in its first week on sale, going on to sell 10 million. Its sales were so staggering that rather than being seen as a success for Adele, or for XL, or for Columbia to whom we licensed the album for the US, it was viewed as a triumph for the music industry as a whole, providing hope, reversing overall downward sales trajectories.

In his eponymous book *John Hammond on Record*, perhaps the greatest A&R man of all time as the discoverer of Billie Holiday, Aretha Franklin and Bob Dylan, and compiler and populariser of Robert Johnson, said this: 'I've never felt I was buying anyone or putting anyone under obligation. Whatever help I've given has been given freely. Money given simply represented opportunity, a chance to get something done that deserved to be done and might otherwise not get done. Seeing it happily and successfully done was all the reward I ever wanted. Anyone who wants anything more, anyone who wants gratitude from or credit for a talent that already exists, is a pain in the ass.'

I was aware that what occurred with Adele was something of a miracle. Our collaboration succeeded beyond anyone's wildest dreams and secured the future of XL. It's hard to run an independent record label. Far more fail than succeed. Many struggle to manage their finances and cease to exist. Adele enabled XL to get to a place beyond this, and I am grateful to her. Equally, we helped her get to a place that is the dream of many.

What does her success mean, and what can an aspiring musician learn from it? From the start, Adele did things on her own terms, never compromising her ideals. She tended not to do what was expected of her. On this basis she achieved success on the biggest imaginable level. For hopeful artists there is no secret, or magic formula, except this: trust your instincts. And be willing to fail, and to continue. The music industry will always contain insecure people who wish to make you conform because they fear the outcome otherwise.

Ignore them!

Following Adele's success we strenuously resisted the possibility of XL getting bigger, seeing it instead as an opportunity for the label to be better, by simply continuing to do exactly what it had done before, which was release a small number of hopefully good records every year, but from a more secure position.

The nineties were eventful for XL, but the label found its feet and fully manifested its hybrid nature in the new millennium. Giggs would explain XL to a peer of his as 'a door into another world', and that captured the essence of what I'd been aiming for.

The small roster was key. XL's structure allowed us to take this approach, in that a multi-faceted collaboration had evolved between XL and Beggars Banquet, by now renamed Beggars Group, no longer a record label but a company providing services not just to XL and 4AD but also the Rough Trade and Matador labels, allowing these indies to remain autonomous but giving them support and back-up, avoiding the inevitable and generally fatal culture clash that occurs when small record labels partner with majors.

By 2006 XL was being taken sufficiently seriously to be on the radar of established artists, and we began to be approached by some big names. I did not generally consider these artists to be a good fit, regardless of their status. Then Thom Yorke, stepping outside of Radiohead alongside the band's producer Nigel Godrich, made the *Eraser* album, casting Thom's voice against flickering, textured, mostly electronic backdrops.

Radiohead were by now the most important and influential rock band of their generation but if anything this album, with its more minimal aesthetic, appealed to me more than any of the band's work to date. Following a suggestion of Nigel's, XL became the home for *The Eraser*, and then Radiohead's extraordinary *In Rainbows* album, for me the band's greatest work up until this point. Following a 'pay what you like' experiment whereby the band made the album available to fans at whatever price level they chose, XL did the traditional work required in the releasing of an album.

Then another horizon became apparent. To gain permission from the EU monopolies board for the sale of EMI to Universal, some of EMI's 'assets' had to be sold to third parties as 'divestments'. Warners stepped in to buy the Parlophone label from EMI. Radiohead's shrewd management saw an opportunity to regain control of their own masters, in that their catalogue of albums could be one of EMI's 'divestments', and saw in Martin Mills a partner to get a deal done and in XL a home for the catalogue and potential future releases.

To everyone's amazement a long-term agreement was reached, fiendishly complicated though it was. A long way from the label's rave roots it was still, somehow, a perfect fit. Given the calibre of artists the label was now attracting, I made the decision to enforce a rule on XL of no more than five album releases a year.

Few truly great albums get made, period. A release schedule of even five albums is a lot, if the quality bar is set high. A record label is committed to most of its album releases before the albums are finished, if not before they are started, so there is always an element of the unknown to the end quality. The discipline involved in a five-album-per-year release schedule forced everyone to really consider what they were doing. The less is more approach is deeply anti-business. It would not fly in any company that has shareholders.

It is a mechanism intended to maintain creative integrity. Independent record labels are free of the concept of 'market share', an idea that fosters an interest not only in your own success, but in the failure of others. The sports world works like this – 'I win, you lose' – and some sort of competitive spirit is normally necessary for excellence, but this type of aggression is not necessarily a good fit with an art form as delicate as music.

When I have attended the Association of Independent Music AGMs, I see a room full of people motivated by a genuine passion for what they do, who at any given time may or may not be making much money, and I am inspired by it.

There is no equivalent gathering in the major-label world. There could not be, because each corporation must be in opposition to every other corporation, whether the people who work there wish it to be this way or not.

I have enormous respect for completely music-orientated endeavours such as Warp, Ninja Tune and Domino. This type of independent label and their output, built on a notion of aesthetic quality, provides a genuinely important function in the ecosystem of music.

Musicians can function effectively without record labels better than ever before, but backing can be helpful. Editing also. Most art can be improved by a trusted editor. And so I believe that the better record companies are, the better music can be. Especially now that they are optional rather than essential.

PART 4

Part 4 Playlist

Kicksquad 'Soundclash (Champion Sound)' (Kickin)

The Scientist 'The Exorcist' (Kickin)

DJ Shadow 'What Does Your Soul Look Like Part 4' (Mo' Wax)

UNKLE 'Nursery Rhyme' (Mo' Wax)

Blackalicious 'Alphabet Aerobics' (Mo' Wax)

The xx 'Intro' (Young Turks)

Sampha 'Blood On Me' (Young Turks)

FKA twigs 'Two Weeks' (Young Turks)

Tyler, the Creator 'Yonkers' (XL Recordings)

Monkey 'Heavenly Peach Banquet' (XL Recordings)

The Valentinos 'Lookin' For A Love' (SAR)

Bobby Womack 'Across 110th Street' (UA)

Bobby Womack 'Please Forgive My Heart' (XL Recordings)

Bobby Womack 'Dayglo Reflection feat. Lana Del Rey' (XL Recordings)

Lana Del Rey 'Video Games' (Interscope)

Damon Albarn 'Hostiles' (Parlophone)

Vampire Weekend 'Step' (XL Recordings)

Descendents 'Theme' (Sessions)

Jai Paul 'Str8 Outta Mumbai' (XL Recordings)

Jai Paul 'Crush' (XL Recordings)

DRC Music 'If You Wish To Stay Awake' (Warp)

Shy FX feat. UK Apache 'Original Nuttah' (SOUR)

Various Production 'Hater' (XL Recordings)

La Roux 'In For The Kill (Skream Mix)' (Polydor)

Peaches 'Fuck The Pain Away' (Kitty-Yo/XL Recordings)

Leila 'Sodastream' (XL Recordings)

Ibeyi 'River' (XL Recordings)

Ibeyi 'No Man Is Big Enough For My Arms' (XL Recordings)

First Choice 'Let No Man Put Asunder' (Salsoul)

rLr 'I Am Paint (Centre Of The Earth Dub)' (rLr)

Lee 'Scratch' Perry 'Bucky Skank' (Upsetter)

Everything Is Recorded 'Close But Not Quite' (XL Recordings)

Giggs 'Whipping Excursion' (SN1)

Obongjayar 'Frens' (Self-released)

Sampha 'The Piano' (Young Turks)

Jay Electronica 'Better In Tune With The Infinite' (Dogon Society)

Everything Is Recorded 'This World' (XL Recordings)

NO OUTSIDE REALITIES

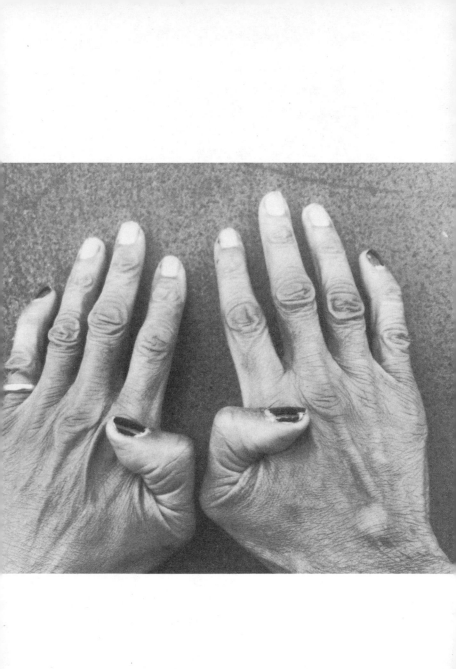

My first attempt to make music in a 'proper' recording facility, in the back room of The Tabernacle on Powis Square, not only led to my initial visit to XL, but exposed me to the kind of set-up de rigueur at the time – a Technics turntable hooked up to an Akai 900 sampler, an Atari PC running Cubase software, one analogue synth, a DAT recorder. Then in the writing room at MCA Music Publishing in Hammersmith I witnessed the many faders. An actual SSL mixing desk.

Once XL was operational and releasing singles, initially there seemed little need for the label to own its own recording studio, as unlike more traditional labels dealing with more traditional music, all artists we worked with were bedroom producers and had their own DIY set-ups, minimal though they might have been. But I had a meaningful encounter with a fellow rave-label boss one day on Portobello Road while visiting the Vinyl Solution record shop.

Pete Harris was the founder of Kickin Records, who released many great early hardcore tunes from the likes of Kicksquad, Messiah and The Scientist, and as we stopped to chat outside his studio he asked me where XL's studio was, and I told him we didn't have one. Pete was horrified, and asked me what, in that case, the point of the label was. If we didn't have a studio, he said sternly, we weren't contributing much to making the music, and that just left marketing, and he rightly pointed out that we couldn't have been much good at that because we were too small, and didn't have much money. The studio, he correctly pointed out, should be the soul of the label.

By 1997 we had resources and I wanted to make two purchases. Both of them were houses, one in Codrington Mews just off Ladbroke Grove and one ten minutes' walk to the east in

Bayswater. My plan was for XL to be based in the Codrington Mews house, and for me to live in the other property.

An illustration of the immense changes that have occurred in London's W11 postcode is that when we turned up to look at the house that is now the home of XL, it was derelict, had been for years, and the estate agents were thrilled at the possibility that anyone was interested in it. Rave cash in hand, it cost less to purchase both the mews house and the house in Bayswater, together, than a single one-bedroom flat in the area would now, and so it's a far more unlikely home for a fledgling independent record label than it was.

When XL moved into the mews it didn't work; we couldn't get the layout or the feeling right. Initially we co-habited the building with James Lavelle's Mo' Wax label. I was ambitious and focused from a young age. James was unbelievably so. Having worked in Honest Jon's record shop on Portobello Road, James had been an understudy to DJ Gilles Peterson and then started Mo' Wax at age eighteen. He had a vision which tied together some of the jazz influences he shared with Gilles, together with skate and rap culture, art and fashion, all seen from an international perspective, as much about Tokyo and LA as it was London.

The packaging of the records, and the fashion tie-ins with brands like Tokyo's Bathing Ape, were as important as the music. I related to the relentless energy James brought to all his activities. At the time I first met him, neither of us was taking ourselves too seriously. And when his licensing deal with A&M records had fizzled out, I saw what I thought might be an opportunity to hasten the growth of XL via a partnership with Mo' Wax. Perhaps I was looking for a short cut. I saw how Martin had thrived via his partnerships with both myself and XL, and Ivo Watts-Russell and 4AD. He made it look easy. But the XL/Mo' Wax partnership, despite the best intentions of all involved, would not prove functional.

Mo' Wax had magic as a shoestring independent; there had never been a record label like it. It was about James's passion, his cultural acumen and the network of creative people he had cultivated. When, with the help of his business partner Steve Finan, he secured funding from Polygram imprint A&M, Mo' Wax used the major label money to ensure that Josh Davis's, aka DJ Shadow's, classic *Endtroducing . . .* album reached the wide international audience it deserved. James then co-opted Shadow to help him turn his own artist vehicle UNKLE into an ambitious collaborative unit, making their album *Psyence Fiction* together.

Debates over credit and who had done what on the album started to create fractures in the already delicate relationships that existed. Still, the label had been doing great. Right up until we tried to work together.

Mo' Wax entered a decline as soon as we were in business, and we were co-habiting in our new west London space at a time when neither label really had their direction properly defined. Less than three short years after the relationship with Mo' Wax began, we had managed to plough a considerable chunk of our *Fat Of The Land* profits into a series of releases that failed to connect in any meaningful way. Whose fault was this? Everyone involved. Just like success, everyone's responsible.

It was not that the music Mo' Wax released in this period was bad or lacked originality. Releases like *Now Thing*, which compiled different versions of a popular dancehall rhythm of that moment, a new album from legendary arranger and composer David Axelrod, and leftfield West Coast hip-hop full-lengths from Divine Styler and Blackalicious were all of interest. But the wind had stopped blowing in Mo' Wax's direction and they weren't used to it. There was a vague feeling of entitlement, and there were lessons to be learned. I had been in wannabe mogul mode with the Mo' Wax relationship, thinking too big too soon, and it did not work for me.

Equally some seeds of success were invisibly sown. When James and Mo' Wax left, two of his people wished to stay behind, Toby Feltwell and Nick Huggett, and they had ideas for the next stage of their careers. They were looking to start their own label called Platinum Projects, and while they would not fully realise their vision for this imprint, it was they who would shortly bring in the white label by an unsigned artist from Bow called Dizzee Rascal.

Toby would then leave, moving to Japan to start the hugely successful Cav Empt clothing line, and Nick would enjoy an incredible A&R run at XL before departing for major-label pastures. Meanwhile, though, a back-to-basics approach was required.

I needed to tap into my own passions and address the label's lack of direction. The solution was right under my nose. There was a garage attached to our property, and initially we had let visitors park in it, until it struck me that this was a waste of a valuable resource. This garage could be a place of musical creation. With Pete Harris's words ringing in my ears, I sat down with XL A&R Matt Thornhill to discuss what needed doing.

Matt, a quiet soul with a large amount of knowledge, had some instinctive acoustic and aesthetic expertise, his father having been a luthier, a hand-crafter of acoustic string instruments.

With newly hired young engineer Rodaidh McDonald on board, we set about creating what was first viewed as a demo room, until I realised that if we saw it as a demo room we'd only make demos there. I announced to everyone involved that we were to refer to the room at all times as a recording studio. The word demo was banned. We would make records there, 'first-class masters'. Now it was a question of seeing who would turn up.

The hardcore revival of 2005, aka 'new rave', was always suspect. Day-Glo was back, The Klaxons covered 'The Bouncer', people partied like it was 1992. With a slightly heavy heart I accepted an offer to play a throwback breakbeat set at an event hosted by a teenage promoter.

There was a good energy on the night but the event was shut down by the Metropolitan Police, and my fee failed to materialise. So it actually had some of the authentic hallmarks of real rave. Regardless of the event's early closing, none of the punters got their money back, and the promoter presumably had a profitable evening despite the various catastrophes. His name was Caius Pawson; he was nineteen years old, and was clearly capable of grasping triumph from the clutches of disaster.

I recognised familiar traits; a driven personality, the type who would have been unlikely to find an outlet at school but might be unstoppable once the correct habitat is occupied. I invited him in to Codrington Mews to develop his own Young Turks label and soon he discovered, via his colleague Katie O'Neil, a group from south London called The xx. Each member of The xx, a four-piece at this time, seemed quiet. Withdrawn, almost. They were not asking for attention, but they got it.

They were soon ensconced in what had until recently been the XL garage but was now the studio, and recording their debut album. It would turn out to be a Mercury Prize-winning classic.

The XL studio mark one was alive, but I began to realise that it was a good recording facility for everyone except me. We were building an increasingly vibrant operation in the mews, and while I was committed to it, I was by now feeling some music of my own starting to come through. The XL building was not the place for me to toil for hours over a bass sound. This prompted me to create a small and dank but great-sounding programming and mix room ten minutes away, at home. Soon, I was recording Gil in Looking Glass and Clinton Studios in Manhattan, and bringing the materials – mainly Gil's vocals and piano – back to this tiny, dark and atmospheric home studio in London to work into what became the album we ended up releasing.

Next, I would need to build a studio that would combine the big live-room feeling with the basement programming vibe, just as I'd previously thought that XL needed to combine the independent label sensitivity with the big-label ambition. XL had made a quantum leap, from being passive backers of others' creativity to creating two classic albums, The xx's remarkable debut and Gil Scott-Heron's swan-song, from scratch, in our own modest facilities. We'd started again and XL felt like a new label.

When I asked Jamie xx to remix the Gil album, threads were tied together in a way that would spark even more energy.

Codrington Mews was becoming a more and more exciting place to be. There were some great interns, the quietest of whom was a south Londoner called Sampha Sisay. He would remind me of his inauspicious beginnings at the label the night he won the Mercury Prize for his album *Process* some eight years later, the second time Caius's Young Turks label had won this accolade.

For the first few months he was present in the building no one had known Sampha could sing, but Tic gradually helped his artistry emerge. Caius's entrepreneurial and artistic instincts were proving acute, and I was helping him as Martin had helped me. With Tic providing his trademark ego-less, elusive assistance, he would help Tahliah Barnett, an artist from south London who called herself first Twigs, then FKA twigs, to begin to carve out her own space on the Young Turks roster.

In 2010 Caius played me the minute-long video for the song 'French' by Tyler Gregory Okonma, aka Tyler, the Creator, of LA skate/rap collective Odd Future Wolf Gang Kill Them All, or OFWGKTA. Tyler had been making beats using Reason and FruityLoops since he was twelve, while wearing a Slipknot T-shirt to school and taking the abuse that went with it. This was a quintessential insider-outsider, influenced by jazz and soul but with a punk sensibility. We did a deal with him to release his debut album, since when he has revealed himself to be an auteur who transcends rap music, and launched TV shows, clothing lines and his own festival to become one of the most unlikely and brilliant artists and cultural entrepreneurs of our time.

In 2019, Tyler propositioned East Coast hip-hop gatekeeper Funkmaster Flex in an extraordinary freestyle on HOT 97's YouTube channel. The rap counter-revolution, from within, was televised, but not in a way even Gil could have foreseen.

Tyler's relationship with XL entailed no hands-on musical involvement on the part of the label. He made and delivered the *Goblin* album and XL put it out for him. The increasingly multi-faceted nature of the label was crystallising around the time we began working with Tyler, and a project that would require more personal input from me was simultaneously manifesting.

Damon Albarn and I met not through any music-related activity but at the local gym we both used to attend off Westbourne Grove. XL was soon releasing the soundtrack to his stage musical *Monkey: Journey To The West*, and Damon was contributing some synth work to the album I made with Gil. Damon had recorded with legendary soul singer and guitarist Bobby Womack on the Gorillaz album *Plastic Beach*, they'd toured it together and Bobby had asked Damon to help him make his own album. In light of my work with Gil, Damon felt like I might be a good production partner to get the best work out of Bobby, who had also not made a record for well over a decade.

The theory made sense. Damon's natural gifts for melody and his expressive piano playing felt like a natural fit with my ideas for rhythms, texture and samples, and we both loved Bobby and wanted to help him deliver something worthy of his immense talents. I knew this would be an opportunity to continue to deepen my learning. And though I had worked hard to get to this point, my creative journey was humdrum compared to the one Bobby had been on, his story reading a bit like that of soul music itself. From the humblest of beginnings, he became integral to a number of key moments in musical history.

A sickly child, Bobby Womack had grown up in grinding poverty in Cleveland, Ohio, walking eight miles to school each day. Both of his parents had fifteen siblings each. His disciplinarian father, Friendly, had been in a gospel singing group called the Voices of Love. Bobby and his four brothers started to imitate them, and seeing this their dad formed them into a gospel group which he named the Womack Brothers. Physical punishment ensued if any of them missed a day's singing practice. Bobby said his father scared the songs into them.

Sam Cooke, one of the most ground-breaking figures in musical history, an artist who broke through racial barriers in the US to have his music embraced by all, signed the Womack Brothers to his SAR label, and suggested that they rename themselves The Valentinos. They moved away from gospel. Their first secular recording, 'Lookin' For A Love', was a huge hit.

Friendly Womack was horrified and felt they had betrayed him and the church. They were ejected from the family home and moved to California. Bobby toured and recorded extensively with Sam Cooke, his idol and mentor, until Cooke was shot and killed on 11 December 1964. Bobby Womack, who played his guitar upside down and, like his friend and peer Jimi Hendrix, left-handed, went solo.

He would go on to create some of the greatest soul music of all time, including seventies classics like 'Across 110th Street' and 'Woman's Gotta Have It' and the songs I first heard on Robbie Vincent's Radio London show in the eighties, such as 'I Wish He Didn't Trust Me So Much' and 'If You Think You're Lonely Now'. Bobby played guitar on landmark recordings for Ray Charles, Aretha Franklin, Sly and the Family Stone and Elvis Presley. The Rolling Stones' first number one hit in the UK, 'It's All Over Now', was a cover of a song he wrote for The Valentinos, of which Bobby said, 'I didn't like them stealing my song until I saw the royalty checks come in.'

Bobby influenced musicians across five decades and didn't seem regretful about anything, but he'd seen a lot. His much older first wife, Barbara, was Sam Cooke's widow. She shot Bobby twice when she found him carousing with her daughter Linda, who to be fair was actually close in age to Bobby.

Linda would end up marrying Bobby's brother Cecil, and forming Womack and Womack with him. In 1974 Bobby's younger brother Harry, the subject of Bobby's song 'Harry Hippie', was stabbed to death by his girlfriend. Bobby went on to lose two sons, one as a four-month-old baby, one to suicide at age twenty-one.

He spent much of the seventies in the company of Sly Stone and Ike Turner in LA and he told us once how the three of them had borrowed a police car and used it to drive to Watts and rob drug dealers. Bobby had been clean for some while by the time we collaborated but had spent a lot of his life extremely high.

He was a musical heavyweight, and while it felt like a gift to be invited into recording sessions with him in any capacity, I didn't take the challenge lightly, or make any assumptions about how easy or otherwise it might be. The reality was that he himself had been anxious about the prospect, not knowing what was going to be expected of him. What he found was that we simply wanted him to be himself. This is what I ask of any artist I work with – that they present their authentic self to the process and thus to the audience.

Bobby's experiences with the business side of music had always been mixed, at best. As well as my working on the album as co-producer, musician and writer, XL was a natural home for it, as Bobby did not have a record deal. He was excited to discover that there were no 'suits' to encounter, no one to question the product he would deliver on the grounds of its commercial viability or otherwise.

Once Bobby grasped that we would be able to deliver an undiluted product, and that we were genuine fans of his music and just wanted to help him present the strongest possible vision, the sessions took on a life of their own, Bobby saying it was the most relaxed he'd ever felt in the studio. And working with Bobby was a more relaxed experience for me than working with Gil. The energy was lighter, partly because I was sharing the responsibility with Damon, but also because Bobby was a less intense character.

I was in awe of his talent, but I'm in awe of the talents of all the artists I've worked with. If I'm not, I shouldn't really be working with them. I continued to explore the textures, snippets of sampled vocal and dusty percussion I'd been investigating as backdrops for Gil. Bobby's phrasing, and the timbre of his voice, were wonderful. There's an audible world-weariness, but the record we would make accurately mirrors the process of making it, in that the sound is airier than the place Gil and I went.

Bobby spoke of spirituals one day, and offered to play us one. At the end of the song 'Deep River', we knew it was a perfect take, and told him it should be part of the album. He asked if it was commercial enough. I told him that didn't matter. Bobby looked at Damon, seeking reassurance. Damon confirmed that he agreed with my view. Bobby, glancing at us both, said something that will always stay with me: 'So y'all are that free?'

I'd sought out liberation through music, and here was one of the greatest musical talents of all time pointing out to me that I had found it. And now not only did I have the privilege of self-sufficient artistic and commercial space, but I was able to extend the benefits of it to someone like Bobby Womack, who had always deserved creative freedom, but never really had it. Meanwhile, the label was also extending that freedom to a young talent like Tyler, the Creator, enabling him to express himself in as radical a way as he saw fit. Bobby's comment gave me a new appreciation of what I had, and of the possibilities of what could be achieved.

I found a sample of Bobby's mentor Sam Cooke talking about the process of ageing as an artist. I knew that this would prompt a response from Bobby, so I introduced it to the sessions as a writing tool as much as anything else, but Bobby fell in love with the sound and feeling of it and we included it on the album itself. It struck me that this song would be best rendered as a duet, and XL A&R Imran Ahmed suggested a new female singer from LA who happened to be in town, an artist called Lana Del Rey, who was yet to release a record but had put a song called 'Video Games' on YouTube.

Imran had originally been a music journalist, and I had been impressed by his articulacy when I saw him on a panel at an event held by AIM, the Association of Independent Music. I had then bumped into him walking through a field at Glastonbury, and convinced him to leave *NME* and try his luck as an A&R person at XL.

Soon, Imran brought a New York four-piece called Vampire Weekend to the label, co-led by Ezra Koenig, a knowing and gifted lyricist, vocalist and guitarist of Hungarian-Jewish descent, and Rostam Batmanglij, an equally talented producer, writer and multi-instrumentalist of Iranian heritage. Their sound borrowed heavily from different sources, and they combined this magpie approach with a bookish intelligence that echoed Talking Heads.

There were initially obvious African influences on their sound.

Rather than claiming authenticity, Ezra stated that he'd been influenced by Paul Simon's *Graceland* album when growing up. It was a provocative yet disarming comment, and when Ezra hopped onstage with Toronto punk band Fucked Up at a twelve-hour marathon hardcore show in New York, wearing his trademark preppy outfit of plaid shirt tucked into belted chinos, said, 'What's up, nerds?' and launched into two incongruous punk covers, it struck me that subtle provocation was a central part of his work.

His confidence and attitude would be key to the band's success. There was much about Vampire Weekend that could be criticised and debated; but they seemed okay with that. There are always going to be a lot of opinions. And just because someone's outraged doesn't mean they're right. Vampire Weekend's sophomore album was XL's first self-released US number one album.

Imran would also introduce Jai Paul to me and XL. Meeting Jai on my fortieth birthday I knew a wizard when I saw one, his music both immediate and unlike anything I'd ever heard, possessed of an otherness which only the greatest musicians and producers can capture. When his unfinished album *Bait Ones* leaked in 2013 (no one was sure how, but Jai said that quite a few people had access to his music between 2010 and 2013) it was a disaster of incalculable proportions to Jai, a sonic perfectionist. He finally felt comfortable to stop stemming the leak in 2019, and the unfinished album was made available. He might not agree but *Bait Ones*, even in its unfinished form, titled *Leak 04-13*, is a masterpiece.

As a fan of soul music Lana Del Rey responded to the question of whether she would like to record a song with Bobby Womack as we had hoped – 'When should I get there?' Her voice and writing were perfect. She had a sultry and enigmatic presence and Bobby loved collaborating with her.

While Bobby's guitar work was by his own admission not as slick as it had been at his playing peak, his singing voice was undiminished. He also proved to be extremely open to modern production techniques, surprising us all with his enthusiasm for pushing things sonically, our having assumed that we might need to be more reverential, and present his voice in a setting that was somewhat traditional.

I managed to include Gil in the proceedings by sampling him talking about TV evangelism on the intro to the song 'Stupid', and the majestic Malian vocalist Fatoumata Diawara joined us on 'Nothing Can Save Ya'. We ended up with a lot of material of extremely high quality, so much so that one of the most successful experiments didn't make it on to the album, a song called 'Hold The River Down'. Bobby is at his most evocatively nostalgic on this recording.

Bobby said that in getting to know me, he had been surprised to discover a musician when he'd expected a record executive, and asked me if I'd be up for touring the record with him. I responded in the affirmative, perhaps not thinking that it would actually occur, but a few months later I found myself rehearsing with Bobby and Damon in New York. Despite the combined experience of the people involved, we were a new band, with the strengths and weaknesses that go with that. We had enthusiasm but were far from a well-oiled unit.

We would get to find out whether what we had put together was working, live on network TV, when we played on *Late Night with Jimmy Fallon* on NBC. This would be my first musical TV appearance since *Top of the Pops*, peak-rave, some twenty years earlier. I knew that no one would really care how I performed except me, that Bobby was the attraction and we were there to make him look good, but some nerves were inevitable.

Bobby arrived on time and in good shape for the afternoon run-through at 30 Rockefeller Plaza. We played the intro to the album's title track, 'The Bravest Man In The Universe', and Bobby missed his cue, completely failing to come in. This was a concern. As his band, now we had something to feel nervous about. We had a short and finite time slot in which to run through our songs, and in the second run-through Bobby was no more present. He sang few actual words and just murmured vaguely along to the music. Bobby seemed to feel nothing was wrong and the camera rehearsal had gone fine, and was off for a rest before the actual show.

I consulted with Damon; what could we do? He was unfazed, and suggested we gather our bandmates, Kwes, Jaleel Bunton (of TV on the Radio) and percussionist Remi Kabaka, get a bottle of wine and spend some time outdoors. It was, after all, a sunny day. I dozed off in Central Park. My debut US TV appearance was taking on an increasingly dreamlike quality.

We rented two tuk-tuks, split ourselves into teams and raced each other through the busy Manhattan streets, resulting in much hilarity and a collision as we neared 30 Rockefeller Plaza. Kwes's knee got bashed up but minor injuries aside we were having so much fun that the spectre of the nerve-racking rehearsal we had experienced receded.

When it came time for the actual performance, Bobby was present and acute in his delivery. I suspect that in some unconscious way he did not wish to waste any of his creative and performative energy on a mere run-through. The fact that this had terrified us as his backing band was not really his concern.

A few days later we performed on the Canal+ music show *L'Album de la Semaine* in Paris. Lana joined us, she and Bobby touchingly holding hands throughout their performance of the song with the Sam Cooke spoken word sample, 'Dayglo Reflection', helping each other through the performance.

It was great, but when we were sitting in a Parisian bar afterwards I suggested that we needed to get out of the sterile TV studio environment, and that Bobby needed a real live audience, in a club, at night.

We were headed back to London to perform on the BBC show, *Later . . . with Jools Holland*. A small show for friends and family was duly booked at Notting Hill Arts Club, home of my favourite club, Yo-Yo. What a night that was, among musicians I had massive respect for, playing for an audience of our loved ones. This mini tour with Bobby was one of the warmest and most unexpectedly beautiful periods of my working life.

An interesting brush with insightful criticism came during

this phase. The album was praised by critics and was named *Q* magazine's album of the year; we had a great day out with Bobby at the Q Awards ceremony. But I was interested that one review, while positive about many aspects of the album, questioned the production techniques used. Specifically, the writer queried how well-suited some of the sounds were to Bobby's voice. This hit home for me.

While Bobby (as well as Damon and I) loved everything we made for the album, at one point I'd wondered if the music suited Bobby as well as it ought - as much as the gentler, warmer sounds that enveloped his voice on his seventies albums. Of course, we didn't want to make something mushy, and we didn't want to compete with the seventies. Our approach was creatively more ambitious than that, and that's what Bobby wanted, a more modern context, otherwise people could go and listen to an old album of his. But from this review I picked up a technique that's stayed with me and informs all my recording work; it's not enough for the singer to love the music - does the music love them?

At the time we met, Bobby had something more to say. He felt that he had been spared to tell his story; all his peers were gone. It's doubtful that Bobby or Gil actually knew that they were making their last records, but then they wouldn't have been unaware of the possibility. In 'Deep River' Bobby sang: 'I ain't got that much longer to stay here.' And Gil's final words in 'On Coming From A Broken Home (Part 2)', the last song on the last album he made, are this: 'God bless you, mama, and thank you.'

CENTRE OF THE EARTH

In 2010 I spent a week in Ethiopia with a crew of Western musicians from different disciplines, from grime artists Bashy and Kano through electronic producer Bullion, to experimental New York musician Joan As Police Woman and Red Hot Chili Peppers bassist Flea. The trip had a deepening effect on my musicality which was hard to quantify but dramatic. The visit was organised by Africa Express, which could be described as an amorphous system of informal cultural and musical exchange. But these words don't really communicate much. Damon Albarn came up with the idea, and it's about experience.

When I told Gil I was going to Ethiopia he asked me why. I said to learn, and to play music. He asked me which instrument I planned to take. When I said my MPC, he seemed amused. 'Show them how that thing works,' he suggested, 'and they might show you the Ark of the Covenant.'

While I was in Addis Ababa, *I'm New Here* was released to great response, and I got a message saying it had become Gil Scott-Heron's first Top 10 album. By now, in collaboration with the cast of characters who were inhabiting the XL HQ in Codrington Mews, we had actually built something close to my once far-fetched vision of a label that echoed Island Records' heyday. It felt good. But there is no satisfaction to be had from standing and gazing at an edifice one has built. The fun is in the process. So, by the time the label existed in the form I had dreamed of, it was time for me to let go a bit.

It was important that XL continued to develop, but I was never actually in control anyway. That feeling is illusory. I increasingly was able to see that things were happening via me, not because of me, and it was actually important to stay out of the way.

All our endeavours, however it may look, are collaborative. My name is on this book but it would not exist without the editor, the agent and all the people who populate it. The artist's solo album is leaning on the engineer, the producer, the manager and all the people the artist has relationships with. A record label is a completely collaborative venture. It's about the team and what you bring to it.

Ethiopia was perhaps my first experience of truly liberated, open and fully collaborative music-making and it changed my whole outlook on creativity.

To visit Ethiopia is to access, by means of a flight taking little more than seven hours from London, a culture of incredible beauty and power, with a somehow feminine energy and a subtly beautiful aesthetic expressed through music, art, food and dance. The capital Addis Ababa was electric, and I was moved to tears hearing manzuma singers in the walled Muslim city of Harar.

I have played various shows with Africa Express since, in venues such as La Cigale in Paris in 2010, where the Cameroon, Ivory Coast and Ghana World Cup soccer teams were part of the wildly enthusiastic audience at this World Cup send-off party, and on stages at festivals including Roskilde in Denmark in 2015 and at the Festa Dos Mundos in Galicia, Spain. I play MPC, synth or any of my variety of electronic noise-making devices and, while I find myself among virtuoso musicians of a level I will never reach, I am able to contribute something, as is anyone with the necessary level of openness. There is a loose spirit of communality and improvisation in these events which can be hard to find in the structured and codified music world. The effect on the musicians who participate is often transformative.

In 2012 we chartered a train and took it around the UK, a hundred musicians playing six shows in one week, in Middlesbrough, Glasgow, Manchester, Cardiff and Bristol, and finally in London's King's Cross. Prior to this Damon had begun to contemplate a trip to Kinshasa, for us to record what became the DRC Music album for Warp records, providing an educational experience for us and a platform for local musicians. The aim was to record an album in one week; because all the producers attending had their own laptop-based recording facilities, multiple sessions occurred simultaneously for the duration of the trip, and remarkably we were able to meet our deadline.

So many elements of this trip were unknown before embarking on it that most producers invited declined to come. It was just too hard for a lot of people to get their head around. But that created a mechanism in itself, in that the producers attending had been willing to take a leap of faith, so there was an atmosphere of creative courage which infused the whole venture. I'm not sure that any pop star in British music history, having achieved mainstream success on the level that Damon did in the nineties with Blur, has used his position to attempt such interesting and unpredictable endeavours, and this venture was typical of that spirit.

Most important of all were the local musicians we met and recorded – Nelly Liyemge, who duetted with Damon on a song called 'Halo', Tout Puisant Mukalo, Jupiter and Bokatola System, Yende Bongongo and Loi X Liberal. There was an open spirit of collaboration and a clear opportunity for everyone involved to learn something. The phrase 'music transcends all language and cultural barriers' would have seemed to me to be a cliché prior to this trip, but to be able to record in Kinshasa, the centre of Africa, the centre of the earth, the birthplace of rhythm, was mind-expanding for everyone. It impacted each of us on a deep level.

If you grew up listening to jazz, blues, pop, rock, rap, R&B or modern classical music, you have heard a large amount of African music. Slave spirituals are the biggest influence on twentieth-century music. It is an example of pain being alchemised and turned into art, as are the songs and comedy written and performed by post-Holocaust Jews.

My ongoing musical education has had a reverse chronology to the order in which the music was created. I heard first pop, and then hip-hop, going on to jazz and blues, and African music. The time spent developing some awareness of these foundational genres has provided me with a deeper understanding of what happens in current music.

I see myself as a student and always will. What any individual knows about music will always be dwarfed by what they don't. Anyone who sees it otherwise is effectively creating a full stop for themselves. As a creative person you can never stand still. Instinct, and the moment, is all. One day in Kinshasa I saw an aged yellow and red sign on the outside of a nondescript apartment block which said 'Residence La Revolution'. I asked the cab driver to stop and I leapt out to photograph it. When I got home, I hired a movie prop company to make an identical copy of it. Now I sit underneath it in my studio every day.

On our return to London, Damon and I didn't stop playing and recording, beginning what became Damon's solo album *Everyday Robots*. As a fan of Damon's more melancholy output, songs like Blur's 'Out Of Time' and 'Green Fields' from *The Good, The Bad & The Queen* album, I was keen for him to express himself in specifically personal terms on this record. I had certain samples that I thought might set the scene.

Damon, a prolific writer, gave me ninety demos and I selected which we would pursue. For the months we spent making the album we cocooned ourselves in Damon's studio, maintaining a hazy and introspective atmosphere throughout. We shut out the rest of the world for the duration of the recording, and the record has a certain specific feeling partly because of this.

Because I was being hired by Damon to produce a record for him that would be released on Parlophone, I also saw this as a break from working for XL, a chance to experience different approaches, perhaps an occasion where I would have less control, and I relished that. Given that this was a Damon Albarn solo album, I was keen that a lot of him, perhaps more than ever before, was audible.

He was also encouraging my self-expression. I had purchased a collection of spoken-word albums from Intoxica on Portobello Road just before it sadly closed down. One of them was by jazz beat poet Lord Buckley, who I'd never heard of before but had influenced artists from Dylan to Beefheart.

His quote, 'We didn't know where we was going, but we knew where we was, wasn't it' seemed to voice one of the themes we were exploring on this album, and his voice is the first thing the listener hears when playing the album, followed by a string loop courtesy of Béla Bartók, before the sound of Damon's piano is heard, my home-made percussion underneath, his chords shifting around the repetitive drone of the strings.

Damon was keen to explore notions of how technology might be starting to pervade our lives in unprecedented ways, and this is explored throughout.

I still did not have my own recording facility, and it was during the course of making *Everyday Robots* that I finally clarified what I specifically needed in my own studio. A small house, a sacred space, entirely dedicated to the process of recording music, that would feel simultaneously intimate and expansive. I spoke to a local property vendor who explained that I would never get permission to build this, and that there were exactly two local properties that could potentially be used for this purpose, and if I wanted, he would ask them if they wished to sell. Neither landlord wanted to, but the owner of The Copper House, a property that met the picture I had in my mind so perfectly that it felt like cosmic forces were at work, said that she would like to meet me nonetheless.

From the moment I walked in I knew this was the site of my future endeavours, and I told her as much. She looked at me quizzically and said that she had been thinking that, for inexplicable reasons, she should move to Scandinavia, and had resolved to wait for a sign that this was indeed the case. I was the sign.

The creation of my own full-service studio within the walls of this house in London was not to be taken lightly. Matt Thornhill had by now helped me execute some unlikely manoeuvres. Seeing a fantastical animated instrument in a Horrors video drawn by Pete Fowler, I told Matt that we needed to turn this imaginary wonder, the 'Pyramid Synth', into a real instrument. He didn't flinch, putting together a team who managed to execute this remarkable technical feat, and this process was a prototype in itself: for the new studio to manifest, we would need to turn fantasy into reality.

In 2011 I had visited Kerala in southern India and passed through an area called Jew Town. I came across some incredible and huge pieces of carved wood, covered in mystical images of Hindu deities and scenes from nature. I gambled that these might work in the studio as acoustic treatment, and would simultaneously lend the place a hallowed atmosphere.

When I first entered the studio on its completion, I put on 'Original Nuttah' by Shy FX feat. UK Apache, and noted that we were missing something at around 20 hertz. These are beloved frequencies, the rates of vibration which are most important in music that thrives on pirate radio and sound systems. An acoustic engineer was duly summoned who confirmed my diagnosis. This resulted, happily, in the installation of bigger speakers. One of the greatest and most overlooked joys of the studio is simply to be able to listen to whatever music you happen to fancy at that moment at great volume and with tremendous clarity. Any day where this occurs cannot be thought of as a total waste of time.

I have spent almost every working day in The Copper House since we converted it into a studio, and have had collaborative, communal experiences there which will stay with me forever. The work we do in this space feels like it is just beginning.

NOW THAT'S WHAT I CALL
MUSIC 2055

Back in the mid-2000s a scene had developed in London around a handful of clubs, including Blue Flowers in Chiswick and Caius Pawson's Young Turks night. The scene itself had no name. People attempted to call it Thamesbeat but this tag was so weak that it didn't stick. The unusual failure of the music press to come up with an umbrella term for this little world may have actually helped the artists involved. They were perhaps more able to create their own identities without being overly associated with each other.

The scene contained young musicians including Florence Welch, Adele Adkins, Jack Peñate and a host of bands including the Mystery Jets, The Maccabees and Larrikin Love. The solo artists were mostly taking their cues from soul music; the bands were following the UK guitar tradition which had proved so fruitful for so long but was starting to reach exhaustion as a resource.

This new London scene didn't have the weight and heft of the grime scene, but it contained some talented and savvy individuals who went on to make a large dent in musical culture. Myspace was starting to play a part in how people heard music, but really this was one of the last pre-internet moments. The four signings XL made from this scene, mainly via A&R man Nick Huggett, illustrate the vastly different eventualities that can occur from a series of related and similar events.

Jack Peñate came first, via Young Turks. He was an excellent song-writer, and would appear onstage performing his compositions alone with an electric guitar in a style that reminded me of Billy Bragg. In the audience a young hopeful called Ed Sheeran looked on, working out a plan that he would execute to staggering commercial effect a few years later. Jack's debut featured his best friend on backing vocals, an artist he was convinced had world-beating talent. Adele Adkins.

As well as playing his part in the development of the two crowning commercial success stories of the current British music scene, Jack signed to XL and released two albums. The first,

RICHARD RUSSELL

Matinee, was well-written but relied too heavily on a style of 'indie' record production that was already beginning to sound dated. Jack would perhaps have been better off recording the songs simply accompanied by his own electric guitar playing, as Billy Bragg did for his first album. I failed to listen to my instinct and battle harder for this approach at the time.

The second Jack Peñate album, *Everything Is New,* was a collaborative affair made with rising producer Paul Epworth, and was a fully realised piece of work that stood up well to anything else of its moment but did not catch on commercially, at least not to the extent of albums by the artists Jack had been associated with and influenced.

The second signing XL made from this scene was Jack's friend, Adele. Then came Tom Hull, a singer-songwriter who called himself Kid Harpoon.

Tom struggled to fully capture the magic of his writing and live performances in the studio. Even Trevor Horn, who ended up helming Tom's debut album *Once,* couldn't quite nail down the material. It dawned on Tom that he may have been better suited to composing than performing. He moved to LA and became a songwriter and collaborator for artists including Florence and the Machine and Harry Styles.

The last of XL's four signings from this scene was Cajun Dance Party, a five-piece band from a leafy part of north-west London. They were led by a magnetic frontman called Daniel Blumberg and a gifted guitarist called Robbie Stern. They looked and sounded great and were brimming with ideas and enthusiasm. They were in their teens and surrounded by ambitious and savvy management, lawyers and parents. The music industry conferred the mantle of 'next big thing' on them, a scrum ensued for their signature and XL was the label chosen to do the inflated deal that everyone else was also desperate to do.

The whole courting process had made me feel uncomfortable. It didn't sit well to pitch the label to a group this young. It seemed desperate. But no one was telling me to do this. I was being led by my ambition and hunger for more success. Ego.

As the deal was about to be signed some part of me knew that it was a mistake. There had been talk of the band finishing their studies, presumably at the behest of their parents. In a situation like this, timing is everything, and sacrifices have to be made. You can't become a force in music while doing it part-time. You have to live and breathe it.

Lead singer Daniel was all-in, and I could see he was committed to the music, but around him I detected rationalisation and compromise. It hit me that they would never achieve the type of success that their deal required, but rather than pulling out of the arrangement at the last moment, I decided to go with the flow and leave it to fate. At the same time I made a decision. I was not going to be involved in this type of scenario again. I was a free man and I needed to act like one.

I don't think I ever would have made an album with Gil Scott-Heron without my going through the demeaning experience of chasing this bunch of teenagers around, well-meaning though they were. I was participating in a process I was not only completely uncomfortable with but actually suspected was doomed to failure. Why was I doing this? Ego.

The huge deal was the peak of the process. It was downhill all the way from there. Eventually, the band was due one substantial final payment; but this was not payable if they split up. So, if that event did occur, they were going to need to appear to still be a unit, just long enough to get the record company to cough up. So keen was I to be done with the whole sorry saga that we decided to act dumb, play along and pay up. We'd made our bed.

Yet somehow all ended well. Daniel Blumberg went on to prove his artistic commitment, launching new band Yuck and subsequently signing to our old allies Mute to record the acclaimed album *Minus* under his own name.

Guitarist Robbie also continued his musical explorations, participating in a number of projects and sitting in on sessions at my studio from time to time, all on a part-time basis while qualifying in the more parent-friendly arena of law.

The raft of signings in this era saw XL wandering far from its original aesthetic, with mixed results, from mediocre to spectacularly great. While the label was engaged in attempting to deliver commercial results on a big level, it felt like something of a saving grace to also continue to release underground records, as it originally was set up to do, and treat them with just as much care as the records with more obvious commercial upside. This policy provided benefits for both types of artist, and was in some ways the ultimate evolution of the hybrid concept of the label I hit on in the nineties.

In 2006 XL released an album called *The World Is Gone* by an artist calling themselves Various Production. The name they chose would pretty much ensure their anonymity and I thought that was in itself an interesting experiment. The two producers who comprised Various were making a sound that reflected grime but incorporated more spacey production and yet deeper bass: some would label this music 'dubstep', and Burial's eponymous debut, released the same year, would also be labelled as such. Dubstep was always a clumsy term.

The moment when the music belonged, more or less, to the FWD>> night - first located at the Velvet Rooms on Charing Cross Road and then at Plastic People in Shoreditch - and a handful of forums felt relatively brief, although there were actually eight years between FWD>> launching and Skream's remix of La Roux charting, which was perhaps the first dubstep crossover moment. This first scene that emerged in the internet era was so quickly exposed, commercialised and Americanised that it seemed to turn into something else before it had firmly established what it was in the first place. It turned out that grime would be the last movement to enjoy the space to incubate in the pre-internet darkness.

On tracks like 'Circle Of Sorrow' and particularly their classic 'Hater', Various married folk inflections with futuristic rhythms to make one of the unsung classics in the XL catalogue, records I'm equally proud of as the hits.

The most special artists are often somewhat unsung.

The first great female artist on XL was a producer and composer of electronic music from Iran by way of West Hampstead named Leila Arab. I have worked with an extraordinary series of female musicians. Merrill Beth Nisker, aka Peaches, made great records like 'Fuck The Pain Away' and her explorations of gender identity were both prescient and fun. MIA, the next ground-breaking female artist on XL, was herself heavily influenced by Peaches. Then Adele arrived, way more political and mould-breaking than she was taken for. I'm currently collaborating with twin-sister duo Ibeyi as they explore spiritual themes of ancestry, faith and race in their four languages of English, Spanish, French and Yoruba, aiming to facilitate them in much the same way Chris Blackwell did for Grace Jones in the early eighties.

Leila had released the excellent *Like Weather* album on Aphex Twin's label Rephlex in 1997, then signed to XL in 1999. She has said that she chose to work with XL because her music was meant to be 'Now That's What I Call Music 2055', and that she could see a link to what I was attempting to do.

But XL was still a dance label at this time, and Leila was making actual art, and we struggled to fully comprehend what she was doing, possibly even making a bit of a hash of releasing her album *Courtesy Of Choice*, though by her own admission she is not a person who always makes things easy for herself, or others. Leila, a sonic visionary and one of the most insightful artists I have ever come across, is by nature a confrontational teller of truths that people may or may not wish to hear. She says that during this period, when I told her that I planned to transform XL into a home for the most artistic, singular and powerful of artists, she thought to herself, 'Joker'.

When this unlikely outcome did come to pass, though, she said, 'Absolutely fucking fair play', adding she recognised my commitment to the thread that linked the seemingly disparate music the label was releasing, and the formidable nature of the partnership between Martin and me.

In 2016 Leila pointed out that XL had never paid her the final part of the advance that had been agreed twenty years earlier for her album, because she had never asked for it. When signing to XL she had requested that we license some rights to EMI/Virgin-backed label Source. They were as keen on her music as XL, and were able to invest a far more substantial sum – five times as much as the XL advance – for the right to release her album in mainland Europe.

She says she chose to keep things cheap for the independent

label, and 'Robin Hood' the major. Subsequently she had never invoiced for the final tranche of the XL funds, saying she hadn't enjoyed the experience of working with us and wished to bring it to a close. But that was then, and by 2016 she had reappraised the situation, pointing out that she had fulfilled her part of the deal, and the record had been released, and she would like the cash. What she said made sense to me. Martin and Ben also thought it was only fair to pay up, and I didn't need to talk them into handing it over. They could see that this was the correct course of action.

XL's original boss, Tim Palmer, was always supportive of me, and I will always be grateful to him for that. Both he and Nick saw that I had potential. Martin Mills was not initially visible to me in his role with the label, and nor was I to him, and he in fact was opposed to Tim hiring another person, which happened to be me.

Previously a talented A&R person in his own right, Martin had sacrificed his personal involvement with artists and record-making in order to facilitate the creative activities of XL and other labels, allowing each to concentrate on working closely with artists. His approach was part razor-sharp business, part big-picture mentorship, part altruism. A born chess master and painstaking negotiator, his thoroughness can seem intransigent in a world where others might do deals on a handshake or the back of a serviette. But the hallmark of his work has always been attention to detail.

Early on I used to take his detachment for indifference, but gradually I began to see him as a sort of Zen master in the material world. Martin and I were from day one blessed with a stroke of luck that any partnership needs: our skill sets are complementary. We are good at different things. He is stable where I am mercurial, patient where I am impetuous. He is possessed of an English gentleman's reserve, where I am governed by emotion; me an idealist with the accompanying lack of pragmatism, Martin a realist. He is ruled by head not heart, and I am the opposite. But we've both always had a high tolerance for risk, and a belief that things must be done the right way or not at all.

Not that our relationship has been without its ups and downs.

It has always been my natural inclination to try to transcend whatever limitations I have perceived to be imposed on me. Sometimes the things that are the making of us appear to be limiting us. Initially I perceived my limitations to be those imposed by outside forces: my family, suburbia and religion. I wanted to exist in a freer, more multi-cultural environment. Eventually, I would come to see all my limitations as self-imposed; this is where a journey of self-actualisation has to lead.

I have been through parallel processes personally and professionally. The label's first limitation was its platform; the scene we came from. We had to stop being a dance label and start being a record label. The scene birthed us but then began to limit us. Rave made us. Then we needed to free ourselves from its shackles.

I saw the major labels, working with a creatively broader roster of artists, enjoying greater commercial success with their releases than XL did. It was understandable but I did not want to accept it. Not when our records were increasingly so good. I wanted XL to be able to compete on every level. So, when The Prodigy achieved the worldwide mainstream success they did, it should have proved to me that given the right artist and circumstances we could achieve anything we wanted.

However, in the early 2000s I started to imagine that Martin and Beggars were holding XL back. I began to project my frustrations on to Martin, and feel resentment towards him. I became negative in my outlook towards the work he and his organisation were doing for us. It would keep me up at night.

Martin, like the two other Taurus types in my life, Adele, and my brother-in-law and collaborator, the visionary designer known as Maharishi Hardy Blechman, is possessed of an unshakable inner confidence that can be hard for a sensitive Piscean type like me to comprehend. The way Martin dealt with my increasing negativity and complaints about the work Beggars was doing for XL was classically Taurean. He simply called my bluff. Until that point, I had not even known I was bluffing.

What I was in fact doing was projecting my fears of failure on to him and expressing them as negativity, doubt and complaints. He wrote me a letter saying that if I was not happy with how our partnership was working, which from my constant complaints he deduced to be the case, we should simply call time on it. His punk roots became visible. If you don't like what's going on, he was saying, end it. No compromise. It was a statement of his own confidence and independence, and his message was clear: despite the many things we had achieved together, and the future endeavours we could probably also successfully embark on, if I didn't believe in our partnership, it should end.

It was shocking but inspirational stuff, and it woke me up, laying the ground for what has so far been another twenty years of fruitful collaboration. Daniel Miller said to me that the reason none of us should resent Martin's success is that Martin has always done the things the rest of us could not be bothered to. Not only does he do that, but he does it with an attention to detail that everyone benefits from. Everyone gets paid properly. That's not to be taken lightly in our world.

Most great partnerships falter and the reason tends to be ego. This is what was happening here, but my ego was put back in check for me. I was snapped back into reality. There is some natural human tendency to behave as badly as we can get away with.

When I felt ready to fully reimmerse myself in music and creativity, the areas I love and where I am happiest and most productive, Ben and Martin were both understanding and supportive. Ben is a calm and steadying presence, like Martin also with strong musical instincts which he does not necessarily shout about or always get credit for. Ben started out as an aspiring dance music producer and DJ, and the practical, audience-focused nature of these experiences has held him in good stead.

He rose from an entry-level promotional position to become managing director of XL and is very much the architect of the ambitious marketing side of the label's activities, contributing much to Adele's stellar success, as she was always quick to recognise. He is possessed of some preternatural calm, and an ability to find and nurture positivity.

NOT DARK YET

Left to right: me, Dad, Jay Electronica, Mum

In June of 2013 I collapsed and was hospitalised. I started losing the ability to move and gradually found myself paralysed. All movement from the neck down ceased. I was forty-two years old at the time and I'd been feeling odd for a few weeks. I had been having some strange dreams. Jack Kreitzman, my grandpa who had died some thirty years ago, had come to me in my sleep one night, serene, perfectly vivid, and said, 'I've got the key if you want it.' In the morning I drew a key on the wall.

A few days later, on Sunday 9 June, Jada and I had been watching *Matilda* at London's Cambridge Theatre. She was four at the time, already showing her mum's strength of character. I was feeling a strange tingling sensation in different parts of my body and was struggling through the performance. During the interval I slumped to the floor in the theatre foyer. I fell asleep when I got home. When I woke up my speech was scrambled, and Esta called an ambulance. I thought I was wandering around the hospital in a fairly cheerful and functional state, when the nurses pointed out that I was falling over more than I was walking, and confined me to bed.

The testing began. My kidneys and liver were not functioning properly and my blood pressure was bizarrely low. There was confusion as to the cause. Some aspects fell into certain medical categories, but each potential diagnosis contradicted the last. I was moved to the Critical Care Unit at University College Hospital. Some signs indicated that I had a neurological illness and that my nervous system was under attack from my immune system.

As well as extremely low blood pressure I had hyponatremia, meaning a lack of sodium in my system. I could not get upright without passing out. If I tried to sit up, my vision faded to black, as if a pair of curtains was being drawn.

After a couple of weeks, the doctors were fairly sure I had Guillain-Barré syndrome, a neurological complaint suffered by perhaps one in every 100,000 people. The initial phase of GBS can be life-threatening for a percentage of people who contract it, but mortality rates have decreased dramatically in recent decades as the syndrome has become more readily identified and thus treated. Most GBS-related deaths come from respiratory failure caused by the paralysis of the muscles necessary to breathe.

It's a serious condition, but if you develop Guillain-Barré Syndrome-type symptoms, a diagnosis of Guillain-Barré Syndrome is good news, in a way. Because if you have these particular physical manifestations, you are far less likely to recover from almost any other illness with a similar profile.

There was no certainty, though. It seemed possible that I was suffering from two other neurological disorders, Miller Fisher syndrome and Bickerstaff's brainstem encephalitis, and the presence of symptoms associated with each of these three somewhat different conditions was creating a confusing prognosis. What was agreed was that I had acute autonomic failure affecting cardiovascular, sudomotor, urinary bladder and gastrointestinal function. In a situation like this, the patient has decisions to make, and if the patient is not capable of making them it falls to their family.

In music industry terms, the patient is the artist. The immediate family member is the artist manager. The hospital is the record company. Your consulting physician is the A&R. The head of the hospital is like the head of the record company: it's unlikely you will ever meet him. He may or may not exist. Contrary to what we hope, and regardless of everyone's best intentions, the hospital will probably only be as good a machine as how it is operated.

Esta was trying to understand a baffling situation with serious implications. She was being asked to ascertain the correct courses of action and treatment, while managing the ongoing needs of our three children, at this time aged four, eight and ten. In this instance the managerial role is more difficult than the artistic one. Because, while medical storms raged around me, I found that things had become quiet. Quieter than at any other time in my life.

I initially thought I was transcending my physicality, occupying a higher plane. In the first two weeks in hospital, I surrendered and decided I was willing to accept any outcome. Given all the pointless things I've worried about in my life, at the point I was paralysed I found myself not worrying about it. I've always been an odd mixture of lazy and determined, and to be serene rather than struggling gave me some extra energy to help combat the illness. Then the treatment started in earnest.

I underwent plasmapheresis, a type of transfusion whereby blood is removed from the body and the plasma is separated from the cells before it is returned. Epidurals, or lumbar punctures, were used to remove spinal fluid. EMG tests were administered, wherein needle electrodes are applied in order to record the electrical activity produced by skeletal muscles.

Our nerves are protected by myelin sheaths, layers of fat that insulate us from what would otherwise be extreme pain whenever we are touched. These myelin sheaths disintegrated in my inert feet and legs. I am a sensitive person anyway. But this was ridiculous. Because I wasn't moving there was a risk of embolisms (aka blood clots) forming, so as well as taking anticoagulants, the nurses had to put stockings on my feet and legs. The donning of these items was an extraordinarily painful process. Just the touch of a sheet brushing my foot would cause acute pain. I would bite on my knuckles and scream silently.

I was normally cheerful in the daytime, but I felt a creeping terror at night, as I would encounter a sort of acute loneliness that I wasn't sure I was equipped to handle. It can be hard to sleep in hospitals, and as each night progressed, I would get more disorientated. Esta slept in a chair in my room some nights, and my close friends also did shifts.

When I mentioned to a doctor that I wasn't sleeping or, for that matter, going to the toilet, he said, 'Hospitals are like that.' I asked him to expand. As he exited the room to attend to what was doubtless one of the many desperately sick people he was trying to help on that day, he said, 'Hospitals are full of people not sleeping or shitting.'

However much hand sanitiser is used, hospitals are still full of germs. I caught ear and eye infections while I was there.

I became acutely sensitive to the nature of each of the nurses and doctors, grateful for their presence but overly alert to their auras, desperately happy to see one nurse or doctor and oddly saddened by another. Before I got ill, I had been devouring books on spirituality and familiarising myself somewhat with the previously alien idea of death. This happened around the time I turned forty. An interest in mortality occurring at this age isn't unusual.

Sogyal Rinpoche's *The Tibetan Book of Living and Dying*, Shunryu Suzuki's *Zen Mind, Beginner's Mind* and Seneca's *Letters from a Stoic* all had an impact on me. Eckhart Tolle's *The Power of Now* and *A New Earth* took on biblical significance. I read and reread these books. I had never consciously considered the spirit before.

The synagogue had played a significant part in my childhood, and the nightclub replaced it in my teens and twenties. I considered these two environments to be unrelated, opposite even, but they were both communal spaces where connection with something higher was sought out.

I had also begun making death-themed visual art, a series of canvases which were based on a directory of all the people I'd known who'd passed away. I'd experienced bereavement before this point, but had always previously put the deceased out of my mind as soon as I could. That I had engaged with the idea of mortality would be useful in accepting some of the feelings I had in hospital.

I believe I'd had some unconscious awareness that serious illness was shortly going to unfold. I'm glad it was not conscious awareness, which would probably have been harder to deal with than the actual events. The thought of bad things happening - the fear - can be way worse than the reality, at which point we're forced to cope.

I knew I had a catheter inserted in my penis to urinate, but that didn't explain everything. I began to wonder how I was defecating. The nurse's answer to my question was intriguing: 'You're not.' When I asked whether that was not a major problem, she said there were more serious issues at hand, and at this point it occurred to me that I was going to have to start actively fighting the illness, which was a far less appealing prospect than the relatively peaceful state of surrender I'd been in up to then. Surrendering is much easier than fighting, but the right strategy is dependent on situation and timing. If I wanted to take a shit – and it seemed like a good idea – I was going to have to work it out for myself. It turned out I wasn't able to execute this activity unaided. No amount of laxatives would work. Eventually, a male nurse had to put his hand up my rectum to extract some faeces. The indignities were piling up. Things were getting gnarly.

My weight was plummeting because my muscle mass was disappearing due to lack of movement. I was prescribed crisps and sweets. The cupboard full of jelly babies and bacon flavour Frazzles was a big upside for my children when they visited, Dexter particularly, his sweet nature matched by his sweet tooth.

Because of the lack of sodium in my body, I was only allowed a tiny amount of liquid per day, administered via sponges dipped in water that I was allowed to suck on. London was experiencing a heatwave in 2013 and I fantasised about glasses of water.

After a while I was told that there was danger of infection if my in-dwelling catheter continued to dwell. It had to be removed, and if I then couldn't urinate effectively without the aid of equipment I would have to self-catheterise several times a day – i.e. stick a tube up my own urethra. Things got competitive. I *had* to successfully urinate unaided. The output would be measured, and if I passed a certain amount, I would be free from catheterisation.

I have never been keener to pass a test – there was a lot riding on it – but I failed, so I had to start sticking a tube in my own member. On first attempt I couldn't get it in the pee hole – it would get stuck and wouldn't go up properly.

At 3am one night a male nurse was trying to get the tube up me, and it just wouldn't happen. It was getting gory. A fair bit of blood was coming from my penis. The fragile male ego struggles with catheterisation. We can withstand worse pain, but there's something about the discomfort of a tube going up the penis which just seems unacceptable.

As I lay there, blood dripping from my member, I had what I now recognise as a flash of insight, what Zen Buddhists call a moment of *satori*. I saw clearly an event that had occurred a few months earlier, performing with Bobby Womack at the Notting Hill Arts Club as part of his five-piece backing band. I was bashing away on my MPC, generating sub bass and crackly hi-hats. Bobby was singing his heart out – one of the greatest sounds ever. Damon was tracing beautiful melodies on his piano.

The audience was comprised of friends and family and the warmth in the room was palpable. I was at my happiest. It struck me that the current situation and the onstage scenario a few months earlier were both just passing moments in our existence. I realised that if you can see these moments for what they are, they are essentially the same. They are fleeting. Impermanent. Nothing is worth getting too attached to; because even the least spiritual person has to recognise that we are really not here for long.

I did not suddenly start feeling cheerful and completely transcend the miserable situation I was in, but I did find some space around the misery. And it pointed directly at something that is intrinsic to Buddhism, the idea that suffering leads to enlightenment. (After this, a Buddhist monk would quiz me about my beliefs and then ask why I didn't call myself a Buddhist, as I clearly believed in all the precepts of Buddhism. I said that I'd already left one organised religion and didn't wish to join another, preferring to inhabit my own bespoke spiritual ecosystem. He responded that it sounded more like a spiritual *ego* system. Cheeky monk.)

One of the more bizarre medical procedures was the tilt table test. Lying flat, I would be strapped to a wooden board that was gradually raised, a degree at a time, until I lost consciousness. The number of degrees achieved, blood pressure, pulse and blood oxygen saturation were measured. As ever, I tried to treat it like a competitive sport but as the table tilted upwards, I would encounter loss first of vision, and then of consciousness.

I was frequently having to blow into tubes so that my respiratory capabilities could be measured; again I went into this pursuing the gold medal every time, but my results were usually poor. I was weak.

The counterbalance to this loss of normalcy was that I felt extremely loved when I was in hospital. By Esta, my parents, my friends, my colleagues. I didn't feel alone.

And while it's seen as virtuous to value your health above your financial position, the financial position I was in (which I had always told myself did not mean anything) was helpful. I wasn't worrying about how to feed my family while I was laid low. It's offensive when wealthy people say money doesn't matter. In this situation it does. I saw it as clearly at this time as is imaginable.

My suffering was less because I was not worrying about my possibly permanent inability to work, as most other people in my ward were. I was in a National Health Service hospital, seeing NHS doctors and nurses, and any person in this country, regardless of their financial situation, is entitled to this care. As my mum had always told me, the NHS is a magnificent thing and any forces that threaten it are malignant.

I was moved to the National Hospital for Neurology and Neurosurgery on Queen Square, founded in 1860, one of the best neurological units in the world. London was there to catch me when I fell.

When I had suffered from depression in my late twenties, I felt isolated, and that feeling was actually worse than a potentially life-threatening condition like Guillain-Barré. Depression sufferers receive little sympathy, but this condition can also be life-threatening. Loneliness is hard to bear. We need each other.

The people around me were so unbelievably giving and generous. Hardy would come at 6.30am, before work, and sit with me. He intuited that I would benefit from massage and not only found a gifted masseur to come to the hospital but when they were not available took it upon himself to perform the task. The only time my legs would move during this period was when someone was moving them for me, so this type of therapy was invaluable.

I asked one of the attending doctors why, given what I saw as my healthy lifestyle, I had been struck with this illness. He seemed tickled. Imagine, he said, you are one of three people at a bus stop. One is a forty-a-day smoker. One is obese. The other is you, with your salads, your yoga. It is you who is getting Guillain-Barré syndrome, because Guillain-Barré syndrome doesn't care how clever you think you are.

Harsh, but fair, his response pointed at why medical practitioners never seem afraid of a drink and a cigarette. A healthy lifestyle is all well and good, but there's a whole bunch of serious afflictions out there that really don't care about our good intentions.

GBS provides the opportunity for a gently brutal return to health which lends itself to an optimistic outlook. At a low ebb one day, my positive mindset failed me and fear and self-pity began to set in. I voiced my sorrow to Dimitri and he dispelled it immediately, telling me if I wanted to complain he would wheel me around the ward and I could try complaining to my fellow patients, all stroke sufferers with a negligible chance of recovery compared to me. This kind of tough love was the most effective approach imaginable. It would not have been helpful for anyone around me to have been confirming to me how bad the situation was, whatever conversations they were having among themselves.

My parents were terrified, and I think in shock. The idea that their son was the one who would need looking after, as they approached their eighties, had understandably never occurred to them. Faith was necessary. Reality is overrated anyway.

There were backward steps as well. After six weeks in hospital I started to undergo tests to ascertain how I would cope with outside life. I attempted to prepare a light meal in a practice kitchen that was set up for this therapeutic function. I couldn't do it. All the physical actions necessary to prepare a tinned tuna salad proved beyond my capability and I became frustrated. It was a moment of reckoning. I was an invalid, and I considered that word. Not valid. I would not accept this.

I was utterly determined to recover, but a balance needed to be achieved. Like with anything else, you can want it too much. I overextended myself in an early attempt to walk unaided one night, deciding that I didn't need to wait for a nurse in order to visit the bathroom. I collapsed in the effort, coming round on a cold hospital floor, lucky not to have sustained a head injury in the fall.

I was allowed to spend a night at home as a test, a kind of dress rehearsal for life, but I passed out in the hallway outside my basement studio and, when I regained consciousness, had to drag myself up the staircase, calling for Esta. At that moment I felt desperate. My condition was that of an elderly, incapacitated person, and any time I didn't accept that reality I experienced an abject feeling of hopelessness. Control was the issue. I had lost control of my physical body, and when I tried to reject that notion a deep terror would grip me. The only option was acceptance. Otherwise a depression would have set in that would have dramatically hampered my recovery.

Initially, the hospital stipulated that access to me was limited to immediate family members, which in my case includes my close friends. When other friends and colleagues got in touch, they were politely told I didn't yet have the energy to receive visitors. The first person to ignore these instructions was Adele. She was upset and wanted to see for herself what was going on, so she simply turned up at the hospital. The effect of being exposed to her energy was remarkable. She had no interest in what she had been told was the correct behaviour; she wanted to see me, so she did that regardless of what the hospital rules were and it was helpful.

Damon was the next pop maverick to arrive unannounced, turning up at the hospital with soup he had made at home, a thoughtful, home-made gift that was welcome now my liquid intake was less restricted. It was somehow fitting that an attempted musical collaboration between Adele and Damon that occurred soon after this was a disaster. Two uncontrollable, beautiful forces of nature possessed of an unstoppable energy. It was just too much.

The surprise musical guest in the neurological unit was Bobby Womack. He'd been ailing himself recently and was recovering, though he would relapse and pass away almost exactly a year later, at the age of seventy. Our recent collaboration had been a pure joy and I had recognised a fellow sensitive Piscean when I met one. So I shouldn't have been surprised to see this giant of soul music turn up to visit me in the hospital, but I was honoured nonetheless. It was as uplifting at that moment as his music had been for me many times previously, and since.

I was initially not able to read, but was still helped out at this time by *The Tibetan Book of Living and Dying*. I'd absorbed this practical and useful tome before I was hospitalised and I could not have made a better investment than the time I spent doing that. Its second half is challenging to Western sensibilities, as the writer's belief in reincarnation is absolute; but my view on this subject changed radically when I considered a question posed in the book - is it any more amazing to be born twice than it is to be born once? And when we try to understand reincarnation by the only methods we have, such as thought and analysis, is it not like dogs trying to consider mathematics? By sniffing? Mathematics exists, but it is way beyond the conceptive ability of the canines. Some things are beyond our limited powers of comprehension but that doesn't mean they are fallacy.

By the time I'd been in hospital for two months I was able to take a few steps. My rehabilitation was underway, but I had become a little institutionalised. I was scared of being in the outside world. This fear somehow pointed at what was necessary. I had to face it.

I knew I'd be better off at home than in the hospital. The Dorset countryside would be the centre of the healing process for me. On 1 August 2013, with the help of Nick Goldsmith and Dimitri Doganis, friends who have been as close to me as brothers for thirty years, I was discharged. Nick gave me a frame containing ticket stubs he had kept from four concerts we went to together as teenagers: Stetsasonic at the Electric Ballroom, LL Cool J at

Brixton Academy, Trouble Funk at Hammersmith Odeon, and Gil Scott-Heron at the Town & Country Club in Kentish Town with a moving message on the back welcoming me back into the world.

It would be a different world. For one thing I was in a wheelchair and it wasn't clear when I would be back on my feet.

The support of my family and friends would play an enormous part in my recovery; Esta's selflessness astounded me and will be with me forever.

Some months later I would visit a fellow GBS sufferer at the same hospital, a younger man who did not have the same level of support as I did, and I could see starkly how much more difficult his situation was. Back at home, the rehabilitation process was often frustrating but always tempered with relief at being out of the hospital.

I knew I had to re-enter the world, frightening though that was. I began to work with physiotherapists, most of whom were incredibly patient and helpful. One was less encouraging. She said that although my myelin sheaths had not regenerated yet, at least they'd only disintegrated in my feet and lower legs, whereas some people were afflicted by the loss of this crucial protection in one half of their whole body. These unfortunates recover from paralysis but it's replaced by something actually far harder to bear. This sounded terrible. When I asked what people did in that situation, she casually said it usually resulted in suicide. I didn't find this information comforting.

I wasn't able to function unaided by pharmaceuticals for a while. I had to take great handfuls of pills several times a day. On discharge from hospital, my ongoing prescription included:

- 10 milligrams of midodrine three times a day to reduce dizziness and help me stand unaided
- 200 micrograms of fludrocortisone each morning for my low blood pressure
- 60 milligrams of pyridostigmine twice a day to treat muscle weakness

- another 30 milligrams of the pyridostigmine each evening
- 150 milligrams of pregabalin twice a day for neuropathic pain
- 7.5 milligrams of zopiclone each night in order to try to get some sleep

I was encouraged to stop taking the zopiclone as soon as possible, as it's easy to establish dependency, but I was not able to sleep without it.

I realise that I could have been traumatised by what happened to me, but I did not suffer emotional aftershock. Unlike most trauma that people experience, I was able to take the time to fully process what happened to me. The nature of the illness lent itself to this healing process. I couldn't work or really do much at all when I came out of hospital, so I was able to work through what had happened to me. This is ideally what a person would be doing after any traumatic life experience, such as a bereavement or serious illness, but life doesn't generally allow it. I used the space as an opportunity to regroup and rebuild.

The processing took many forms. I went on journeys with artists I'd always wanted to spend more time with, some actual and some virtual. I watched every movie Stanley Kubrick ever made. I prayed with the rapper Jay Electronica, at that time relocated from New Orleans to west London, both at the Hindu temple in Neasden and at my parents' house, where my mum and dad welcomed Jay and me to celebrate Hanukkah, the Jewish Festival of Lights.

I was moving slowly and the whole period now has a hazy and dreamlike quality for me. I was not depressed, being so relieved to be out of hospital and in the comfort of my home, but nonetheless I kept weeping. I wasn't sure why this was happening. I went with it. Crying is one of the greatest healing activities we have at our disposal. Some inner intelligence was telling me to use it, as a child uses it. The shedding of tears releases oxytocin and endorphins, and my tears helped heal me.

Sickness and recovery have changed my existence. I had to mourn the passing of the life I had before, but my new reality is better. I still have various types of pain, particularly in my feet and hands, but I've become aware of just how many people live with pain, and how feasible that is. Pain and suffering are different things. The suffering is caused by resistance to the pain. The pain can be acceptable - if you choose to accept it.

A few months after I left hospital, Hardy mentioned something he felt might occur in ten years' time, and I noticed myself thinking that this wasn't relevant to me, as I wouldn't be around a decade from now. It then struck me that I may well be around in ten years, or in fact twenty or thirty years. Fifty years even. I momentarily thought the long term was irrelevant to me because at some point during my illness I accepted the possibility of dying. I had somehow embraced death as part of my future, and not even my distant future.

I felt a wave of the most extraordinary elation and gratitude. I had been given the ultimate gift. My own life had been returned to me. I could now see how unbelievably precious it was and I planned to revel in it. The joy of the seemingly mundane aspects of life - to be able to work, to walk to Portobello Road and get a cup of coffee, to put Jada to bed - was suddenly abundantly clear.

Before the Guillain-Barré experience I might not have appreciated the magic of these aspects of my existence. My illness opened my eyes.

FAITH LETS YOU FALL INTO HER ARMS, WITHOUT A WORD

Some six months after I left hospital I found myself at my new studio listening to an Afro-Cuban duo from Paris called Ibeyi, comprising twin sisters Lisa and Naomi Díaz, daughters of famed Latin percussionist and Buena Vista Social Club member Angá Díaz, as they performed their songs using piano and cajón – the percussion instrument Naomi picked up and started using when her father died in 2006, when she and Lisa were eleven. Angá was a Grammy Award-winning master of this box-shaped drum, and Naomi was continuing a musical family tradition.

Prior to this, I had been complaining to Martin that all the new young artists I was seeing on YouTube at this time seemed to be inhabiting a spiritual void. That since older artists had now started making better records than we used to expect them to, perhaps there was less room, or less need, for young artists to have much depth. His response to that was to say that a friend of his in Paris had sent him a link to a new artist he thought I might like. This was the first and only time in our nearly thirty-year relationship that he has pointed out a new artist to me. I believe he normally avoids doing this so as not to tread on anyone's toes, or invade their curatorial space. I was pleased he breached his normal protocol.

When Ibeyi came over from France to play me the songs they were writing, while I was not ready to work yet, I knew this was the first artist I should record in my new habitat. However, I had to first issue a disclaimer. I said that I needed to wait six months before I was strong enough for studio life again, and so I completely understood if they wished to proceed with another producer meanwhile.

They were teenagers and six months is a long time, but they chose to wait. The process of recording their debut eponymous album was a joyous one, and the record, and particularly the song

'River', in which we employed the 'no music' production formula and dispensed with all elements except voices and drums, was enthusiastically received.

Our attempts to incorporate a sample from an interview with Nina Simone wherein she articulates her powerful feelings about the religions of the world ('they are all necessary') on the album were hampered by legal issues. But although we were unable to obtain clearance, the sample still provided inspiration for elements of the work Ibeyi did on their debut.

Ibeyi continued their explorations on the follow-up album *Ash*, which along with a ceaseless touring schedule won them an audience of devoted fans.

Whereas the first album was made only by the three of us, on the second album we collaborated with other musicians, including Meshell Ndegeocello, a musical hero to us all who played bass on 'Transmission', the most ambitious song we had embarked on to date. Recording at my house in Dorset, the sessions started the day the 45th president of the United States was elected. No one considered their choice of clothing that day, but everyone wore black.

I found a sample of a speech given by Michelle Obama about female empowerment that I knew Lisa and Naomi would relate to, and which would fit perfectly with a song they had written entitled 'No Man Is Big Enough For My Arms'. The former First Lady granted us clearance, and Lisa would later meet with her in London and discuss the use of her words. On that same song a classic sample from the Paradise Garage era came to mind: 'No man in the world', taken from First Choice's 1977 track, 'Let No Man Put Asunder'. The song title itself was another sample, coming from a phrase in *Widow Basquiat*, Jennifer Clement's account of her time with Jean-Michel Basquiat, a book Lisa picked up in my house during recording.

During the period of recording the debut Ibeyi album, and helping them take their first steps into their recording career, I was drawn towards a sonic wizard who had a lifelong influence on me and countless others, but I had never personally encountered before. At 2am on 23 November 2014 I found myself at Lee 'Scratch' Perry's house in Lausanne, Switzerland. He and I had spent the last few hours hand-painting 12-inch record sleeves. Hardy was on hand to art-direct Lee and me in our attempts to paint each of the 250 sleeves. The photographer and filmmaker Ed Morris was also with us, capturing the events, whatever they turned out to be.

I was still ill but felt good nonetheless, and began to ruminate on how I got here, and said to Lee, dub pioneer, the Piscean magician behind a lot of the most influential record productions of my lifetime, that I think I'd been having my own private revolution and it was starting to work. 'It must work,' he said.

The DJ Benji B had got in touch with me a few months earlier and asked me to do an hour-long mix for his excellent radio show. A decade earlier I'd have given myself two days to do this and executed it in a tremendous rush. In this instance I gave myself two weeks and enjoyed the experience tremendously. I included a new musical experiment called 'I Am Paint', a song I'd recorded quickly using a sample of Lee 'Scratch' Perry talking, from a documentary film about him called *The Upsetter*.

The song had sounded good enough in the mix I did for Benji that I decided to clear the sample and then press some vinyl. When I'd played the song to Ed Morris, who had recently shot the excellent 'River' video for Ibeyi, he had responded by making an 'I Am Paint' painting. This sparked the idea of hand-painting the 12-inch vinyl sleeves, and when I'd mentioned this to Hardy he'd said, 'That's a good idea, if Lee does the painting with you.'

I got in touch with Lee and to my delight he was up for this; having booked our flights to Switzerland, where Lee resides, I got around to reading the book *K Foundation Burn a Million Quid*, which details what happened when The KLF, a hugely successful late eighties Discordian rave duo, decided to burn all the money they'd made from music. I came across this quote in the book: 'Money is the shore to which the vessel of man is tethered, and will remain tethered until man finds a more spiritual form of exchange.' This resulted in a eureka moment.

Once we had hand-painted the sleeves, selling the records would not be a sufficiently 'spiritual form of exchange', we needed to swap them; and only for items people had made specifically for the purpose. The trip to Lake Geneva to see Lee was a pilgrimage, some sort of shamanic journey. It turned out that by law you can't bring paint into Switzerland, so Hardy, Ed and I gave ourselves an hour to go paint shopping on arrival. Having selected all the colours we needed in a paint shop we had located online, the emergency services turned up to evacuate the shop, as there had been a severe gas leak. But we were not leaving without our paint. This led to our being threatened with arrest for failing to evacuate a Swiss paint shop. We negotiated and eventually the paint was ours.

We had struggled to work out how we were going to paint all 250 sleeves in the one evening we had with Lee. Hardy pointed out that if each sleeve took a conservative estimate of five minutes to paint, the process would take around twenty hours, and Lee may or may not want us occupying his home for that long. We had no choice but to let events take their natural course.

On arriving and explaining our predicament to Lee, he instructed me to paint the soles of his feet, and promptly walked all over the 250 sleeves. They immediately started to look like his work. He gave me simple instructions on how to hand-letter the sleeves, turning me into his apprentice, and by the early hours we had all 250 records artworked.

As I prepared to leave the house, Hardy decided he wished to stay. Lee's place reminded him of Sun Inn, the family home in Bournemouth he grew up in with Esta. Lee and Hardy waved us off at 3am on 23 November 2014.

Back in London we rented a PO Box, set up a website, and the swaps began to turn up. The only criterion was that you had to make something specifically to swap. You couldn't submit something you had already made.

An astonishing selection of items started arriving. We received a perspex cube with a hand-made bird inside, denoting freedom. A box containing, it said, John Lennon's air. Tributes to Lee in the form of oil paintings, sculptures, hand-made items of clothing, voodoo dolls, a hand-made puzzle, jewellery. A golden 3D printed Pegasus.

Studio engineer John Foyle submitted an incredible hand-made music box which played the 'I Am Paint' tune. The swapping climaxed in a hand-tooled leather-bound book arriving from RZA of the Wu-Tang Clan and his collaborator Cilvaringz, telling the story of their adventures in a similar realm, when they made one copy of a new Wu-Tang album and sold it to the highest bidder (with unexpected and controversial results). The book included a part about our own 'I Am Paint' experiment.

The experience of receiving these items brought nothing to mind so much as receiving birthday presents when I was a child. Total excitement. We were encouraging our creativity and in turn other people's, and nudging them out of their comfort zone.

Our 12-inch was named by the Vinyl Factory as the most valuable record released that year, so everyone who went to the trouble of making something ended up receiving something of tangible material value for their troubles. But I'd like to think this is not all they got.

My experiences in Lausanne unlocked something within me. It was akin to a hallucinogenic experience, nudging my perspective to the side. Collaborating with Lee 'Scratch' Perry while I was recovering from illness, when I was so open, really impacted on me. I found myself making my own collaborative album at my studio, the Copper House. I would use the collective name *Everything Is Recorded*, inspired not by the studio process but by the life review described in *The Tibetan Book of Living and Dying*, which also inspired the title of this book. I've worked in different roles on many musical projects. This was the first time I'd put myself at the centre.

The photographer Ed Morris was around for the three-year duration of the recording process, capturing what happened and always contributing something to the sessions. This is his recollection:

343

There wasn't a lot of light upstairs, where I had to take photographs. There was no overall agenda. There was Giggs's mum's food. There were unrecognisable electronic instruments everywhere, like the Pyramid Synth. There was laughter; my favourite laugh was Maya's. There was the humbling and respectful awareness of Richard's recovery. There was Peter Gabriel drinking a cup of tea in the sunlight. There was something magical, even numinous about Peter. There was vinyl and joss sticks, and incense and green tea. There was always the brief text from Richard the night before.

There was Obongjayar's full-beam smile. There was the wall we covered in the photographs. There was the IDMC gospel choir. There were quotes Blu-tacked about. There were moments in the sun, sat in the front garden with its swaying bamboo, steep steps and white pebbles. There were times when I was asked for my opinion about the music. There were names like Syd, Tic, Wiki and Kaner. There was a great day-to-day mutual respect to be felt. There was no point talking to Rich about hip-hop, you'd be out of your depth immediately. There was no knowing who would show up next. There were days off I'd spend printing in the little darkroom in St John's Wood. There was that connection you only get between musicians when they play together. There was a lot of that. There was Dooom, who was always happy. There was Moog, Oberheim, Roland, Critter and Guitari. There was, long after his passing, still the presence of Gil Scott-Heron in the room, anchored by the small portrait of him in the delicate silver frame on the windowsill. There was Infinite's infinite intrigue and beauty, and then out of that the voice. There was a very direct approach towards the work that felt at times like we were building a bridge or shelter on an island. There was the day, orchestrated by Hardy, that we all painted record sleeves in the driveway and smoked and talked while they dried in the sun. There was always sunlight and good ideas around Hardy. There was rum on a Friday. There was Eno's grin and his boyishness. There was a trance I went into when

Lisa Díaz spoke. There were bursts of great and enthusiastic conversation over lunch that would meander and find their way eventually back to the music, back upstairs to play and sing. There were moments of no music, thumbing through records, quiet reflection, even chanting. There was Giggs's silver Audi in the drive.

There was Young John and his contradictory air of maturity. There was a sense of love, warmth, generosity and good spirit. There was this most from Warren Ellis. There were the restorative naps Rich took in the small bedroom while we kept our voices down or carried on recording upstairs. There was the trip we took to see Eckhart Tolle. There was Pauli hunched over a keyboard with a scarf over his head. There was to my knowledge never a moment's pretence or prima donna bullshit. There was the way Kamasi Washington sat so comfortably with the sax in his lap. There was an astonishing and abundant flow of musical creativity. There were people whose names even had rhythm, like Fabiana Palladino. There were the books on the shelf in the bathroom; I remember one title, *Pain, Sex and Time*. There was, to the best of my knowledge, no pain, sex or time at the Copper House. There was always a scattering of sheets full of handwritten lyrics. There was Tic teaching yoga to a pregnant Mela Murder. There was Lily's hand-made diorama of The KLF's burning of a million pounds on the island of Jura. There was her blue hair. There was discussion of Jews and Jamaicans in the history of music. There was the mirror in the loo that I always stared into questioningly every time I took a piss. There was the time we all did DNA ancestry tests.

There was the honour of being present and able to witness so closely as great artists reached into their soul for expression. There was Naomi's sass and silver Chanel jacket. There was the 1925 Gibson that I always wanted to play, with its black lacquer finish and perfect balance in the hand. There was the arrival of the record collection that once belonged to Ilhan Mimaroglu with a sticker on each record – 435 West 119th Street, Apt 9C,

New York. There was the electronic gate, boiled water straight from the tap and a huge yellow door standing up against the wall that someone told me Bob Dylan had touched. There was the theme of Richard's paternal role among fatherless artists. There was the constant debate about album title and artwork. There were trips out for coffee, ice cream and jerk chicken. There was Green Gartside's silver star ring that blinked as he played. There was a piece of paper on the wall with 'MORE BASS' scrawled across it. There was Sampha at the piano. There was his very likeable shyness and kind of ancient humility. There was a gift, an album by Alice Coltrane, thanks for that. There were those that smoked weed and those that didn't. There was Albarn's stubble, tattoos and beautiful choice of notes. There was Rich's obsession with samples. There was always my frustration at not being able to join in, musically, like a eunuch in a harem. There was the cupboard that didn't want to shut and the quote on the studio door from the wall of the Android's Dungeon. There was the distinctive and reassuring brassy click and wind of the Leica. There were the track lists on a flip chart that got crossed, shuffled and rewritten on a daily basis. There was the need to go about my task without intrusion. There were the songs that didn't make the album – 'No America', 'The Heart Cannot Think', 'On My Mind'.

There was the day a Buddhist monk showed up. There were some that liked the camera and some that didn't. There was the day Roger Linn was there, the inventor of the Linn drum and the MPC. There was an almost holy reverence for him. There was Seb Chew's obvious and incredible ability to listen, conversationally and musically. There were combinations of these things overlapping all of the time. There was the implicit agenda to contribute in any way we could to reach the goal. There was the bassist with the dreads, the striped trousers and the purple suede shoes. There were times I left with a real feeling of elation that needed to be managed; there was the come-down. There was an email I wrote to Rich that he stuck on the wall.

There were people that came to heal. There was a general sense of healing. There was the day Richard handed me a copy of the album. There was the yellow vinyl version. There was my love and respect for the time, the people, the work, the living and life of it all and of course for Rich. There was the little table covered in pots of paint, brushes, photographs and a typewriter.

The making of the record was unforgettable but even the promotion of the album provided memorable moments. Seeing that Sampha, Wiki and Ibeyi would be in LA at the same time, we gathered there to shoot a video for the song 'Mountains Of Gold'. I suggested that we invite any LA heroes we could think of to attend the shoot. Quincy Jones was top of my list and remarkably he materialised.

Turning up at the shoot for his cameo performance, he somehow immediately identified me as a fellow Pisces, told me I looked like I'd seen a few things and had four words he wanted to share with me about Gil Scott-Heron: 'He was so great.' Well into his eighties, Quincy's energy was infectious.

The following night, the shoot wrapped, everyone involved in making the video hopped on a rented bus together and we had a jubilatory night out seeing Kanye West perform at The Forum in Inglewood.

Around the release of the album in February 2018, I invited everyone to come together for two performances in east London, stage- and art-directed by Toby Ziegler, at a then unused venue which was shortly to reopen as Evolutionary Arts Hackney, around an installation by Toby. I had no idea how a public recreation of the album would work. I just knew that whatever we did needed to be a celebration, and that I had to have faith that something special would manifest. The principle I tried to stick to was that the absence of doubt would lead to success. Commit to the process, don't waste time thinking about whether it will or won't work, and execute to the best of your abilities. The rest will take care of itself.

When we performed some songs live for Radio 1 from the BBC's studios in Maida Vale the night before our show, everyone was open about their nerves, and once you accept these feelings, they fuel the creativity and the performances. The fear is necessary and understandable, and most performers are dealing with stage fright of some type or another. You're not meant to feel good before you perform. You probably will after.

Giggs, though, does not seem to suffer from any type of performance anxiety, so I decided to share mine with him, and he offered the following advice by text:

Relax it'll be fun.

Then:

What's there to be scared of?

Then:

We'll be runnin riddims and bussin jokes.

There was a transcendent quality to the shows, achieved by the combining of the remarkable talents involved, all of whom were devoid of ego and helped each other to create a communal experience. It was a 'happening', inspired by sixties events I'd read about. We performed live four times, once for friends and family, twice for ticketed audiences and once for a radio session, and each time I felt that special quality that comes from the heightened concentration that live performance demands.

My fingers were bleeding by the end of the last show and that in itself felt symbolic and necessary. The responses from the people who attended were extraordinary. The album was chosen as one of the Mercury Music Prize albums of the year, and we regrouped to perform live on TV at the ceremony, which took place at the Hammersmith Apollo, where I have seen so many gigs that have been of great significance to me.

We performed 'Close But Not Quite', featuring Sampha, which had become the most popular song on the album and includes a sampled line from Curtis Mayfield's song 'The Makings Of You': 'These words I try to recite, they are close but not quite.' I was touched that while Sampha is the only vocalist who performs on the song, Ibeyi, Obongjayar, Infinite and Mela all turned up to provide backing vocals for our Mercury performance. It was to be a beautiful conclusion of the first phase of this project.

On the recording of 'Close But Not Quite' I had used Brillo pads to create a specific texture preceding each snare sound. I suggested to Tic that he play Brillo live as part of his percussive duties. When I stumbled across some multi-coloured and potentially telegenic Brillo pads in a kitchen shop on Westbourne Grove the day before the show, I knew the performance would be special. Coincidences are 'God's way of staying anonymous'. They are a reassurance that there is a flow and it's useful to note and appreciate them when they occur.

In times of strong creative flow, I see coincidences all around me. During the recording of the album one day I had a strong urge to leave the studio, get on the Northern line and go to Edgware. I had no idea what the purpose of the trip was but felt I shouldn't question it. Arriving at Edgware station and walking down Station Road, the street that was my route from home to the rest of the world when I was growing up, I began to notice things that were oddly relevant to my current life. I saw the step I used to sit on before school with my first girlfriend. I noticed for the first time that it was outside number 92, the house number I now live at.

Passing the hairdresser's, there was a photo of my current next-door neighbour in the window, modelling a haircare product. I walked past the site where Loppylugs used to be, and saw that the road that ran down the side of the shop was Heron Grove. Next to this was a block of flats, the name of which was the same as the tiny village where I stay in Dorset. Another street sign, remarkably, carried the name of the house there. I headed towards my childhood home and thought that I recognised the figure about to cross the road a few metres ahead of me. It was my father. I took his arm to help him cross. He thanked me without registering my identity. On realising it was me, he showed no surprise.

A year or so after the album's release, I was listening to Benji B's Radio 1 show on headphones as I walked into the West End. Obongjayar was guesting, having spent the year since he performed on my record building his own career to great effect. As I walked into town, immersed in the sounds in my headphones, I heard him say of his own studio process:

'It's all about bringing people in. That sort of environment where everything is raw and natural and you feel free. Experimenting. It's not closed off to being in your head. You want the experience to be as inclusive as possible and have fun doing it. That's all credited to Rich. A lot of my production process and music-making process comes from him.'

Hearing this confirmation that I was providing inspiration to other musicians felt like achievement. I am indebted to the people from whom I have learned how to make and capture music, both those whose music I have listened to and those I have worked with directly. I've spent a lifetime absorbing other people's lifetimes of music-making. So, for any artist, of any level of experience, to feel that I have helped their creativity – that is the affirmation I need, and we all need affirmation, that I'm travelling on the right lines.

Obongjayar said of *Everything Is Recorded*: 'I was lucky to be a part of it. It shouldn't but it sounds very cohesive. It was done so naturally; it's a beautiful thing.'

As I complete this book, the second *Everything Is Recorded* album takes shape, to be entitled *Friday Forever*. This collaborative project has given me the opportunity to work with a range of artists simultaneously broad and connected, from newcomers like Manchester rapper Aitch and Irish vocalist Maria Somerville to some long-term, legendary musical heroes like Penny Rimbaud of Crass and Wu Tang Clan's Ghostface Killah. It includes a song called 'Walk Alone' featuring up-and-coming vocalists Berwyn

Du Bois and Infinite Coles, Ghostface's son, based around Man Friday's 'Love Honey, Love Heartache', as originally produced by Larry Levan and released on Charlie Grappone's Vinylmania label.

Endless threads.

I try to let my instincts dictate what work I do and how I do it. In my musical/working life I cannot help but push myself. This hasn't always been a good thing. But I want to make music that can exist on the same extraordinary plane as the work that inspires me. Usually the goal is unattainable, but the pursuit is enough.

There are moments when it seems easy – when Sampha walks in the studio and I play him an instrumental and he improvises a vocal on it which he is channelling from somewhere else and I know that we will have something that might outlast us. Or when someone plays me a song they have been working on and struggling with and I know exactly what they should do, something that will solve the problem. Or when a sample-based instrumental manifests in moments while I work alone in the studio. These moments of yield always feel like a gift.

There is a great power in tempering your desires. XL did not resemble the thing I wanted it to until I stopped wanting it to quite so badly. Delusions of grandeur don't lead to grandeur. I had notions of creating an influential record label before I had developed any real breadth of vision. It was ego-based.

When I stopped wanting things for the wrong reasons, they became possible. Now that I'm based full-time in the studio, and developing the necessary craft to be truly effective, the label most closely reflects my idealised vision of it.

I let go to concentrate on actually making records.

The people at the label are empowered and effective. All over the world, people can listen to any of the music released by XL over the last thirty years, anytime they like. I never saw that coming.

In our best moments we are all capable of practising a type of alchemy. Pain becomes art. That the worst experiences of a person's life, the causes of their sorrow, can be turned into the making of their music, is a process possessed of an unutterable, fleeting beauty. It's why the studio is a sacred environment for me; the most magical place in the world.

I am deeply grateful for my experiences, for everything I've learned and for the freedom music has given me.

EPILOGUE

Some of the characters who populate this book are no longer with us. Gil Scott-Heron died at the age of sixty-two on 27 May 2011, and Bobby Womack would pass on 27 June 2014, aged seventy. Dave Domleo would pass away soon after he graciously allowed me access to Island Records in its heyday. Rafi Sigarney, aka MC Lord JT, the first rapper I ever worked with, lost his life in a car accident in his early twenties. Marts Andrups also passed in his twenties.

My colleagues Jazz Summers, Pete Harris and Mike Champion are all gone.

The year I began working on this book, 2016, saw some of my musical heroes depart – George Michael, Prince, David Bowie and David Mancuso. Paul 'Trouble' Anderson passed away during the writing of this book at the age of fifty-nine after a lengthy battle with cancer, having previously suggested that his 150,000-strong vinyl collection be buried with him, 'like a pharaoh'.

Their contributions are ever more resonant, and their work outlives them.

When Jada was showing me a celebrity birthday website early in 2019, I noticed the date Keith Flint was going to turn fifty, and in his case this birthday somehow seemed particularly special. I added the date to my diary so I could surprise him with a call. It had been a while. Mike Champion had only recently passed away, his liver giving way on New Year's Eve 2018.

Mike had not been The Prodigy's manager for the last decade, but Liam always credited him with his contributions to the band's success, saying to me that he felt that the three of us, in our moment, were 'the fuck-you team' who created the space for the band to burst through whatever barriers were perceived to exist. Liam once said he has a whole book of stories about Mike that people would simply not believe. I hope that book gets written one day. We were all shocked and saddened by Mike's passing, but perhaps able to be philosophical that he had made it to the age he did.

On the morning of 4 March 2019 I learned of Keith's suicide, aged forty-nine. He had taken his own life by hanging. I had long, bewildered conversations with Liam, Maxim and John Fairs, feeling their infinite sadness.

In an effort to still my thoughts I tried to write about how I felt, but there was no way to process what had happened. I was stuck on the idea that there is a time when we are meant to go, and we are not meant to take that into our own hands. We are no more supposed to be in control of our end than we are of our beginning.

I was doubtless one of many people wishing, hopelessly and pointlessly, that they could have somehow changed the course of events. Surely this was an avoidable tragedy? That a person who was a source of joy and excitement to so many ultimately found his own pain unbearable seemed, in itself, unbearable. I was bewildered by the randomness of it all.

If only Keith had not taken his own life at the time he did that night, perhaps he might have felt differently twenty minutes later? Days later I began to wonder, most likely in order to comfort myself, if this was perhaps an inevitable part of Keith's journey. He had run his best ever time in a 10k race the day before. I wept, and thought that by the time Keith's funeral occurred I would have done all my weeping and would be able to maintain a stoic facade. That was not possible.

But the funeral was extraordinary, many fans turning up to rave in memory outside the church. This was John Fairs' 1,051st Prodigy gig. It's not really fair to call him a tour manager, as he is so much more to the band, but nonetheless he is the best tour manager in the business, and with his customary thoroughness he visited many local churches until he found one with a vicar open-minded enough to let Keith's life be celebrated authentically.

The recollections expressed that day were real and Keith's presence was tangibly felt. The Prodigy were Keith's permanent family. I am lucky to have shared many peak experiences with them. When John Fairs, Leeroy, Maxim and Liam entered the church, leading the coffin bearers, Liam sporting Keith's 'Champions Of London' live belt over his shoulder, Keith's dog Cyrus among them, I felt a mixture of pride and deep sorrow.

Liam referred to Keith that day as 'my loyal friend' and, indeed, Keith would have done anything for his bandmate.

But he could not live on for him. It was an extraordinary service, the send-off that Keith deserved. Although Keith only sang on a handful of songs, his spirit can be heard in every Prodigy record.

BIBLIOGRAPHY

Adam Ant, *Stand and Deliver* (Sidgwick & Jackson, 2006)

Chris Brook, *K Foundation Burn a Million Quid* (Ellipsis London Ltd, 1997)

Dan Charnas, *The Big Payback* (New American Library, 2010)

Brian Coleman, *Check the Technique* (Vol.1: Villard Books, 2007; Vol. 2: Wax Facts Press, 2014)

Freddy Fresh, *Freddy Fresh Presents the Rap Records* (Nerby Publishing, 2004)

Nelson George, *Hip Hop America* (Penguin Books, 2005)

John Hammond, *John Hammond on Record* (Penguin, 1981)

Herbie Hancock, *Possibilities* (Viking Press, 2014)

Adam Horovitz and Mike Diamond, *Beastie Boys Book* (Faber & Faber, 2018)

Norman Jay, *Mister Good Times* (Dialogue Books, 2019)

Sacha Jenkins, *Ego Trip's Book of Rap Lists* (St Martin's Press, 1999)

Grace Jones, *I'll Never Write My Memoirs* (Simon & Schuster, 2016)

Tim Lawrence, *Love Saves the Day* (Duke University Press, 2004)

Alan Light, *The Skills to Pay the Bills* (Three Rivers Press, 2005)

Ed Piskor, *Hip Hop Family Tree* (Series: Fantagraphics)

Rakim, *Sweat the Technique* (Amistad, 2019)

Christopher Sandford, *Bowie: Loving the Alien* (pp. 157 and 176 re. Hitler; Sphere, 1997)

Huston Smith, *The World's Religions* (HarperOne, 2009)

Jazz Summers, *Big Life* (Quartet Books, 2013)

Graeme Thomson, *George Harrison: Behind the Locked Door*
(Overlook-Omnibus, 2016)
Bobby Womack, *My Story* (John Blake Publishing, 2014)

ONLINE DOCUMENTARIES AND CLIPS

David Bowie: Finding Fame (BBC Four, 2019)
Bowie on fascism: https://www.youtube.com/watch?v=zX0ZVQhEnEc
Larry Levan and Paradise Garage documentary: *Maestro* (2003)
Marley Marl, *Classic Recipes – Recreating Eric B. & Rakim 'Eric B. Is
President'* w/Akai MPC: https:youtube.com/watch?v=hvob_fcrRZs
Keith Flint and Richard on rave: https://www.youtube.com/watch?
v=waAkAlbmu-k
Jerry Barrow, *The Secret History of Public Enemy's* Yo! Bum Rush The
Show: https://www.okayplayer.com/news/secret-history-public-
enemy-yo-bum-rush-the-show.html
Robbie Ettelson, *Ultimate Breaks And Beats*: https://medium.com/
cuepoint/ultimate-breaks-beats-an-oral-history-74937f932026
Christopher R. Weingarten, *An Oral History of House of Pain's 'Jump
Around'*: https://www.spin.com/2012/02/house-pain-look-back-
20-years-jump-around/
Gil Scott-Heron interview on *The Fader*: https://www.thefader.
com/2010/11/30/feature-looking-to-the-future-gil-scott-heron-
rejoins-the-present
Freddie Foxxx on Rakim: https://youtu.be/QoeyyHnslDY

CREDITS

PICTURE CREDITS:

The author and publisher would like to thank the following for the use of their images in this publication: p.3: XL Recordings/Rob Ricketts; p.29: Bauer Media/Smash Hits; pp.19, 39, 66, 67, 131, 161, 241, 279: Richard Russell; p.101: Trevor Jackson; Edward H Morris pp.171, 297, 337 (t, b); p.209: Ewan Spencer; p.225: Everynight Images/Debbie Bragg; p.241: Aliyah Otchere; p.307: Leila Arab; p.319: Cherise Payne; p.353: Camera Press/Phil Nicholls.

Use of album covers and flyers with kind permission: Eleven Management, Chris Griffin, Sony Records, Third Man Records, Tommy Boy Records, Warner Music UK, Warp Records, XL Recordings.

Excerpts from *Vinyl Maniac* magazine used with kind permission - Charles Grappone; excerpts from *The Fader* magazine used with kind permission - *The Fader* / Matthew Schnipper; facsimile on pp.186-7 used with kind permission - the estate of Gil Scott-Heron; excerpts from *Sound on Sound* magazine used with kind permission - *Sound on Sound* / Tom Doyle

SONG CREDITS:

p.5: CASISDEAD, 'Pat Earrings'; p.17: Adam and the Ants, 'Kings Of The Wild Frontier'; p.27: Notorious B.I.G., 'Juicy'; p.37: Coldcut, 'Beats + Pieces'; pp.51, 148: Ultramagnetic MCs, 'Give The Drummer Some'; p.63: Ultramagnetic MCs, 'Watch Me Now'; p.64: Ultramagnetic MCs, 'Critical Beatdown'; p.65: London Posse, 'How's Life In London?'; p.76: Derek B, 'Get Down'; p.125: House of Pain, 'Still Gotta Lotta Love'; p.169: Gil Scott-Heron, 'Parents (Interlude)'; p.239: M.I.A., 'Bucky Done Gun'; p.245: Neneh Cherry, 'Manchild'; p.251: Giggs, 'Cut Up Bag'; p.264: Adele, 'Daydreamer'.

THANK YOU

Sam Copeland for suggesting I write a book. Lee Brackstone for patience and understanding. Laura Stefu for help above and beyond.

Mum and Dad for everything.

Esta forever.

Ed Morris for his photography and his account of the *Everything Is Recorded* LP1 sessions.

Liam Howlett, Giggs, Maya Arulpragasam, Leila Arab, Mike D, Rick Rubin, Cage, Ian Montone, Charlie Grappone, Martin Mills, Seb Chew, Nick Halkes, Matt Thornhill and Tim Palmer for their time and insights.

Dimitri Doganis and Matt Thorne for detailed feedback.

Alfie Allen, Hardy Blechman, Nick Goldsmith, Trevor Jackson, Ben Beardsworth, Patrick North and Jake Simmonds for their visual contributions.

I'm particularly grateful to Tim Lawrence for *Love Saves the Day: A History of American Dance Music Culture 1970-1979* and to Brian Coleman for *Check the Technique: Liner Notes for Hip-Hop Junkies*. I leaned heavily on these insightful, informative and important books for historical background. I strongly recommend them.

Richard Russell (b. 1971) is a British record producer, musician and the co-owner of the British record label XL Recordings. He has nurtured and guided some of the most influential recording artists of our time, including Adele, Dizzee Rascal, The Prodigy, MIA and Giggs. As a producer and musician, Russell has made albums with the likes of Gil Scott-Heron, Bobby Womack, Damon Albarn and Ibeyi, and most recently launched his own artist project, *Everything Is Recorded*, whose self-titled debut album was nominated for the 2018 Mercury Music Prize.

Further praise for *Liberation Through Hearing* and Richard Russell

'The music business is full of kneejerk hyperbole, but XL Recordings, the independent London label run by Richard Russell, remains the most extraordinary enterprise ... a refreshing account of how a tremendously successful record aficionado gradually worked his way round to a kind of Zen humility'   Kitty Empire, *Observer*

'The book is a hugely enjoyable personal trip through Russell's life as a producer, artist and label boss'   *Electric Sound*

'Remarkable . . . manages to offer far more erudition and insight than is generally encountered in rock writing'

Angus Batey, *The Quietus*

"Russell is a great memoirist. This excellent autobiography combines pure fandom with great artist anecdotage'

Craig Mclean, *The Face*

'Richard Russell's vision as a producer and guru to countless artists has always been progressive. This memoir is required reading for anyone who cares about the recent history of British music'

Gilles Peterson

'I love XL. I use them as an example of how a brand is built. On great taste'   Jay Z

'Rich is the fucking boss. Man has no shoes on'   Giggs

WAYMER—The annual Pigeon Day shoot held here on Saturday, was declared a rousing success by the event's organizers. More than 300 sharpshooters—"not all of them so sharp," quipped one official—took aim on some 5,000 birds released on the Memorial Park soccer field.

Proceeds from shoot entry fees, plus revenue from the weeklong Family Fest, netted the community almost $34,000 for maintaining its park.

An unexpected episode occurred during this year's event. At one point in the late afternoon an unidentified boy dashed onto the shooting field and retrieved a wounded pigeon. Shooting was immediately halted, and the reckless lad, perhaps seeking an unusual pet for himself, was allowed to leave the premises with the bird.

Certainly that lucky pigeon had not fallen under the aim of Howard Eckert. Eckert, 36, a dairyman from Harmony Farms, won this year's Sharpshooter's trophy as best marksman.

Said Eckert, "Anybody can hit a clay pigeon. These babies, you never know which way . . ."